PERSONAL AND CONTROVERSIAL

BY PAUL BLANSHARD

PERSONAL AND CONTROVERSIAL

AN AUTOBIOGRAPHY BY

PAUL BLANSHARD

BEACON PRESS   BOSTON

Copyright © 1973 by Paul Blanshard
Beacon Press books are published under the auspices
of the Unitarian Universalist Association
Published simultaneously in Canada by Saunders of Toronto, Ltd.
All rights reserved
Printed in the United States of America

9 8 7 6 5 4 3 2 1

Library of Congress Cataloging in Publication Data

Blanshard, Paul, 1892–
    Personal and controversial.
    I. Title.
BL2790.B5A3   322.4'4'0924 [B]   72–6225
ISBN 0–8070–0514–2

"The Prelate and the Commissar" by Bertrand Russell first appeared
in *The Humanist,* September–October 1953, and is reprinted by
permission of *The Humanist.*

*Dedicated to the memory of nine
great American liberals
who, at one time or another,
were my bosses*

NORMAN THOMAS

FIORELLO LA GUARDIA

JOHN DEWEY

SIDNEY HILLMAN

A. J. MUSTE

OSWALD GARRISON VILLARD

ARTHUR GARFIELD HAYS

JOHN HAYNES HOLMES

CHARLES W. TAUSSIG

CONTENTS

PERSONAL AND CONTROVERSIAL

1. DOUBLE PRODUCTION

FROM THE RURAL CONSERVATISM of my youth to the hesitant radicalism of my declining years, three things have been of paramount interest to me—religion, politics, and sex—and this book is largely devoted to those subjects. In my zigzag career I have been transformed from Christian fundamentalist to humanist atheist, from stodgy Puritan to sexual rebel, from doctrinaire socialist to socialistic pragmatist. Whether I am a patriot or an anti-patriot is a question I will leave to the reader to decide. I think it is possible to love one's country and to hate it at the same time. The reasons for that love and hate are part of my life story.

To begin at the beginning, as my mother wrote her sister Sadie:

On the day before the event, I gave three lessons in shorthand, a music lesson, played two games of croquet and had seven callers, some of them until late in the evening. I felt splendid until two o'clock in the night, and then Oh how I did suffer! I got all numb and paralyzed and Frank got hot water and rubbed my limbs but I didn't dream my time had come. I thought it was inflammation of the bowels. But Frank ran for the lady doctor and she got here at 5 A.M. I was Oh dreadful bad until the first boy came at 9 o'clock and the next a little before 10. I pleaded for them to give me chloroform but the doctor poured whiskey and some other stuff to bring on pains. I had an awful lot of grit until the first was born but when I heard the doctor whisper to the nurse that there was another coming feet first, I tell you my

hopes flew and Frank's face blenched with terror. He was
in the room and helped to hold me all the time. . . . They
are so good looking. Everyone says they are the prettiest
twins and healthiest they ever saw. They each weighed 6½
pounds naked. I hadn't many clothes made even for one but
got at the end of three days 6 lovely suits, 3 shirts, 2 flannel
skirts and 2 white neckties. Wasn't that cute? We sent to
Chicago for a double crib, Yankee invention, with two
departments, and it doubles all up or makes a cradle. . . .
Our professional nurse left this morning. She only charged
75¢ a day. She said our babies were so good. She never worked
under $1 for anyone else. They sleep and nurse and sleep
again, just fine. I have enough milk for both. I had an awful
time with sore nipples. It took three to hold me when the
babies nursed; I suffered worse than having them. I got a
breast pump and 3 different kinds of breast shields and Frank
drew the milk himself several times. However they are healing
nicely now and I don't scream much.

In 1892, in the administration of Benjamin Harrison,
this is the way it was in the Blanshard household in a little
town in northern Ohio called Fredericksburg. Today Fredericksburg, with a population of about five hundred, is not
discoverable on any map except a very large and detailed
road map. It has a post office, three churches, a high
school, an abandoned mill, a statue of a Civil War soldier,
and a drugstore which opens for four hours a day.

In the 1890's even with good stethoscopes doctors could
not always tell when a double birth was in the offing.
About forty-five minutes after the woman doctor of the
village had picked me up by the heels and given me a good
shaking, my brother Brand pushed his way into the world.
He was not quite as vigorous as I was and he had a somewhat smaller head, but years later it was the head of the
head of the department of philosophy at Yale. My own
head has never achieved so high a ranking.

My father, pastor of the village Congregational church,
was so proud of the double production that he grew a

special set of muttonchop whiskers, and he had the whiskers and the twins immortalized by the local photographer. In that first picture Brand and I look very much alike, but we are not identical twins. Throughout the years our mannerisms have been similar, but there the resemblance ends.

For a few months my father and mother lived a radiantly happy and idyllic family life. My father was enjoying that sense of authority which comes to a young preacher in his first pulpit. In the community he occupied the position of an advanced liberal because he actually contended that Darwin's doctrine of evolution *might* be true and, as everyone knew, this was in defiance of the first part of Genesis. His congregation in Fredericksburg stood behind him because it was that kind of a congregation, organized in 1878 after a grand theological row over hell and infant baptism in the local Presbyterian church. The minister of that local Presbyterian church had been the Reverend A. N. Alcott, a relative of Louisa May Alcott, and he had publicly declared that, contrary to the Presbyterian creed, unbaptized infants were not destined to go to hell, a conclusion with which the majority of his congregation disagreed. So Alcott had left and taken part of the congregation with him to found the church my father later served, the First Congregational Church. The new congregation was small but very proud and determined. The members built the finest stone church in town and with it went a large white parsonage. It was in this parsonage that Brand and I were born to the Reverend Francis George Blanshard and Emily Victoria Coulter Blanshard, two naturalized Canadians who had already become very loyal Yankee citizens.

I suspect that my mother was especially proud in her glorious motherhood because she had waited so long and so patiently to marry. She and my father had met when they were students in high school in Weston, Ontario, now a part of Greater Toronto. For eight weary years of their engagement they had written weekly love letters to each other, always circumspect and pure. My mother waited for marriage until she was twenty-seven. She had come from a large and sturdy family of farmers, the only one of the eleven children in the family who ever attended college. Walking five miles to high school through Canadian blizzards, she had won entrance to Hamilton Ladies College, now part of the University of Toronto, and she had worked her way through that institution by teaching shorthand. In an old tin box in the attic of my Vermont farmhouse the other day I found two Governor General's medals she had won in a single year, one in English and the other in mathematics.

When Brand and I were eleven months old, my father and mother took us back to Canada to show us off to the Coulter family on the old farm in Richview. It was a proud summer. We were the only twins the Coulter family had ever produced and the relatives flocked in to see us. In the old pink brick house on the hill my mother helped joyously in the work of the farm. Every day she would dash down to the cellar to skim cream from the big pans of milk that sat on a long shelf along the wall, and help to churn the yellow butter in a large wooden churn that sat on the dirt floor. One day, late in the afternoon when it was growing dark, she started down the old wooden stairs with an oil lamp in her hand. Tripping on her full skirt, she plunged downward head first, the oil spilling over her luxuriant hair. Instantly her whole head was a mass of flames. Screaming, she ran out the cellar door into the wind. She died in my father's arms the next morning.

It is difficult for me to write with any detachment about Orminda Adams Blanshard, my paternal grandmother, who moved into my father's household with her husband, Shem Blanshard, a Methodist preacher who had just retired. (Shem died shortly afterward, and I have no memory of him.) Grandma Blanshard was the fierce, possessive, loving, dominating factor in my life throughout my childhood, and for most of the time until I was twenty-one she took the place of both father and mother. She had been born on a farm near South Grimsby, Ontario, one of eleven children, seven of whom died of tuberculosis before they were twenty-four. She herself had suffered from "consumption" in her early twenties but had miraculously survived. Her father and mother believed that "night air" was the chief cause of tuberculosis, so they had closed all the windows at night while their children grew up and died.

Grandma's Adams family may have had something to do with the family of John Quincy Adams, but when I mentioned that possibility one day, she rejected it indignantly. "John Quincy Adams was a Unitarian," she said, "and I don't have anything to do with Unitarians." Her church was primitive Methodist. She stood firmly against dancing, love songs, card-playing, and theater-going. The Bible was for her the beginning and the end of moral sublimity, although she always avoided the sexual passages. On those rare occasions when she mentioned sex she would hiss the word "lust."

But this picture of Grandma is one-sided. She had an alert and restless mind, hungry for information about the world. She had a deep affection for her twins, and she lived for us and glowed with pride over every one of our accomplishments. She had a fierce belief in the middle class and an overweening ambition for the success of her twins in that class.

She was a rather handsome woman with a proud, commanding face and deep-set blue eyes. In many ways, in spite of her poverty, she was a middle-class snob, looking down at the yokels who had sat in the pews of Shem Blanshard's churches through the years. H. G. Wells' mother as seen in his autobiography reminds me of Grandma. She was "an incorrigibly bad cook"; she had a powerful "instinct for appearances"; she ordered us "never to mix with common children."

I think that Grandma's union with Shem had been less than joyful. He was a stodgy, heavyset man with long whiskers, much older than she was. He had come from Yorkshire to Ontario in his thirties as an unordained

Methodist minister without any college training. The Yorkshire Blanshards were Huguenots who had come over from
France in the great Catholic-Protestant wars. The literate
Blanchards spelled their name with a *c;* the rest spelled it
Blanshard. And oh what a nuisance that variation in spelling has been for us! Almost no telephone directory or
stenographer or bank gets the spelling correct on the first
three encounters. Brand and I considered changing the
spelling to the ordinary one when we were in high school,
but with Grandma alive and indignantly opposed to any
change, we soon abandoned the venture.

There is nothing distinguished in our Blanshard past.
The immediate Yorkshire Blanshard tribe was afflicted
with too much religion, mostly primitive Methodist religion. Shem Blanshard's father was a local Methodist
preacher in Yorkshire, so it was natural that Shem should
come as a Methodist circuit rider to Ontario, where he
served for thirty-five years at an average salary of $350
a year.

For thirty-five years Shem and Orminda trundled back
and forth across the dreary wastes of northern Ontario,
never having a reasonable income or a single church all to
themselves or any substantial recognition by the upper
echelons of their church. Usually Shem had to travel with
his horse and buggy—or horse and cutter—to three tiny
rural churches each Sunday, giving the same heavy, biblical sermon to three different congregations of sleepy farmers, morning, afternoon, and night, gathering in the tiny
cash collections which the farmers grudgingly bestowed
upon him. Once, Grandma told us, a gold piece suddenly
appeared in the collection plate. Shem felt obliged to announce from the pulpit that if any donor had intended to
give a penny instead of the gold piece, he could make the
exchange at the end of the service. A sheepish hired man
came forward.

Perhaps there was in Shem's life some moment of stolen
sin. When my father was a tiny infant, just after the
death of his baby sister, Shem one day brought home a

baby girl and told Grandma that he had adopted her. He had not even consulted Grandma and he refused to reveal anything about the ancestry of the new child. She grew up to be the Annie of my childhood, my father's younger sister who became Ada Evelyn Blanshard Stevens. Annie came to believe that she was a child of Shem and that Shem had adopted her in this fashion to mitigate his guilt. Perhaps Grandma believed this too. She hated Annie with a profound and jealous hatred, and in moments of rage she would shout, "That's your French nigger blood that is showing through." So far as we knew, there was no Negro blood anywhere in the picture, but there had been rumors of a willing French servant girl, and in Grandma's lexicon of evil anything French was almost as bad as anything black. Annie graduated from Oberlin Conservatory of Music and married a Michigan farmer, but she never had any children. Grandma's taunt about French nigger blood had scarred her whole life.

I am always amazed when writers talk about their re-actions before they were four years old. I can remember almost nothing before I was six. Was this because I had an overly protected childhood? Perhaps. I was shielded by the fierce guardianship of Grandma. Our father was a shield until we were ten, a moral leader of the community whom we worshiped as a kind of god. Brand shielded me because he was a little more mature than I was. As twins we formed a special kind of community of our own, wearing the same models of clothes until we reached high school, getting about the same grades in school, never lacking company or suffering from loneliness.

From Oberlin, where we went for a time after my mother's death, we moved to Grand Rapids, Michigan, where my father had his first and last city pulpit. I re-member Father taking each one of us by the hand and crossing the railroad tracks on the way to our first session of school while the crossing-tender waved his red flag to hold the locomotive back; I remember the gold stars we both got on the blackboard for attendance and scholarship; I remember the first little girl whose pants we took down to see what was underneath; I remember our father running up to our bedroom with a newspaper and the big headline MAINE SUNK IN HAVANA HARBOR; I remember the tiny image of Admiral Dewey far in the distance receiving the keys to the city; I remember the watch-night prayer meeting in our church ushering in the twentieth century and how the congregation laughed when I ran down to the pulpit to get a penny from my father to put in the collection plate.

During that brief Spanish-American War the country went crazy with expansionist patriotism and self-righteousness, but to a small boy it all seemed good—and exciting. McKinley was forced by public clamor to demand from Spain for the sinking of the *Maine* such humiliating concessions as no honorable and proud nation could have accepted. And when Spain actually offered most of these concessions after a three-day ultimatum, McKinley did not even wait for their arrival but, under the whiplash of the Hearst press, took us into war anyway. The American flag won, and (perhaps) Teddy Roosevelt charged up San Juan Hill. Anyway he became our school hero.

By this time Father had started to cough and had left his Grand Rapids pulpit to take over a small church in Helena, Montana, so that he could benefit from "the dry air." He went west alone, and we rented a house in Grand Rapids for $8 a month, where Grandma took over and supported us from her Methodist pension of $250 a year. I remember the day when Grandma had just five cents left in the house, but she was too proud to ask anybody for help.

From Grand Rapids we moved south to a little village in north central Ohio, which was to be my father's last charge, Edinburg, located in Portage County, seven miles from Ravenna. It had a school, a post office, a grocery store, a town hall, a blacksmith shop, and about ten houses. Every night the farmers came from miles around for the mail, although there was rarely any mail for them.

They hitched their horses to the hitching posts in front of Gause's general store, sat on the store porch, and spat their tobacco toward the road. It was a terrible blow to them when the postal free delivery was introduced during our years in Edinburg and they no longer had an excuse to come down to the center.

Edinburg had plenty of religion, Protestant religion. There were white wooden churches for Congregationalists, Methodists, and Disciples. My memory is that there were no Catholics or Jews in the village. Although Father's Congregational church was the largest of the three, it always had a hard struggle to keep going, partly because it was just a little too intellectual for most of the farmers and it never staged a revival meeting. My father was a Republican, of course, since everybody in our village who remembered the Civil War was a Republican, but he subscribed to the *Outlook* and he didn't say that evolution was heresy. That set him apart from most of the farmers and puzzled them a little because otherwise he seemed like a good loyal American.

I remember Edinburg: the potbellied coal stove in the old wooden schoolhouse where Brand and I served as school janitors for $5 a month, splitting the kindling and pushing it down into the sooty belly of the stove to start the soft coal burning at about seven each morning; the great pans of boiling syrup in Bingham's sugarbush, where Mr. Bingham, a deacon in Father's church, let us dip; the great stallion in Dec Davis' yard and the way Dec jumped into the corral and steered the stallion's penis into the mare so the semen wouldn't all leak out. And I remember how the stallion whinnied at a new, passing mare immediately after he was through with one. I remember the boy who said he could show us his white milk if we wanted him to take down his pants but we said no because we were afraid that Grandma would come; the shit piled so high in the backhouse at school that no one could sit down there; the way Mr. Burns' horse swelled up and died right before our eyes even after the vet had reached into his bowels and brought out a brown mess that reached up to his elbows; the way our father shot our pet cat through the brain with a rifle bullet when the cat went crazy; the way Daisy, our cow, broke from a heavy chain and rushed wildly back to the barn when her calf was born too soon; the crowded schoolroom, containing six grades, where we sat so close to the potbellied stove that we had to put our big geography books in front of our faces to keep off part of the heat; the way the bigger girls, going self-consciously to the backhouse, felt the backs of their skirts to see whether the safety pins were holding up; the way the wire rats in their pompadours sometimes showed through; the way William Moore stank when he came to school after working in the stable; the way the older boys and girls used the big dictionary in the middle of the schoolroom for passing love notes to each other; the great price war over milk when Mrs. Tuttle insisted on selling milk for four cents a quart while Mrs. Davis stood by her price of three cents a quart.

Father's cough got worse and he began to use a blue spit bottle wrapped in a handkerchief even when he was in the pulpit. But he still looked like a healthy man because he had a bright red beard that hid his sunken cheeks. And he seemed to us to be a good preacher. I suppose the whole course of my life was affected by that boyhood conviction about good preaching. My father was the Good Man, the most respected in the village. I suppose that I have pursued that image all my life even when I finally arrived at the stage of preaching against preaching.

Ultimately my father left for Albuquerque, New Mexico, in search of "dry air," but not before Grandma and he had tried every quack nostrum on the market. Peruna, one of the most famous cures for catarrh, had replaced Paine's Celery Compound as the most potent remedy in the country for almost anything that ailed you, and both had plenty of alcohol. Peruna sold for $1 a bottle. (Samuel Hopkins Adams later told how a person could make Peruna for himself for eight cents a bottle.) And Peruna was good for convulsions, mumps, colic, women's complaints, and rheumatism. Its chief competitor, Lydia Pinkham, with twenty percent alcohol, appealed to suffering woman- hood. Liquazone, "liquid ozone, that is all," sold at an even higher price and was found to contain ninety-nine percent water and one percent sulfuric acid. I remember that it tasted very potent. Father tried most of these things, end- ing with a small black tube which was practically guar- anteed to cure consumption. The patient drew in his breath through the tube, then expelled it slowly while a little ball in the tube checked the process of expulsion. This gave the patient "the full benefit" of the oxygen in the air.

When Father left us for Albuquerque, he kissed us quickly at the railroad station, climbed on board the train, and didn't look back. A year later, alone in a tent he died and was buried in a sandstorm. There was no stone marker on his grave. A few days before he died he wrote Annie that he had bought the lumber for a chair for $3, built it himself, and sold it for $6. "It is the first money I have made in a year," he said. When he was found dead in his tent, the doctor said; "It seems rather peculiar. He seems to have died of an overdose of sleeping pills, but I don't know."

Did my brother and I face a life of agony as deprived orphans? If so, we were never conscious of it. No happi- ness has ever seemed to me more complete than the happi- ness of Edinburg. We had each other and we had the open country. In school we were almost always at the head of the class together. Brand was a little ahead of me, but no one ever told me that, so our rivalry was never jaundiced or jealous. We had food of a sort, nothing but oatmeal for breakfast and often nothing at night but a large bowl of canned tomatoes. But we never knew that we were under- fed, and we always had plenty of milk.

For magazine literature we had the *Youth's Companion,* and for books we had the pious Pansy books from the Congregational church library, all the Alger books, and all the books of G. A. Henty. Grandma tried to keep us from

reading anything on Sunday except the Bible and the
Sunday School Times and nominally we accepted her rule,
but on lazy Sunday afternoons we ferreted out the sex
passages in the Bible and read hungrily about how Lot lay
with his own daughters and how David loved Bathsheba
unwisely and too well. There never was a time in my
memory when I did not dream of some girl, even when I
did not have the courage to speak to any particular girl.
In my prayers at night in Edinburg I always ended by
saying, "And help me to grow up and marry Pauline
Hudson." Pauline was the pretty girl in the class just
behind us.

In those Alger books which we devoured, Bob Trueheart,
son of the widow Trueheart, usually won out because he
helped Squire Kind Heart to defeat Squire Cold Heart,
who was about to foreclose the mortgage on the Trueheart
house. Corny? Yes, but I have never scoffed with Horatio
Alger's critics. I suspect that his awful corn was good
medicine for boys who had to earn a living by hard work
in the American capitalist system.

Came adolescence and Bay View, Michigan, a Methodist summer resort south of Mackinac where Grandma
moved us after Edinburg. I suspect that Grandma moved
us partly because she had acquired the habit of moving
every two or three years in her wanderings with Shem.
Perhaps she had heard of the great price war between
passenger boats on Lake Erie. At any rate we crossed Lake
Erie from Cleveland to Detroit on the way to Bay View for
twenty-five cents each. At the Union Station in Cleveland
Grandma asked for a doughnut for our dessert, expecting
to cut it up in three parts for the three of us. When the
man told her that it would cost five cents, she indignantly
returned it and called him a robber.

Brand and I quickly became the most noted boy entrepreneurs in Bay View, starting in the Howard House
wiping dishes for $1.50 a week plus meals. This was
during the summer in which we began to shave with
Grandma's old corn razor. Then we painted Miss Black-

wood's cottage for ten cents an hour. Then we became the town's bootblacks and newsboys, operating a big and profitable newsstand on the "campus." Then we punched tickets for all the Assembly lectures for $15 a week. Then we launched our favorite enterprise, a daily Bay View news column in the *Petoskey Resorter,* where, for a total of $5 a week, we were allowed to experiment boldly with the English language. We interviewed everybody of consequence who came to town, ranging from Ernestine Schumann-Heink—she ended her concert with "The Rosary"— to William Jennings Bryan.

Bryan had a magic kind of talent based on two assets, a uniquely orchestrated voice and the capacity for repose on the platform. He stood foresquare in his black alpaca coat with scarcely a single gesture until, toward the climax, he would lift an arm slightly, bringing it down with the authority of Jove. On the printed page his words looked like Tomfoolishness—he was an idiot in matters of currency and fundamentalism—but nothing could negate the mysterious power of that voice. In the days before the loudspeaker his diaphragm was his own loudspeaker. And, on the platform, he was swift-footed, knowing just when to shift from hortatory generalizations to homely humor. Once when he came to Bay View there had been a mix-up in the announcement of his topic. One announcement had listed the subject as "Woman Suffrage," another as "Prohibition." He began the session by putting the question to a vote of the audience. Which subject would they prefer? The show-of-hands vote was about evenly divided. "Very well," he said, "I will give both." And he proceeded to weld together those two lectures so smoothly that I, watching in fascination, could not tell where one left off and the other began.

Another orator I heard in those days helped to shape my whole life. By this time we had gone to live in Petoskey, a small city two miles away from Bay View, and entered the high school there. One night there was a notice in the paper of a free lecture on socialism at the Baptist church.

When we got there a cherubic man with a perpetual smile and a shiny bald head stood up to speak, Eugene Victor Debs. He was already famous as leader of the Pullman strike of 1894 and as Socialist candidate for the presidency in 1904.

It has become popular now to downgrade Debs as sentimental and superficial. He was both of these things, but he was also something more, a radiant secular saint, the most infectious socialist evangelist who ever graced a platform. Daniel Bell has described him as "the true protestant . . . [who] stood at the end of the long road of the Reformation," and at that particular moment in my career his semi-secular protestantism inflamed my imagination. If he drank too much and gave away his overcoat to the nearest tramp, it did not show in his lectures, at least in the one lecture which made him famous, a star lecture on the struggles of the working class. He had polished and simplified that one lecture until it attained the perfection of a superlative vaudeville act with evangelistic overtones. I heard that speech for the first time in Petoskey, Michigan, in 1906. Some fifteen years later I heard the same speech at a political conference in Chicago, and it was even better the second time.

Debs made me feel for the first time that I belonged to a lower—and more virtuous—class, "the workers of hand and brain." It was a question of feeling, not of reason. I was poor and these others were poor, and I began to feel that we belonged together. Debs' most famous sentence was pure poetry: "So long as there is a lower class, I am of it; so long as there is a soul in prison, I am not free."

Debs and Bryan and the image of our father made Brand and me feel that oratory was the secret of success in the world. We made the high school debating team, and Brand won a silver medal from the WCTU with an oration which ended with the sentence: "I hate the liquor traffic." Brand built a little pulpit in the open meadow back of our cottage in Bay View and practiced repeating the speeches of Edmund Burke, Wendell Phillips, and Daniel Webster to the open breezes. I followed suit.

Perhaps it was natural that in this period we should come to God by way of an evangelistic sermon. A large-bellied evangelist came to the First Methodist Church of Petoskey, where we had become members, and in a special mass meeting for men only he dwelt on the sickness and horror of sexual sin. He appealed for all who wished to escape from the devil's trap to accept Jesus. "He that lusteth in secret is doubly sinful," he shouted. I stood up and said, "I accept Jesus as my savior." I felt very sinful, although I didn't even know what masturbation was and didn't practice it until long after my first marriage. I knew about Mrs. Corey's whore house near the fair grounds and I knew the boys in high school who got "clap" from the three whores when they went there. But Brand and I never went there. We were Good Boys, somewhat apart from the mainstream, a little snobbish, priggish, and unpopular with regular guys. For several years in Petoskey we went to the Methodist church five times on Sundays, to morning service, Sunday school, Junior League, Epworth League, and the evening sermon.

Sex was something to be shunned and Brand and I never talked much about it. There was in Petoskey a re-tired preacher who had on several occasions taken me for a ride across the snowy country in his cutter. Another boy had warned me to watch out for him. When an accident obliged us to sleep together in a farmhouse for one night, he reached out his hand early in the morning and covered my genitals. I promptly jumped out of bed and professed to be wholly uninterested in further sleep. To this day I retain a certain revulsion for the pervert or the irregular. Is that because I had in myself some latent homosexual desires which I wanted to suppress? I think not. I think if there had been any such desires in me they would have revealed themselves sometime during my twenty years of intimate life with Brand.

I was a Methodist but it never occurred to me to be specifically anti-Catholic. We lived a life separate from most of the Catholics in Petoskey simply because they went to a separate, parochial, school. We had a few

Catholics in our school too, and one of them, Chuck Foley, was our particular hero because he dared any boy in the school to fight with him. There were no takers. There were a few Jews, and somehow I began to feel a special affinity for them. They seemed interested in ideas, and they were outside the Establishment, and so was I. That feeling has lasted all the years.

But I must not read too much into those early days. We were intellectually serious but our main interest was in play. We learned to play tennis; we manipulated a $5 scow in Little Traverse Bay; we played Flinch because Grandma would not allow "gambling cards" in the house; we attended the nickelodeon in Petoskey and watched Pearl White slide down the rope to safety; we learned to play chess, which later was to become my primary recreational vice, more fascinating to me than any other game.

2. GROWING UP IN THE MIDDLE WEST

FOR OUR LAST TWO YEARS in high school Grandma took us to Detroit, where we graduated from "the largest high school in the world." We had heard of an exciting feature in Detroit Central High School, a house of representatives where students debated in imitation of the national Congress. In Detroit we lived in three rooms in an old wooden tenement with running water in the kitchen, a water closet in the back yard, and one bare electric bulb in the middle of each room. We studied hard and soon reached the top of our class. We made the school debating team and I became speaker of our house of representatives.

Brand was made class poet, by which there hangs a tale. Years later when he was at Oxford he took a walking vacation with two other Oxford students, T. S. Eliot and a third friend. To make their vacation profitable they assigned themselves a triple literary task. One was to do a poem, one a play, and one an essay. The man chosen for the poem was not T. S. Eliot but Brand. Eliot was so shy and silent about his poetry in the early days that even his most intimate friends did not know of his poetic talents. Later Bertrand Russell had him as a pupil in a philosophy seminar at Harvard and afterward Russell commented: "I did not know at the time that Eliot wrote poetry. . . . [He was] extraordinarily silent."

In describing my high school education it is hard for me to be temperate. Aside from a reading of the newspapers and our intensive work in debating, our education was almost totally irrelevant to the world in which we lived. Throughout America important things were happening.

Upton Sinclair had published *The Jungle* in 1906, and in 1907 William D. Haywood, defended by Clarence Darrow, had been acquitted of the murder of Governor Steunenberg of Idaho in what was probably the greatest labor trial in American history. In Wisconsin a short man with a bristling pompadour, Robert La Follette, had started his campaign against the railroads.

In Detroit itself, a few blocks from our school, a nervous, wiry tinkerer with bicycles, Henry Ford, had started to make "horseless carriages" that were cheap enough for common people to own. Wealthy dowagers were driving Baker electrics down Woodward Avenue but Ford wanted something different. He was experimenting with a thing called mass production by means of assembly lines and, with his higher wages, he was beginning to break down the whole concept of craft unionism.

During the year we arrived in Detroit, Edsel Ford, who went to school near us, had persuaded his father to become interested in using a Model T engine for an airplane, and the first model was constructed with a wood fuselage and a tricycle landing gear. Detroit was in turmoil in those years, with the Detroit Federation of Labor going down to defeat before the power of the Employers' Association. There was even a "May Day riot" created by the police when they attacked a demonstration of workers from the Ford factories who were protesting the prevailing wage of $1.89 a day. (Ford did not spring his $5-a-day surprise until 1914.) But none of these issues was ever brought into the classrooms of Detroit Central High School. Brand and I got up at five o'clock in the morning to bone up on Latin, German, algebra, and theoretical chemistry. There was no course in social problems or current events.

It was natural that we should go to the University of Michigan after Detroit. It was a great people's university and the tuition was only $30 a year for residents of the state. For four years at Ann Arbor, living in three off-campus rooms heated by soft-coal stoves, we cut our own hair, washed our own shirts, and ironed our own collars— the Hoover style of detachable collar was then in vogue.

Grandma cooked meals for us. I never ate a meal away from home at college until I was a senior. We almost lived in the college library and reveled in its riches, counting ourselves among the blessed of the earth and coming out somewhere near the top of our class as a result.

We were "barbs," that is to say we were openly opposed to fraternities, and we were also rather openly hostile to all the forms of social organization that seemed to distract students from study and build up a false set of competing values. Many years later, as one of the editors of *The Nation,* I wrote:

Practically every college in America has its undergraduates over-organized in a hundred varieties of "student activity" which assume a higher place in the estimation of the students than classroom distinction. In most colleges thought outside the classroom is positively unpopular. . . . At the time of graduation it is true that the college senior begins to realize the sham and insignificance of the "pep meeting," the club membership campaign, the fraternity presidency, and even the varsity letter. But then it is too late. In the last half of the senior year he will vote for Phi Beta Kappa as the one genuine distinction at college, but for his first three and a half years he would sell a thousand scholarships for one fullback's sweater.

As an appraisal of the University of Michigan in 1910–1914, that was too harsh. It was a big, bustling school, the best of the new state universities of the Middle West that had been built with taxpayers' money. It offered even to undergraduates some of the most stimulating scholars of the time. We did not, before our senior year, have personal contact with top professors outside of the lectures, but that is a failing of all big American universities. In their operating machinery they are super–high schools with advanced textbooks, taught by young scholars on the way up while the older scholars are working on "publish or perish" projects in order to guarantee their own promotion. But the lectures at Michigan were good and the library was even better, and toward the end we were given permission to roam without limit through the miles of shelves. For a bookworm there is no other privilege like that.

It was natural that Brand and I should go in for debating and oratory, and in these fields we were fortunate. Each of us won the university oratorical contest in successive years, I captained the university debating team, and by a mathematical miracle we each won in successive years the National Peace Oratorical Contest, in which almost one hundred colleges participated.

The great event of our Michigan years came in the spring of 1913 when we were juniors. The Oxford scholarships established by the will of Cecil Rhodes had become famous but they seemed very remote for most American students because an applicant in those years had to show proficiency in both Latin and Greek. Who wanted to specialize in dead languages? Certainly I didn't. But Brand studied the requirements very carefully, decided that he had a chance to win a scholarship, and spent several weary years in mastering the classics. When he came before the Rhodes scholarship committee he had the backing of many of the leading department heads of the university and he had an endorsement for his baseball skill from our baseball coach, Branch Rickey. More important, Brand had studied the philosophy situation at Oxford so carefully that when the examiners asked him why he wanted to go to Oxford to study philosophy, he did not generalize. He answered like a Socratic marvel that he wanted professor X for such and such a specialty, Professor Y for another, and so on. When he came running up the stairs of our house that afternoon and told us that he would be a Rhodes Scholar at Oxford for three years at $1500 a year, I looked at him as if I were looking at Vincent Astor. Such wealth seemed to me incredible.

We did not know, of course, that the war was coming. Brand was caught in it in the middle of his Oxford course. He spent two years with British forces in Mesopotamia and India, then came back to serve in an American medical corps, then got his M.A. at Columbia, his Ph.D. at Harvard, served Swarthmore as professor of philosophy for seventeen years, then ultimately became Sterling Professor of Philosophy at Yale. I think his oratorical training served him well. I remember visiting a class of his at Yale with six hundred students. He held them spellbound through the hour without a note, managing to discuss the most difficult philosophical problems with easy clarity.

Perhaps it was good for me that Brand won that Oxford scholarship. I was compelled to stand on my own. I became much more sociable, outgoing, and aggressive. I was almost elected president of my graduating class. Circumstances transformed me from an introvert to an extrovert. I managed to become a successful salesman during the summer months in the most difficult of all fields, the door-to-door selling of books. The books constituted the most fantastic combination of piety and hokum ever offered to guileless housewives by a college student. They were Dr. Stall's *Self and Sex Series,* bound in eight red-backed volumes and called *What a Young Boy Ought to Know, What a Young Girl Ought to Know, What a Young Man Ought to Know, What a Young Woman Ought to Know, What a Young Husband Ought to Know, What a Young Wife Ought to Know, What a Man of 45 Ought to Know,* and *What a Woman of 45 Ought to Know.*

Before I arrived in a town to sell these books, I prepared the ground very carefully. I secured from the publishers the names of all the local purchasers of any one of the books. Before I knocked at a door I had usually acquired the name of the lady of the house from the lady of the adjoining house. I would begin my spiel by saying, "Good morning, Mrs. Jones. I am a student from the University of Michigan and I am in Laingsburg on a purity crusade. May I come in and see you for a moment?"

Since I was fairly presentable and quietly courteous, I usually got in the door. I had hardly seated myself and begun my descriptive speech with pious words about informed purity when I would casually pull out from my

pocket a roll of paper about six feet long, looking very
much like a roll of toilet paper, and fling it across the
floor. "This," I would say, "is a list of the people in this
town, most of them your neighbors, who have some or all
of these books." The list was not only impressive in length;
it excited curiosity about neighbors and sex. Any prospective customer could almost always find many names she
knew. With the list came warm endorsements of the books
by the chancellor of the University of Kansas, by Judge
Ben B. Lindsey, and by a great many Protestant preachers.
Most of the prospective customers probably thought that
"Doctor" Sylvanus Stall, the author, was a medical doctor.
He was in fact a doctor of divinity, a Baptist clergyman
whose knowledge of sex was approximately equal to that
of Saint Paul. Kissing and dancing, he averred, were
dangerous for any nice girl, and a husband should not
have intercourse with his wife during pregnancy. Birth
control, of course, was not mentioned. A woman of forty-
five should be treated tenderly. Men of forty-five gradually
lost their sexual potency. When I told that to a vigorous
prospective customer of fifty, he slammed the door in my
face.

During those college years I arrived at two decisions
about myself. I would be a socialist and I would enter the
Christian ministry. In retrospect the first decision seems
entirely natural, almost inevitable; the second decision
was the worst blunder of my life.

At that particular period Christianity and socialism
constituted one sentimental meld in my thinking. When I
gave the class oration at our university commencement
I startled the august ranks of listening parents by saying
that the world needed "Christian socialism." It was an
absurd combination but I had some authority for it. Bernard
Shaw—he was my particular hero at the moment—had
written "Preface on the Prospects of Christianity" for his
Androcles and the Lion. In it, although he proclaimed that
he knew "a great deal more about economics and politics
than Jesus did," he could still invoke Jesus' spirit for his

own particular brand of social revolution by saying: "I see no way out of the world's misery but the way which would have been found by Christ's will if he had undertaken the work of a modern practical statesman."

This conditional appropriation of Jesus for the cause of socialism was quite the rage among American liberals for several years. In England R. J. Campbell and in the United States Walter Rauschenbusch served as intellectual pioneers in the Christian socialist movement. Their sentiments were as wholesome as their thinking was fuzzy. Some of them became famous, especially George R. Lunn, mayor of Schenectady, and Stitt Wilson, mayor of Berkeley, California.

H. G. Wells had a profound influence on me at that time. His *A Modern Utopia* fitted into the mood of the period. I was even more impressed with an essay on sociology that Wells had produced, partly because I was considering sociology as a career. Wells proposed to dump the sociological theories of the past and make sociology into the science of the future. Man, he argued, should devote his energies consciously to building utopias. What was intelligence for?

That line of thinking, of course, had been suggested by Edward Bellamy in his *Looking Backward* in 1888, a very poor book but a great sociological romance. I was romantic in my approach to the scheme of things partly because my Christianity was very romantic. I had read a few pages of Karl Marx and listened to my economics professor, Fred Taylor, "demolish" Marxism in three easy lectures, but both Marx and Taylor left me rather cold. The forces moving me toward socialism were outside the textbooks. The period of my college life, 1910 to 1914, was a period of prodigious restlessness in America and I shared in the restlessness.

The great Triangle fire in New York in 1911 had resulted in the death of 146 persons and the exposure of the American sweatshop. The IWW, gaining a membership of at least fifty thousand, had been partially successful in a textile strike in Lawrence, Massachusetts, in 1912, where the Italian poet Arturo Giovannitti (later my friend) had gone to prison on a framed-up murder charge. In the Ludlow Massacre of September 1913, following the refusal of the Rockefeller interests to accept unionization, some twenty-five persons had been killed, including eleven children and two women. In the election campaign of 1912 Teddy Roosevelt tore party establishments to pieces in his fight against Wilson and Taft, carrying Michigan with his confused patchwork of "reformed" democracy.

Down in a dirty little hall in Ann Arbor I attended a Socialist Party meeting and heard an eloquent speech by a former clergyman, Alexander Irvine. He could not find a hall on the campus in those days for a socialist speech. A few months later I joined the Socialist Party and I retained my membership most of the time for nineteen years until 1933, when I joined the La Guardia administration in New York.

It is hard for me now to understand why I chose the ministry as a career. It was, I suppose, partly my father's image and partly the constant pressure of that Methodist upbringing. Also I had been captured by an eloquent, deep-voiced general secretary of the student YMCA, and he had made me president of the University of Michigan YMCA, in which post I bustled around actively and importantly, with my own stationery, my own office, and considerable publicity. Youth can be bought by subtle flattery and the sense of being useful. My experience at that time helped me later to understand how Catholic priests win recruits for their profession from boys of fifteen, who are evangelized into a world of illusion by older men who have themselves been evangelized into a world of illusion.

I think sexual continence had something to do with it. Also I am not sure I would have been inveigled into the ministry if I had had plenty of money to go on with secular graduate study. I wanted to take graduate work at Princeton but I lacked the money. Harvard Divinity School offered me everything free. Thus sex—or the absence of it—Christian socialism, and poverty all united to start me in the wrong profession. The Michigan history professors asked me to come back and serve as an instructor in American history but I surrendered to the evangelistic impulse.

Love did come, but it came too late to head me off from that mis-choice. It came at the end of my senior year, in the springtime. She was sitting in an upstairs seminar room in the old college library one afternoon. She and I were the only persons left at a great, round study table. She dropped her pencil and I picked it up. She smiled broadly and thanked me. She apparently knew who I was, but I had never seen her before. She had light brown hair and warm brown eyes and a slender beautiful figure.

We started talking to each other and we talked and talked. Miraculously, three nights later, we sat next to each other when we were both inaugurated into Phi Beta Kappa: The name of Julia Sweet Anderson was alphabetically next to that of Paul Beecher Blanshard. She was the orphaned daughter of an Illinois Congressman, George Anderson, who had been district attorney of Quincy, Illinois. I was rather frightened when I found that she belonged to one of the more posh sororities, but she was apparently as poor as I was and shared my ideas.

Somehow I summoned the courage to ask her to go for a walk with me one night, and she said yes. Three weeks later, after much poetry reading from the *Oxford Book of English Verse* and a little holding of hands, she said another and more important yes—to our marriage. I had never even kised her—or any other girl—until the afternoon when she said yes, and even then I never went beyond the fondling of her soft young breasts. I was a very proper and a very good boy, and she, with a Presbyterian background, was almost as proper as I was. We found that the double miracle in our meeting was geographic. Before we met we had both arranged to be in Boston the next year, only a few miles apart, she with the Curtis Publishing Company and I at Harvard Divinity School. Fate, we agreed, must have had something to do with that.

3. MARRIAGE AND MAVERICK CHURCH

THE HARVARD WHICH I ENTERED in the fall of 1914 was not a serene place in which to settle my troubled doubts about religion. The war had made repose and reflection seem almost like a cowardly escape. Some of my fellow divinity students quit the seminary to fight in France and one of my classmates was killed there.

The student body in the Divinity School was very small, but the great names of Harvard's faculty were still available. The historical associations of the place awed me. Emerson's room was just down the corridor from mine in Divinity Hall. William James had died and Santayana was away, but Josiah Royce was there. Suffering from a stroke, Royce still managed to limp across the Yard several times a week, looking like an unemployed janitor, and talk to our small class in philosophy with the lucidity of a master.

I soon realized that, although the technical level of scholarship in the seminary was very high, the whole seminary teaching process was based on verbal evasions. The institution was what Mark Twain would have called a theological cemetery. The professors were "objective" in presenting facts. They never drew the logical conclusions from those facts, the conclusions that would have downgraded Christianity. My church history professor described quite candidly all the silly little theological quarrels that had split the Christian church in earlier centuries, and then he proceeded to appeal to "the unity of Our Lord." He did not dare to go even as far as Gibbon had gone in his famous chapter on Christianity in *The Decline and Fall of the Roman Empire*. His tone was consistently reverential.

He was helping to train men to occupy pulpits with congregations of believers, and there had to be some remainder of acceptable myths for the congregations to chew on.

I suppose I would have abandoned the idea of the ministry almost immediately if it had not been for a great surge of activity, a substitute for thought. I started practice preaching in the Andover chapel with other students and found, somewhat to my surprise, that I could preach easily. I fell into the biblical rhythms without strain. My long saturation in religious ceremonies and studies had paid off. I could even run off glibly and ad-lib the "haths" and "doths" of traditional Protestant prayer.

It was the tradition at the seminary for students to place themselves for Sunday work as ministerial assistants at some church in the Boston area. For me it was a big "socialist" Congregational church in East Boston directed by a dynamic young radical, Albert Rhys Williams. I was delighted beyond words when Williams, shortly after I entered Harvard, asked me to be his assistant at $10 a week. The name of his church was the Maverick Congregational Church, named for a Congregational benefactor, not for a stray calf. Oddly enough, the name came into public prominence many years later when it was disclosed that Joseph P. Kennedy had become the youngest bank president in the United States and that his bank was located on Maverick Square in East Boston.

East Boston, once the island home of many of Boston's wealthy Wasps, had degenerated economically over the years until it was a slum, and the population had changed from Congregationalist to Catholic. Williams, a big eloquent preacher of Welsh descent, had temporarily saved his church by transforming it into a kind of labor temple with a Sunday night service operated like an open forum. There was applause for the lecturers and questions from the floor.

Almost immediately Williams heaped heavy responsibilities upon me, asking me to preach frequently in his place. I was too young for such a role and the memory of it has left scars upon me. To this day my most gruesome nightmare concerns Maverick Church and a sermon I am trying to deliver to a fading congregation. I am talking glibly when suddenly I notice that my notes have disappeared. While groping for them I extemporize frantically. The congregation displays signs of restlessness and starts to walk out. I wake up in a cold sweat, feeling like Coleridge's Ancient Mariner.

But in those first awful months in the pulpit I did learn a number of useful things about preaching. I learned that the method of speech may be almost as important as the content, at least for the average congregation. The quiet, confident delivery is all-important. Even if a preacher reads his sermon, he must not appear to read it. I agreed with Sydney Smith in his attack on "the stale indignation" of written sermons: "Pulpit discourses have insensibly dwindled from speaking to reading; a practice of itself sufficient to stifle every germ of eloquence. It is only by the fresh feeling of the heart that mankind can be powerfully affected." I never wrote out a sermon in my life but I learned to prepare it as carefully as if I had written and memorized the text. Every Saturday night before preaching I would take my notes into the large empty church, stand up in the pulpit, and talk my sermon with only the Irish Catholic janitor as an audience. While he dusted the pews, I would talk from my notes until every phrase was indelibly impressed on my memory.

My work at Maverick Church soon became so engrossing that I moved over to a room in East Boston and returned to Cambridge only for classes. Soon Williams left his pulpit and I served as full-time acting chief minister of the church for more than a year. I chose to join the Socialist Party of Boston rather than the Harvard Socialist Club, although I had heard many good things about the club's first president, Walter Lippmann.

I preached more socialism than Christianity in my first year in the pulpit, relying more on Bernard Shaw and H. G. Wells than on Saint Paul. This combination of Christianity and socialism had become fairly common among young clergymen in that pre-war period. David Shannon in his book on the American Socialist Party says that in the pre-war years "practically all Socialists were in a sense Christian Socialists" and that in 1908 there were three hundred American clergymen in the Clergymen's Socialist Alliance. I joined that alliance in 1915 and carried an alliance sign in the Boston May Day parade. After I was arrested by an East Boston policeman and held in jail for a few hours for "obstructing the traffic" by picketing in a knit-workers' strike, I preached a sermon to the strikers on "How to Be a Millionaire," which quite accurately represents the blend of naïveté and dedication of my first year in the pulpit. This part was quoted in a Boston paper:

Millionaires are more dangerous than anarchists. The anarchist tries to wreck society from the bottom, the millionaire crushes society from the top. Once it was an honor to be a millionaire, but that time has gone by.

There are three ways of being a millionaire: to be born one, to be lucky or to steal. Most millionaires steal. The system in which we live is responsible for the thieving by the millionaires. In that system gambling is at a premium, labor is at a discount and wrong is more precious than human life. While a small circle of millionaires in Wall Street control billions of dollars, the average American workingman is starving himself and his family on less than $600 a year.

The church of Jesus Christ must choose between the millionaire and the workingman. It cannot serve God and Mammon. Like the priest and the levite in the parable of the Good Samaritan, the preachers and the church members pass by on the other side while the laboring man is being robbed by the capitalists, the politicians, and the courts. The church must learn that salvation begins with boots and bread and that a Christian has as much right in a strike as in a prayer meeting.

After that the New England Socialist Party sent me into several strikes as a kind of clerical agitator. During one of these forays I had my first contact with Bartolomeo Vanzetti. In that bitter winter, a great strike had broken out in one of New England's largest mills, owned by the Plymouth Cordage Company. It was a spontaneous strike without formal leadership. The striking workers had become polarized into three competing groups, affiliated with the American Federation of Labor, the Industrial Workers of the World, and the Italian anarchists. Informally the strikers were asking for a minimum wage of $8 a week for women and $12 for men for a ten-hour day. The company, refusing to yield to the demands had hired strikebreakers and armed guards at $5 a day and expenses. When I arrived in Plymouth the situation was very ugly. The *Boston Post* called me "the head of the strikers," but I was nothing more than an intervening agitator.

After talking to all factions in the strike and also to the employers, I decided that the strike had no future because of the divisions among the workers, and I stood up at a great mass meeting of two thousand strikers in a skating rink and recommended that the strikers accept the offer of the employers of a five percent wage increase and a guarantee against punishment for any striker. Far over in one corner of the skating rink a small man with a walrus mustache stood up and made a speech against me while I was speaking. "The Reverend Blanshard," he said, was a "mere reformer." He was "joosta sama priest" who would sell out the workers or ride on their backs. They told me that he was an anarchist and that his name was Vanzetti. I won the strikers' vote and he lost.

When he died in the electric chair in August 1927, along with Nicola Sacco, for the murder of a payroll employee in South Braintree, I was as horrified as the next liberal by the anti-alien prejudice evoked by the case. But I was not quite so ready as some of my friends to recognize sainthood in Italian anarchists. Upton Sinclair himself, who described the strike in his novel *Boston,* later leaned to the notion that perhaps Sacco was guilty. Ballistic evidence produced after the trial seemed to show that the chief murder victim could have been killed by a bullet from Sacco's revolver. Sacco and Vanzetti were both carrying loaded revolvers when they were first arrested, and their first explanations were confused and contradictory. They admitted at the trial that they had lied repeatedly.

As the war approached in 1915, the peace forces were badly divided. The American Socialist Party was firmly opposed to our entrance into the European war, and our leaders were puzzled and horrified when the socialist parties of Europe, which had made so many anti-war pledges, quickly succumbed to nationalistic appeals and joined their respective national armies. We had a difficult time explaining to nonsocialists this collapse of international sentiment among European Socialists. The German Social-Democrats had been admired by American Socialists as the most successful of the European Socialist pioneers not only because they had built a large political party but also because the threat of their power had been partly responsible for the advanced social legislation developed under Bismarck. Now these very Socialists had failed to rally the German working class in the move to stop the war. Some of their leaders had become German chauvinists.

The defection of the French Socialists was almost as horrifying. We American Socialists tried to explain away these defections as the result of capitalist pressure. We made a great hero of Jean Jaurès, France's most eminent Socialist, who was murdered in 1914 as a direct reprisal for his anti-war evangelism. But how few Socialists there were in Europe who had the courage of Jaurès! When war came, all their international sentiment seemed to be incinerated in national chauvinism. Red flags stood in the corners of virtually every Socialist headquarters in Europe. But when war came they were thrown out, and the comrades died for national honor.

The executive of the American Socialist Party held true to its standard position in August 1914 when it declared that true socialists were opposed "to this and all other

wars, waged upon any pretext whatever." In 1916 the
party nominated for the presidency a relatively obscure
journalist, Allan L. Benson, whose chief claim to leadership was that he had written good anti-war editorials in
the old *Appeal to Reason*. At one time during his campaign
Benson even suggested that if war came, any legislator
who voted for war should be conscripted first, which served
to remind the public that in most wars old men send young
men to die for them.

In the middle of all this furor Julia married me. Probably it saved my life since I was losing weight from over-
work and my digestive processes were almost in a state of
collapse. Years later X-rays seemed to show that I had had
a touch of tuberculosis.

We bought some second-hand furniture with $300 I
had won in a Harvard essay contest and moved into the
upstairs flat of an old wooden tenement in East Boston.
We were a little disturbed by the "luxury" which we were
accepting on my salary of $1500 a year. A government
report had just been issued showing that the average
American factory worker got only $15 a week. Was it
moral for us to take more? We finally decided that we
could accept the $1500 scale of living because we were
acting for the church and the church needed a ministerial
establishment with "luxury."

We decided also that it was wrong for us to be married
with the usual Christian pledges. We had seen a copy of a
document called "Marriage Ceremony for Revolutionists,"
put out by an Episcopal socialist clergyman, Bouck White,
who had presented Jesus as a socialist in his book *The Call
of the Carpenter*. He had once gone to jail on Blackwell's
Island for invading a Rockefeller Baptist church. In his
revolutionists' ceremony, the bride and groom pledged to
live together only as long as love should last. I found an
Episcopal socialist clergyman in Philadelphia who was
willing to marry us with this ceremony and he read it all
with such singsong clerical solemnity that nobody in the

audience realized the revolutionary significance of his words. In a sense we were buying term insurance for our marriage instead of a straight life policy, but the variation was recorded in such small print that nobody bothered to read it.

After all this juvenile and "advanced" gerrymandering, our honeymoon was a farce. I had taken Sylvanus Stall and his ideas about "hurting" your bride too seriously, and it was more than a week before we accomplished what the Catholics call "consummation." It was many years before I was to realize that such honeymoon messes are very common among young people, especially among religious young people, and that they sometimes do permanent damage to sexual adjustment. Studies seem to indicate that sexual failure is twenty percent higher for women with husbands who have come to marriage as virgins than it is for women who come to their honeymoons with experienced mates.

But I soon made up in zeal for what I lacked in knowledge. And there could not have been a more suitable wife for me than Julia. She joined me on picket lines, attended labor mass meetings, and with me signed up in the Socialist Party. After the restraints of my boyhood with Grandma it seemed to me an amazing and blessed miracle that I had a woman who loved me both day and night, who shared my longings of mind and body, and who fed me better than I had ever been fed before. And the congregation loved her shining personality as much as I did.

Julia helped me to bring many famous women to Maverick Church. Perhaps the most important was Margaret Sanger, who became a warm personal friend for fifty years. I think that our East Boston church was the first church in which she spoke after serving a short term in a New York jail where she had been put at the behest of Cardinal Hayes. (I ridiculed the Cardinal by quoting his famous pronouncement: "Children troop down from Heaven because God wills it.")

Although Margaret was nearly scared to death whenever she had to make a speech to a large audience, she almost always captivated her audiences completely. She was pert and winning in her nurselike approach. She did not, however, dare to mention a single contraceptive article in her speeches. This was Boston, the most benighted Catholic city in the United States, where birth control was to be "against God's law" until the 1950's. Even I, in my fervid speeches for birth control, did not once attack the Catholic Church directly for its campaigns of calumny and misrepresentation about birth control. When a Protestant-Catholic dispute about birth control broke out in Boston in 1916, I pontificated in the *New England Socialist:* "War, religious bigotry and industrial despotism are the three great opponents of free speech. Instead of fighting each other, Catholics and Protestants should fight these great enemies of society."

I was a little more forthright when a wealthy young man, Van Kleeck Allison, was arrested by the Boston police for "disseminating obscene literature" in the form of a pamphlet favoring birth control. I presided at a mass meeting for him in our church and helped to form "The Allison Birth Control League," with Stuart Chase as treasurer. I think that Boston's Superintendent of Police Crowley, who had announced that he was determined to protect the purity of the city's working girls, was a little startled when, at the Allison trial, the courtroom was packed with some of the most famous professors, clergymen, and social workers in America.

The upper class had started to move into the birth control battle and even the Hearst newspapers began to change their tune. Hearst's Boston daily actually carried a special article from me under the heading "Pastor Blanshard Declares Persons of Education and Wealth Have Long Been Informed; Asks Free Speech." "If the truth were made public," I proclaimed, "and the laws which prevent the spreading of even oral information about birth control were strictly enforced, how few of the married society leaders, judges, doctors, ministers, and business men would be outside the prison dock! . . . the mothers of the poor are kept in such complete ignorance that they believe the whole subject is obscene."

In these days when acceptance of birth control is almost universal it is hard to realize how successfully the Catholic Church frightened the politicians and even many Protestant leaders in the birth control controversy in the early years. The principal Boston newspapers and major radio stations refused to accept dignified advertisements calling for the revision of the antiquated Massachusetts law. The Catholic hierarchy of Holyoke prevented an address on the subject by Margaret Sanger at the First Congregational Church at that city by threatening a boycott of Congregational businessmen. The leading Catholic priest of Springfield, Massachusetts, announced, "Margaret Sanger with her pail of filth . . . is coming to interfere with the laws of our Commonwealth. She is coming to enlist the aid of dog-loving women in changing the fundamental laws of our state."

In her early years Margaret Sanger was far more anti-Catholic than I was. She had come from a free-thought environment. Her father was an Irish socialist and friend of Robert Ingersoll, and she was quite realistic about the timidity of clergymen, both Catholic and Protestant. Her anti-Catholicism endured even into the Kennedy administration. During the 1960 presidential campaign she announced that if Kennedy should be elected President she would leave the country. She could not believe that a member of the Catholic Church would give the birth control movement fair treatment. When she saw how reasonable Kennedy was as President, she decided to change her plans and remain in the United States for another year and "see what happens."

It was at Maverick Church that I first knew Helen Keller, when she accepted our invitations to speak for our congregation several times. My old Michigan classmate Peter Fagan, who had been a reporter on the *Boston Herald,* was then serving as her secretary. Under his influence Helen had become both a pacifist and a socialist. Anne Sullivan Macy, who was beginning to break away from her literary husband, John Macy, was sympathetic with left-wing pacifist thought and quite ready to help Helen in her progress as a radical speaker. We were in the war period, but before America's entry, when Helen proclaimed: "Let no workingman join the army that is to be organized by order of Congress. . . . [The army] has already proved itself an enemy of liberty. It is an army that can be used to break strikes as well as to defend the people. . . . I look upon the world as my fatherland and every war has for me the horror of a family feud." My own socialist pacifism was only a little less naïve than that.

On July 4, 1915, two months after the sinking of the *Lusitania,* I persuaded more than one hundred members of my Sunday evening congregation to sign an anti-war pledge which read: "I pledge myself as a Christian never to enlist in any army or navy, or to assist any army or navy in murdering my brothers." It was not surprising that the *Army and Navy Journal,* coupling me with John Haynes Holmes, who had promoted a similar pledge in New York, declared: "Any man who attempts, without justification, to prevent or discourage the high duty of sharing in the public defense casts the gravest possible doubt upon his fitness to guide or advise the young in any respect." The *New London Telegraph* put it more bluntly. Its editorial was headed "Traitors."

4. TAMPA, GOD, AND WAR

AFTER I HAD SERVED for more than a year as the acting head minister of Maverick Church, it was natural that the Congregational home mission board which helped to finance the church should suggest that I return to the seminary, complete my theological education, and seek regular ordination. The board, composed largely of conservatives, had been very charitable to me. It was unusual to give as much authority to one who had not even completed his full theological course.

Also there were some misgivings about my open Socialist partisanship. I had gone even further than my predecessor, Albert Rhys Williams, in identifying the church with left-wing labor. One of my sermon topics, plastered on the large signboard in front of the church, was "Socialism and the Kingdom of God," and in that sermon I equated the two quite consistently. I quoted Karl Marx to the effect that "The social principles of Christianity preach cowardice, self-contempt, abasement, submission, humility, in short all the qualities of the canaille," but I was careful to point out that *that* type of Christianity was not mine. I preached the romantic Jesus of social revolution.

The thought of returning to the seminary full time filled me with dismay. Theological classroom work seemed utterly irrelevant in my new world of strikes and pacifism. Should I abandon the ministry altogether? Julia made no attempt to influence me one way or another. She had no religion herself but she was scrupulously fair to my conglomerate socialist-Christian faith. Like me, she had a more firm allegiance to socialism than to Christianity.

I was miraculously saved from the dilemma of my split faith by Dr. Henry Atkinson, then national head of the social service division of the Congregational Church. He told me one day of a church in the South which was looking for a socialist minister, or at least a minister with socialist leanings. It was the First Congregational Church of Tampa, Florida, and—double miracle—it not only had a largely socialist congregation but it had an endowment, left by some innocent philanthropist who had never imagined that in the South any church could become infected with anything so nasty as socialism. Atkinson thought that with my biblical studies at Michigan and my work at Harvard I could be ordained in Florida without more training. (I actually completed my seminary work later on at Union Seminary.) The congregation wanted me. I accepted the bizarre opportunity with a whoop and left East Boston on a coast-wise steamship in 1916 for one of the most novel assignments ever offered a young clergyman.

Tampa was then a bustling boom city afflicted with land speculators, mosquitoes, and terrific heat. It was bursting at the seams with a conglomerate population of Florida "crackers," northern escapees, Cuban cigar makers, and Negro helpers. The city, of course, was racially segregated, but segregation could not be absolute because of the many Cubans of mixed ancestry who were needed to make cigars. Cubans were usually consigned to live in a partially segregated section known as Ybor City, where their status was similar to that of the Puerto Ricans of today in New York City.

Somehow the simplistic socialism of Eugene Debs had penetrated part of the working class of this city. A Socialist local had been started and the movement had grown swiftly because of the seething discontent over high prices produced by the war in Europe. When reports of political corruption rocked the local Democratic machine, the Socialists jumped into the political breach and almost elected a mayor who, incidentally, was treasurer of the church which I was to serve. The Socialists, in the interim between pastors, had moved in and "captured" the church, electing their own board of trustees and holding their meetings in the church basement. The church membership was all white but its social gospel was multi-racial.

The ruling white churches of Tampa, dominated by the Southern Baptists, were fundamentalist in theology and stand-pat in economics. Their ministers looked at me and my church with raised eyebrows, not knowing what to make of such a northern heretic. Congregationalism was at a disadvantage because it was known as a northern religion, and socialism was in the same class as communism and anarchy. Socialists were also villains because they opposed preparedness, and the United States in 1916 was aflame with preparedness sentiment.

Julia and I moved into this troubled atmosphere with all the confidence of romantic youth. In the operation of the church I transferred—or tried to transfer—to this Southern city all the techniques I had used in a labor temple in Boston. There were mass meetings with sensational liberal themes, publicity in the local papers and vigorous participation in every local movement for social reform. I became a noisy social catalyst in the community. Fortunately, the local editors regarded me as such a refreshing sensation that for a time they gave me all the publicity I wanted, a headline almost every Monday morning with a pointed attack on something or other. The old-line preachers in the city never took the pains to market their wares in journalistic form. I beat them to it by typing out the most newsworthy parts of my sermons every Sunday night and taking the carefully finished copy personally to the city editor of the leading daily. Usually he had some unfilled space to assign to my philippics, and the result was that I gained for my church an importance out of all proportion to the size of its congregation.

Usually I concentrated on social problems but sometimes I wandered over into the field of straight theological heresy. "Doctrine of Hell Is an Insult to Deity," proclaimed one of my first headlines. "God is not a policeman," I said with great assurance. "The doctrine of hell makes Him more vindictive than Nero. If you had a child that disobeyed you and questioned your authority, would you take that child into the cellar, build a big fire in the furnace and throw him in?" This was rather strong meat for a state where Jesus-saves evangelism was so popular that some public schools were dismissed in order to allow their pupils to attend Protestant revivals. (William Jennings Bryan had already begun to serve as a salesman for Florida real estate and the Bible as early as 1915.)

When the Tampa Ministers' Association staged a big cooperative revival under fundamentalist auspices, I refused to unite in the project although I was a member of the association. I rented a tent formerly used by Pentecostal evangelists and conducted an opposition "revival" of my own, calling it a Social Service Revival. Speaking nightly for a week to large audiences, I ridiculed Billy Sunday and advocated social reconstruction to eliminate poverty and racial injustice. I ranged over the whole field of social reform from "Graft and Patent Medicines" to "America Starving."

In the midst of all this clamor came my ordination. All things considered, it is quite remarkable that I was ordained at all. The Congregational clergymen of southern Florida were summoned to my church by Dr. Henry Atkinson to pass judgment on my fitness for the Christian ministry. There is no doubt that I was unfit, but when I was examined in an open hearing the ministers failed to ask those questions that would have exposed my unfitness. No one asked me if I believed in the Virgin birth—I did not— or in the bodily resurrection of Jesus—I did not—or in the complete uniqueness of Jesus—I did not. Instead, the ministers happened to ask me several questions on theology and church history which, by pure chance, I was prepared to answer quite correctly and with an adequate display of ecclesiastical learning. As I knelt at the end of the proceedings to become, by the laying on of hands, the Reverend Paul Blanshard, I had such an inner sense of tension and conflict that I almost stood up and said: Look here,

gentlemen, I agree with your moral aspirations and I love
the concept of the church as a center for moral discussion,
but I am much more of a heretic than you think and I
really don't belong with your bunch at all.

Later on I was to discover that a large proportion of
young ministers come to ordination with the doubts I had.
They balance their intellectual misgivings against their
potential usefulness in a moral institution and the intellect
usually comes out second best. After all, man is only partially a reasoning animal.

I buried my doubts temporarily in very strenuous activity. I led a parade of grim and hungry Cubans from Ybor
City to the City Hall, demanding from frightened members
of the city council some drastic measures to halt the rising
cost of living. I launched a newsletter on labor issues and
sent it free to all the labor weeklies in the Southeast. I
published a raucous pamphlet called "Why Workingmen
Hate the Church," with the picture "The Carpenter of
Nazareth" by Art Young on the cover.

Tampa at that time had a large and official vice district,
and I pointed out in the press that the evil was tied up
with segregation as well as with poverty; the houses of
prostitution "were backed up against Negro churches and
Negro schools." I cited the statement of a Tampa physician
that ninety percent of Tampa's Negroes had venereal disease. But I had almost no personal contact with the isolated and desperately poor Negro community.

Midway through my experience in Tampa, my old
friend and Michigan classmate Peter Fagan came to visit
us and announced that he was planning to elope with
Helen Keller. Helen was staying with her family at their
home in Alabama and, according to Peter, was ready and
anxious to marry him but was being held a virtual prisoner by family members who opposed the marriage. She
had no way of telling the outside world what she really
wanted because all communication by mail or otherwise
was controlled by the family rulers.

Peter and Helen had "secretly" taken out a marriage

license in Massachusetts before Peter had come down to
Tampa, but when a Boston reporter found out about the
license and published the news, Helen's mother ordered
"the upstart" Peter out of the house. Helen, totally blind
and deaf, apparently continued to want marriage with
Peter but was helpless to carry out her wishes. Although
Peter had successfully served her as assistant and secretary, the family regarded him as an unemployed adven-
turer who wanted to exploit her. It is true that Peter, about
seven years her junior—she was thirty-six at the time—
was not technically employed at the time he came to
Tampa and had no cash reserves. He had to borrow money
from me for his marital project. But he was not without
prospects and he had great plans for Helen's future, which
might have given her even more fame and influence than
she ultimately attained. He was a brilliant intellectual,
perhaps the most brilliant in my time at Michigan, and
later on he was to achieve success as an editor and public
official in his home state.

Peter's plan was to "kidnap" his willing Helen from her
Alabama house on a Sunday morning when almost everybody was at church. The plot was arranged by correspondence between them, using a simple secret code. They
innocently imagined that the code would not be deciphered
by the family because it was done in Braille and the meaning was "disguised" by striking each key on the Braille
typewriter just to the right of the key which showed the
real meaning of the letter. Apparently this rather juvenile
technique of camouflage was quickly decoded by some
guardian in the Keller household, but no one told Helen
that her secret was known.

Since I had not yet been ordained when the great "kid-
naping" was planned, I secured as the prospective officiat-
ing clergyman for the marriage ceremony my friend Dr.
George Waldron, then superintendent of the south Florida
Congregational churches. Peter and Waldron went off in
an automobile to Alabama all ready to "capture" the willing
bride on her family's porch, spirit her away to a legal

wedding, and then bring her to our parsonage. They drove up and down, up and down, in front of the Keller porch for hours on a Sunday morning but no Helen appeared. No Helen ever appeared, and Peter came back to Tampa utterly discouraged.

The full, tragic story of Helen and Peter has never before been told, although Helen herself published some parts of the Boston end of the story without ever using Peter's name. Peter lived for a time in the Macy-Keller house in Wrentham, Massachusetts, as a public relations specialist. Late in 1916 Anne Sullivan Macy was suddenly taken ill and had to be rushed to a hospital while Mrs. Macy's assistant, Miss Thompson, was away. Peter became Helen's sole assistant for several weeks. He had mastered her finger language perfectly and a great rapport had developed between them. One night, holding her hand in conversation, Peter began telling her that he loved her and wanted to make her career his life work. At first she was shocked, then her whole attitude changed.

She described the change in her own words later: "His love was a bright sun that shone upon my helplessness and isolation. The sweetness of being loved enchanted me, and I yielded to an imperious longing to be part of a man's life. For a brief space I danced in and out of the gates of Heaven, wrapped up in a web of bright imaginings." She wanted to tell both her mother and Mrs. Macy of the new miracle of love but Peter dissuaded her and asked for delay in the announcement. He knew that Mrs. Keller detested him and his ideas: Was he not a socialist who wore a flowing black tie?

When the story of the Keller-Fagan marriage license was printed in a Boston paper, Helen, in a desperate panic over the thought that her beloved mother would be brokenhearted, chose to deny the whole story. Her mother spirited her away to the family home in Alabama without even telling the bedridden Anne Macy anything about the great love secret.

Before Helen died in 1968 at the age of eighty-seven,

she said quite bitterly that if she had ever been able to see she would have married "first of all." She wanted love and she wanted children and she was deprived of both by the conventional prejudices of her mother. Peter Fagan, with all his shortcomings, might have turned out to be the "bright sun" she needed to illumine a darkened life.

The period in Tampa was for me a period of great intellectual agony in two respects. I did not know what to do about the war when it actually came, and I did not know what to do about continuing as a clergyman in a Christian church. During 1916 and 1917, before America entered the war, the propaganda against the Kaiser and the German atrocities increased in intensity month by month. It became more and more dangerous to support the Socialist position, particularly in the South.

In the election of 1916 we dutifully voted for Allan L. Benson but our hearts were with Woodrow Wilson in his bitter struggle with Charles Evans Hughes. After all, there was a great deal of sense in supporting Wilson against Hughes on the basis of Wilson's published statements. In 1914 he had described the war as a "war with which we have nothing to do." Early in 1916 he had said, "I pledge you my word that, God helping me, I will keep this nation out of war if it is possible."

Julia and I were so anxious to see Wilson elected that we almost forgot our doctrinaire Socialist obligations in the crisis. On election night we stood up all night in Tampa's chief public square to watch the returns come in on the giant screen where stereopticon slides recorded the fluctuating electoral tides—first Wilson, then Hughes, then Wilson, then apparently Hughes for sure. Hughes went to bed thinking that he was the next President of the United States, but California changed the result.

We did not know then that within a few weeks Wilson would be promoting a great national preparedness drive and that he would be primarily responsible for getting us into the war which, fifty years later, Archibald MacLeish described as "the most murderous, hypocritical, unnecessary, and generally nasty of all recorded wars." I did not know enough about the origins of the war and the manipulations in Washington to pass such a judgment on it at that time, and neither did MacLeish, who joined the army himself in a burst of patriotism that engulfed most of us liberals.

The war "information" that flooded America in 1916 and 1917 was heavily loaded with pro-British propaganda. The German apologists were not granted equal time or equal consideration. Germany's announcement of unrestricted submarine warfare on February 1, 1917, was a frightful blunder, but the German policy was not wholly without technical justification. As Senator George Norris, one of the six Senators who finally voted against the American declaration of war, pointed out on the floor of the Senate, the United States "had accepted the defined British war zones and refrained from sending American ships into them. On the other hand, American ships had insisted on steaming into German war zones and so into German torpedoes." In truth, the United States government was never genuinely neutral in 1916 and 1917.

In the winter and spring of 1916–1917 most of the churches in both the North and the South and most of the great labor unions swung over to support a declaration of war against Germany. Dr. Lyman Abbott called the anti-war Senators "escariots." In Beecher's old church in Brooklyn, on a "War Sunday," Newell Dwight Hillis preached a sermon "Why We Should Go to War with Germany." More than 150 New York City churches came out for conscription. Samuel Gompers swung his American Federation of Labor to the support of a pro-war resolution.

In Tampa nearly all the ministers were caught up in the war fever, especially after several American steamers had been sunk by German submarines with the loss of the lives of women and children. I preached against our entrance into the war all through the winter and spring of 1916–1917 and praised the intransigence of the "little group of willful men," led by La Follette and Norris, who blocked the move to arm American merchant ships. I quoted Norris as saying: "We are going into war on the command of gold. . . . I feel that we are about to put a dollar sign on the American flag."

When the United States actually entered the war in April 1917, this kind of propaganda was too much for the Tampa newspapers to take. At first I kept right on talking in this way. When the drive for the first Liberty Loan began in June, I did not buy any bonds myself and I supported, in the name of American liberty, the right of a local German-born shipowner to refrain from buying them. This marked my demise as a decent citizen. A quiet boycott against me began. My congregation dwindled. The city editor of the leading Tampa daily informed me that he had been glad to get my stimulating sermons as part of his Monday morning copy, but "We do not condone treason." For several months my name was unmentionable in the Tampa papers.

In those agonizing months I was not certain in my own mind what my course should be. The constant pounding of one-sided Allied propaganda shook my convictions. At times the verbal magic of Wilson's rhetoric mesmerized me. Letters from Brand affected me. He was then with the British troops in Asia and he strongly emphasized the moral superiority of the Allied cause. The word "slacker," entering the American language about that time, made me wince. Was I evading my moral responsibility in clinging to a doctrinaire Socialist position?

At that moment came conscription, with compulsory registration for all males between twenty-one and thirty, and my name was listed in the first call for the draft. Should I be a conscientious objector? I had been a secular pacifist but never a religious pacifist; perhaps I should have been labeled a semi-Marxist pacifist. I didn't know what would happen to me if I appeared at a draft board as a conscientious objector, at that time the laws about conscientious objectors were very much muddled. I felt like a trapped animal looking for a door out of a cage.

At twenty-four I was a reasonably able-bodied young man who had no children to support. Julia could, if necessary, have supported herself. Finally I decided to register for the draft but to claim freedom from conscription under the provision exempting ordained ministers in active church service. For me it was a most humiliating course because I had never believed in extending special civil privileges to clergymen. I was promptly exempted, and I felt profoundly ashamed of myself.

The Socialist Party at that time was going through some of the same torments that afflicted me. It developed a split personality in regard to the war. For several months, even after America's declaration of war, the party maintained its intransigent opposition. Its famous St. Louis resolution, passed a few days after America's entrance to the war, branded the war as "a crime against the people of the United States" forced upon the people by "the capitalist class." Morris Hillquit, the most important leader of the party at that time, remained formally anti-war. When he ran for mayor of New York City in 1917 on an anti-war platform, he polled 145,000 votes, nearly 100,000 more votes than the Republican candidate. He helped to father the anti-war resolution at St. Louis along with Eugene Debs and Victor Berger. But a great many of the party's most important leaders resigned in protest, including Upton Sinclair, Jack London, J. G. Phelps Stokes, Charles Edward Russell, and William English Walling. Gene Debs remained firm and ultimately went to a federal prison for ten years for opposing the draft. From prison he ran for President in 1920 and polled 900,000 votes.

Our little Socialist local in Tampa kept on faithfully opposing the war but we could never tell when we held a meeting whether some new and enthusiastic member was a government spy. Throughout the Southeast the labor unions were virtually unanimous in support of the government. Since I had been identified as a war-resister, my labor newsletter suddenly died.

In spite of all these agonies I think I would have stayed in the Tampa pulpit if it had not been for other difficulties.

The congregation was most kind and asked me by unanimous vote to continue as pastor. I finally decided to leave for a very odd reason: I read the New Testament through carefully for the first time in my life, trying to read each passage with the independence of mind of an outsider or unbeliever. This may sound like a startling confession for an ordained clergyman but I do not think that my experience was unique. I had been saturated with the Bible all my life, but I had never read it with a critical eye, and I am convinced that the majority of Christian clergymen never read the Bible with their minds awake. They reverently intone it and pluck from it spiritual ammunition for moral warfare in support of bourgeois goals.

In this connection I am reminded of the experience of George Eliot, who at twenty-three suddenly abandoned an intensely orthodox Christian outlook and became a free thinker because she examined for the first time some scholarly works of higher criticism of the Bible. Although she never abandoned her deep interest in churches as moral institutions, she sloughed off forever all the ordinary illusions of Christian supernaturalism. My transition was slower partly because I had more at stake; I was a professional preacher and I was slightly intoxicated with my own success. I had found that preaching came to me naturally and I did not want to give up the sense of power that it brought me.

Several things helped me to arrive at the conclusion to leave the Tampa pulpit. I read Sir Leslie Stephen's *An Agnostic's Apology* and its urbane integrity won me over completely. I conducted funeral services for several persons of doubtful moral character and I almost gagged at the ritual guarantees of personal immortality which I felt obliged to repeat over the caskets.

Then, gathering my skeptical thoughts into organized form, I produced a secret manuscript of six chapters which I called "The Immoral Reflections of a Preacher," and, somewhat to my surprise, it was accepted for publication by Paul Carus, editor of the *Open Court* magazine of

Chicago. At that time the *Open Court* was a magazine of considerable intellectual standing in the philosophical world. Ordinarily I would have been flattered to have anything published in its pages under my own name, but I was so uncertain about the validity of my conclusions, as well as the amateurish quality of the whole, that I had the articles published under the pseudonym of John Denmark. I never acknowledged the authorship even to my closest friends. The book—although it never became an actual book—was dedicated to "all those who seek a religion beyond Christianity" and in it I tried to demolish in simple prose the leading theological claims of orthodox Christianity. Three months later I left my pulpit.

Landing in New York in November 1917, Julia and I were almost penniless. She was wearing hand-me-down clothes given to her by our Tampa organist, and I was not caparisoned in any better fashion. We located a small room near Columbia for $5 a week where we had to wait in line in the morning for the only bathroom on the floor. A thirty-cent table d'hôte dinner at a nearby German restaurant was our only large meal each day. Julia started working for $11 a week as a telephone operator at a Congregational building.

I had decided that I wanted an M.A. at Columbia and ultimately a Ph.D. in sociology, with a university teaching career as my ultimate goal, but I had no money to pay the rather high tuition. So I enrolled for several courses at neighboring Union Seminary and, under the arrangement then in force, secured all my tuition for courses both in the seminary and in Columbia.

Sociology in those days was in a condition of uncertainty and confusion. Squeezed between political science and psychology, it was fighting for its life. Even its own savants did not quite know where it belonged or where it was going. At Columbia my head professor, the large-bellied and red-bearded Franklin Giddings, who was then the most famous sociologist in the country, seemed to spend his time fitting society into neat pigeonholes with special Giddingsesque labels that were no more realistic than the labels of Saint Thomas Aquinas.

In 1918 my protest against the relative uselessness of academic sociology was muted and personal. There was no academic group of protesters to share my rebellious point of view to the public. C. Wright Mills, coming to Columbia many years later, blew the lid off conventional sociology, and his caustic, though often mistaken, debunking produced a whole school of anti-sociology sociologists who changed the character of the science in the 1960's. In a way I am glad that sociology was in such a traditional mess during World War I because if it had been in a healthy condition I might have committted my life to it.

All of us who studied at Columbia during that first year of my graduate study there felt the terrific pressure of the war. The stories of atrocities by German soldiers were given daily headlines. Seventeen members of the IWW had been tarred and feathered near Tulsa, Oklahoma. An effigy of La Follette had been burned in Madison, Wisconsin. During the following summer, 101 members of the IWW were convicted of interfering with the conscription law, and their leader, Bill Haywood, was sentenced to prison for thirty years. I watched in court as the government tried to send Max Eastman, Floyd Dell, John Reed, and Art Young of *The Masses* to prison for sedition, but two juries divided on the question of their guilt and they were finally freed. German music was banned in many places and sauerkraut became Liberty Cabbage.

The persecution of anti-war leaders spread even to Columbia, where Nicholas Murray Butler was our czar. In September 1917 two Columbia professors were dismissed by the trustees for their anti-war utterances, J. McKeen Cattell and H. W. L. Dana. In protest against their punishment, Charles Beard resigned from the faculty.

In spite of such irrational suppressions, I gradually swung over to support of the war effort. Mary Pickford, Charlie Chaplin, and Elsie Janis finally persuaded me to

buy some Liberty Bonds. Wilson's Fourteen Points, published in January 1918, helped to change my position on
the war, and also the influence of my brother Brand was
substantial. After service in Mesopotamia and India, he
had returned to New York to take an M.A. at Columbia
because the war had made his work at Oxford impossible.
He had tried to enlist in the American army but because
of poor eyesight was rejected until the closing months of
the war, when he was sent to France as a sergeant.

A little later, Brand and I were thrown together in an
amusing adventure in 1918, beginning in Columbia and
ending abruptly in the slums of Philadelphia. We had both
been chosen to attend a very special small seminar in advanced philosophy under John Dewey at Columbia, and
one of the individuals attending the seminar was a re-
spectable-appearing elderly businessman named Albert C.
Barnes of Philadelphia. We soon learned that he was the
famous millionaire who had made his money from the
antiseptic solution Argyrol and had then developed in
Philadelphia one of the finest collections of modern art in
the world. He was a fanatical, almost unbalanced, admirer
of both John Dewey and Bertrand Russell. He wanted to
use his money to advance their ideas in a practical way.

Suddenly he offered to take the whole seminar to Philadelphia for a summer of special study, concentrating on
a district which was composed mostly of Polish immigrants. The suggested assignment was very vague. We
were to apply the principles of John Dewey and Bertrand
Russell to this area in any way we saw fit. He would rent a
house for us and pay all the bills. John Dewey accepted
the project, to be operated nominally under his jurisdiction, and the rest of us gratefully concurred. The group
included, among others, Brand and myself, Irwin Edman
of Columbia who later wrote up the adventure in his
Philosopher's Holiday, a Russian-born female novelist
named Anzia Yezierska, and Frances Bradshaw of Smith
College, a charming young lady who later married Brand
and still later became dean of women at Swarthmore.

After several weeks of seemingly fruitless talking we did not seem to be getting anywhere. Barnes kept popping in and out and making rather wild and impractical suggestions. In an attempt to achieve some systematic results I persuaded most of the group to start a house-to-house survey of the area, ringing door bells and asking the people several key questions about their economic conditions and social concepts. Barnes was furious and declared that I was diverting the project from its original purpose, whatever that was. Suddenly I was fired. I was both chagrined and relieved. The group finally produced a few magazine articles which could just as well have been written without the establishment of a temporary settlement house.

The debacle did not undermine my great admiration for the two heroes of the project, John Dewey and Bertrand Russell. Dewey continued to be a good friend and I continued to regard him as one of the great seminal thinkers of our time. Many years later when my *American Freedom and Catholic Power* came under heavy fire from the Catholic and neutral press, Dewey came to its rescue with a handsome endorsement, declaring that it was done "with exemplary scholarship, judgment and tact." In the great battle over Catholic power in that period Dewey was more than a passive friend. He went out of his way to underscore the intellectual's case against Catholic policy, describing the church as "a powerful reactionary world organization" promoting "principles inimical to democracy."

But my experience under John Dewey produced a surprising conclusion about his personal merits. He was a great thinker but a wretched teacher. He was rambling and vague in his presentation of textual material, and he had no gift of oral emphasis, no capacity for simplifying his very difficult theories. He became famous not because of his teaching techniques but in spite of them. I am not alone in this opinion. His greatest admirer and closest associate, Irwin Edman, once described his reaction to the first lecture he ever heard by John Dewey. It was, he said, "quite a shock, a shock of dullness and confusion."

The other star of the Philadelphia story of 1918, Albert C. Barnes, became almost as famous as Dewey, for different reasons. After assembling one of the finest art collections in the world in his private gallery in Merion, he would not let anybody enter it except a few favored individuals, who first had to run a gauntlet of inspection. He quarreled with everybody, including his original idol, Bertrand Russell. "He is a man," said Russell, "who likes quarrels for no reason that I can fathom." A desire for flattery and obeisance seemed to dominate his life. Several years after the Philadelphia experience, Barnes made a five-year contract with Russell to lecture at the Barnes gallery in Philadelphia, then suddenly revoked, or tried to revoke, his contract for no apparent reason. Since Barnes was a millionaire many times over and Russell at that time was a poor man, ostracized by the British and American establishments, Russell sued Barnes for specific performance of his contract and finally won.

By the time I had finished my stint in that weird "philosopher's holiday" in Philadelphia, my wartime conscience was troubling me more than ever. Where could I be useful? I had come at last to the conclusion that Wilson's concepts of self-determination and an association of nations to prevent war were worth fighting for even if the fight involved service in capitalist battalions. The Socialist Party had pretty well disintegrated because of the successful propaganda campaign for the "moral goals" of the war.

The newspapers said that America desperately needed more ships—Liberty Ships was the appealing label. I went to work as a machinist's helper in a great shipyard near Newark, living in a crowded rooming house— crowded with prostitutes and bedbugs. I scarcely knew the difference between a hammer and a screwdriver but I knew enough to tighten bolts and pass tools along to a qualified machinist.

Came the Armistice, fake and real. The fake armistice, based on a premature United Press dispatch from Roy Howard, was far more real than the real one. Julia and I joined the wild throng near the great stone lions in front of New York's public library, a throng that danced, screamed, kissed, and hurled great handfuls of confetti. Julia, then working in an office near the public library, was already pregnant, having abandoned birth control when she thought her restless husband might disappear into the trenches before she could bear him a child.

At this juncture I was saved from Jersey bedbugs by my old friend Henry Atkinson, who offered me a job with the League to Enforce Peace, headed by William Howard Taft. I was asked to help organize labor groups in support of a League of Nations with power to enforce peace, if necessary by armed power. I liked the concept, and I still do, but we were faced with the psychology of a war-weary nation which was sick of oratorical idealism and ugly death. We were also faced with the unholy and selfish political conflict between a dogmatic Presbyterian idealist in the White House and an equally dogmatic partisan in the Senate, Henry Cabot Lodge. Wilson could have forced a just peace upon our allies but he did not have the nerve to do it. Europe was in the throes of a hang-the-Kaiser campaign and at home Theodore Roosevelt held to his demagogic line, "Let us dictate peace by the hammering of guns."

At first our campaign for a League of Nations seemed to have real chances of success. There was enough in common between Taft's concept of a League to Enforce Peace and Wilson's League of Nations to make temporary co-operation practical. We staged a great pro-League mass meeting in New York's Metropolitan Opera House with Wilson, Taft, and Al Smith as the speakers and Enrico Caruso singing the "Star-Spangled Banner." We arranged a tour of the country for Taft.

At first the audiences were large and enthusiastic. Then everything seemed to collapse at once. Lodge and Borah sabotaged the League concept in the Senate. America, it seemed, was getting entangled in alliances that would impair the national sovereignty. Wilson, overexerting himself on a speaking tour, collapsed after a stroke and for about

seventeen months the country was governed illegally by
Edith Galt Wilson. Various ethnic blocs in the great cities
began to attack the Treaty of Versailles, with much justification, because it had not treated their home countries
fairly. People of German extraction were furious. In New
York City a young Italian leader, Fiorello La Guardia,
whipped up the sentiment of both Germans and Italians by
emphasizing Wilson's "great betrayal." He was elected
president of the board of aldermen as a Republican in a
surprise victory in 1919 largely because of his campaign
on the issue of Versailles injustice.

Taft kept on speaking but his audiences became thinner
and less enthusiastic as the months went on. By the time
of his last mass meeting in Albany, which I had arranged,
he stood up to speak in a vast auditorium with almost no
audience. "I feel," he said, "as if I were speaking to the
wide, wide world." Within a few weeks the League to
Enforce Peace was obliged to suspend for lack of funds.
The era of post-war idealism was over, the United States
refused membership in the League of Nations, and presently Warren Gamaliel Harding restored "normalcy."

5. PICKET LINES AND JAIL

WHERE WOULD I GO FROM HERE? I had plenty of offers of work but this time I determined that I would not be fitted into a wrong slot in the establishment. I would not return to the church because I had ceased to believe its central gospel. My resolve on this point had been strengthened by the fact that my unfinished M.A. thesis at Columbia concerned the rise of the free thought movement in America. I received a rather surprising offer to serve as executive director of an anti-vice committee in New York but I finally turned it down because I did not want to spend my life getting prostitutes arrested when I believed that the vice of poverty was the most fundamental cause of prostitution.

Providentially at that moment an old friend, A. J. Muste, telephoned. Like myself, Muste was a liberal Protestant clergyman who had become thoroughly disillusioned with the religious establishment and had joined the Socialist movement. Later on for a time he became a Trotskyite, then switched back completely to a sentimental Christian pacifist position, and in his post as leader of the Fellowship of Reconciliation he became, before his death in 1967, the most noted pacifist in the United States. He was a hawk-nosed, lean-bodied saint who, with his rimless glasses and thin lips, looked as if he had just stepped out of a monastery. He was frequently called an American Gandhi.

Muste was neither a great writer nor a great speaker, but he had a matchless gift for inspiring a spirit of dedication in his fellow-workers, and he was a good administrator. He had proved his courage in some long and bitter labor struggles in New England textile mills when a great

strike in Lawrence, Massachusetts, dramatized the grievances of the workers: They were getting an average wage
of $11 a week for a fifty-four-hour week. Muste had been
one of three Protestant clergymen to be beaten by the
police in that strike, and later on all three became leaders
of the new textile union formed in the industry, the Amalgamated Textile Workers of America. None of us ex-
preachers had ever worked in a textile mill in our lives.
Our union was independent, outside the American Federation of Labor, largely financed by another independent
union, the Amalgamated Clothing Workers, headed by the
rising young Chicago labor leader Sidney Hillman.

Muste's voice on the telephone said: "We want you to be
an organizer for the Amalgamated Textile Workers. All
of us are working for $35 a week. That would be your
salary." That was only about half of the salary I was then
earning but I jumped at the chance. The choice was harder
on Julia than on me, partly because we now had a baby
son, Paul Jr. We packed up our few belongings and began
an itinerant life, going to Fulton, New York, then to Allen-
town, Pennsylvania, where Paulie slept in the open lid of a
trunk while we lived in one room, then to Utica, New York,
where we located a grim little apartment over a barber
shop in the Italian end of town.

Utica, a great textile center, was then, as now, sharply
divided along ethnic lines. The Wasps owned the factories
and banks; the Italians and a few Polish immigrants held
the low-paying assignments in the mills; a few German
and Anglo-Saxon skilled workers held the top positions in
the manual working categories and sometimes protected
their privileged status by joining the small A. F. of L. craft
unions.

It is difficult for anyone who has grown up in the era
of union recognition, when collective bargaining is protected by law, to appreciate the atmosphere in the United
States in the summer of 1919 when Julia and I landed in
Utica. An organizer of industrial unions was an outside
agitator branded a "Bolshevik" by both the authorities of

the law and the leaders of conventional organized labor. Under Wilson's war policy labor unions could claim some rights of collective bargaining as long as the war lasted, but when it was over the great employers and the political reactionaries, led by Attorney General A. Mitchell Palmer, closed in on all the "Bolsheviks." The ghost of the Russian Revolution was used as a club to beat down any vigorous move by labor for the rights of the underpaid workers. Palmer's famous "Red Raids" on the headquarters of labor organizations in 1919 and 1920 singled out the "alien enemy" as the major target of every attack. Palmer's assistant in subversive matters at the time of the raids was a young man named J. Edgar Hoover, who was then only about twenty-six years old.

We in the Amalgamated Textile Workers and the Amalgamated Clothing Workers were especially vulnerable not only because our most important leader, Sidney Hillman, had been born abroad and our clientele was largely foreign-born but because our union constitutions spurned conventional techniques of improvement within the capitalist system as inadequate and proudly proclaimed: "The industrial and inter-industrial organization built upon the solid rock of clear knowledge and class consciousness will put the organized working class in actual control of the system of production, and the working class will then be ready to take possession of it." This aggressive declaration had been adopted at a moment when the Russian Revolution seemed to be a beacon light for all working-class movements. We all, Socialists and incipient Communists, rather naïvely accepted its glorious promise, and I graciously allowed the capitalist system about twenty-five years to endure.

The year 1919, when we came to Utica, was a crisis year in labor discontent. Violence was in the air. Returning soldiers found that their victory had not made America safe for even the simplest forms of labor democracy. The cost of living had soared fifty percent between 1914 and 1918 and at the same time advertisements were appearing in the papers for factory workers at $12 a week. In February in Seattle there had been a five-day general strike with labor guards patrolling the streets and with ultimate defeat for the unions involved. In September came two of the most famous strikes in American history, the steel strike led by William Z. Foster, later Communist candidate for President, and the Boston police strike whose accidental hero was Calvin Coolidge. (After the police went on strike, Coolidge had waited until their defeat seemed inevitable and then had sent his historic telegram to Samuel Gompers: "There is no right to strike against the public safety by anybody, any time, anywhere.")

Foster's steel strike lasted for seventeen weeks at the very time when I was leading a strike in Utica for union recognition and a wage increase. Foster's strike, involving 365,000 workers, received almost all the headlines. During the steel strike Judge Elbert Gary, executive head of United States Steel, refused even to meet with union leaders at a time when his corporation had jumped its surplus profits from $135 million to $493 million and his workers were still working the twelve-hour day and the seven-day week. "Jesus Christ himself," said the mayor of Duquesne, Pennsylvania, "could not speak in Duquesne for the A. F. of L."

In Utica in the summer and fall of 1919, Jesus Christ would probably have been permitted to speak, but I am sure that the editors, mill owners, and police would not have listened to him. This was not because these editors, mill owners, and police were any worse than others of their kind. They were ordinary establishment Americans who were frightened. They were frightened by the bitterness of returning, working-class soldiers who were at last free to express their grievances. They were frightened by exaggerated anti-Bolshevik alarms coming from Washington. And the sudden collapse of war orders had left the textile mills almost without orders.

Muste sent a group of us organizers into Utica to canvass from house to house and build up a corps of potential shop leaders. We knew that we were being shadowed by spies, but we were as recklessly bold as the disillusioned returning soldiers. When all was prepared, two of our men submitted to the mill owners a demand for a twenty-five percent wage increase and union recognition. The employers replied by discharging as agitators the leaders who had asked for the increase, and the strike was on. It lasted four months and, although we won a substantial wage increase, we never had a chance to win the only thing that would have guaranteed reasonable working conditions in the mills—union recognition. At times we had picket lines nearly two miles long, marching single file past the mills. We showed that the textile workers were getting about $19 a week. We headed our picket lines with returned soldiers wearing their war medals. It was no use. Our cause was overwhelmed in the great national wave of anti-Bolshevik hysteria.

At first the police did not molest me, perhaps because I was the leader of the strike and they feared an emotional reaction; also I cooperated carefully with the police officers in limiting picket lines to single-file processions, which were peaceful when I was present. The police started with five other organizers, seized them illegally, and shipped them out of the city without any pretense of due process. When I invited Sidney Hillman to address a great mass meeting, they met him at the railroad station, put him back on the train, and shipped him out of the city with a ticket paid for by local businessmen.

They were less formal with the other organizers, seizing them roughly and rushing them out of town with no publicity. Usually the organizers came back quietly and went to work until they were captured again. When this had happened two or three times to one of our union organizers, Frank Coco, I performed the only act of "violence" in my entire labor career. Two police officers had just taken Coco by the arms outside our union office and told him that they were taking him to the railroad station. I hurriedly gathered a mob of strikers, surrounded the two officers and Coco, and announced: "You will take Coco to the police station, arrest him legally and allow him to get a lawyer or I will start a riot right now and take him away from you. And I won't be responsible for what happens to you." The police were frightened and agreed to "accept" my demand. They marched us all through the middle of town to the police station, but there they secured reinforcements, turned on us, drove our crowd away, and shipped Coco out of town according to the original plan.

This was their procedure for dealing with organizers who did not live in Utica. This procedure was not applicable to me because Julia and I lived in Utica, so the police turned to the courts for an injunction. This was in the days before the Norris–La Guardia anti-injunction law when a labor leader accused of violating a writ could be sent to jail without a jury trial by the same judge who had issued an *ex parte* injunction.

It was the tenth week of the strike, and I was very, very tired, having spoken almost every night to strike mass meetings for those ten weeks. The strikers were getting more and more impatient under the abuse of the police and the adamant refusal of the employers to deal with us. One day I received a court order restraining me and all other union members "from congregating together in such numbers as to intimidate any employee or person seeking employment . . . from hostile and menacing demonstrations of any kind intended to intimidate the employees." I laughed and stuck the paper into my pocket. We had been served with six injunctions already, and this was just one more.

My speeches at strike meetings had become quite inflammatory. I had to speak a kind of pidgin English because so many of the strikers were Italians who had not yet learned much English; we always had an Italian orator for them also. In the audience each night, conspicuously flanked by two detectives, sat a young man I took to be a police stenographer. He took down every word I said in shorthand. One night he recorded me as saying "They are mad at us because we frightened their dear little, nice little scabs." On another occasion the stenographer quoted me as saying: "We will have a [picket] line that will resemble a big snake winding its way along Broad Street past the Skenandoa, Oneita, and Mohawk mills. Then the hearts of the scabs will be beating like a triphammer and they will be sick in the stomach and tell the bosses that they will not be in to work." The court took no notice of the fact that these inelegant but persuasive words were followed by the injunction: "Don't intimidate them and don't use any violence." (I always directed the strikers to obey the police.) I did not know that the young stenographer at the meetings was really an agent hired by the mill owners and protected by the police while he masqueraded as one of them. I did not know either that the mill owners had two paid spies on our strike committee.

Under the injunction I was summoned before a Supreme Court justice in another city and charged with "intimidation," although I had not directly advocated violence and no violence had resulted from anything that I had said. In fact, the only serious violence in the strike occurred while I was in jail. I was so angry over the whole procedure that I insisted on defending myself without a lawyer. I appeared alone, with a Phi Beta Kappa key dangling on my stomach, and I revealed a very self-righteous scorn for the abuse of judicial power involved in *ex parte* injunctions. The dignified judge was not impressed. He ruled that the purpose of our picket line was to "frighten and intimidate" the strikebreakers, and he sentenced me to thirty days in the county jail and a fine of $100 for contempt of court. There was, of course, no opportunity for a jury trial.

As soon as I was in jail the real trouble began. The strikers were so angry that they started to riot in front of the largest textile mill. The police fired 250 rounds of ammunition, and six strikers were shot. In the fury of reprisal, the chairman of the strike committee, it was said, planted some gunpowder on the porch of a Polish priest who had opposed the strike. He was tried, convicted, and sentenced to twenty years in the penitentiary. (Several years later I went to Albany and persuaded Al Smith personally to commute his sentence.) The strikers paid my $100 fine in pennies, one penny from each striker.

I regarded my month in the Utica county jail as something of a lark. It gave me a good chance to rest. I worked so hard on Italian that I was able to give an Italian speech to the strikers when I got out. Julia spoke in my place at strike meetings, took up big collections, and wheeled Paulie, shaking a rattle, in a baby carriage at the head of the picket line. She was allowed to talk with me frequently through the bars and to send in meals to me. I was treated with all the elegance of a civil prisoner because the sheriff was up for re-election and sorely needed Italian votes.

One day I smuggled to Julia a document with the request that it be published as a strike leaflet. It was called "An Injunction Against the Capitalist Class of Utica," and it was a bitter, egotistic document which, eighteen years later, almost cost me my admission to practice law as a member of the New York bar. On the cover it had an unfortunate picture of myself, looking like a neurotic radical. In mock imitation of the injunction under which I had been sent to jail, I described "the working class of Utica as Plaintiff" and the mill owners, the city administration, the newspapers, "and all those cooperating to destroy the rights of labor" as defendants. Reciting the long list of grievances of the strikers, I ended with a flourish by declaring that "the defendants are hereby restrained" from, among other things, "paying starvation wages and then posing as models of Americanism," "assaulting and deporting organizers of the Amalgamated Textile and Clothing Workers without legal warrants," "saluting the American flag while blacklisting returned soldiers," "denying to the workers that industrial democracy for which our soldiers died in France."

All things considered, it is rather surprising that the same state courts which sent me to jail in 1919 ultimately admitted me to the post of "officer of the court." The explanation lay in the changed atmosphere of American life in the 1930's, especially after the passage of the Norris–La Guardia anti-injunction act. So many labor leaders had worn contempt-of-court jail sentences as badges of honor that the "disgrace" had lost its sting.

In spite of the courage of the strikers and the technical rightness of our cause, we finally had to admit defeat. Indeed the whole movement of the Amalgamated Textile Workers went down in defeat within a few years and Sidney Hillman had to abandon his dream of a semi-vertical, left-wing organization in the textile field that would challenge successfully the old-line unions of the A. F. of L. His own union, the Amalgamated Clothing Workers, achieved national success. Most of the textile workers of America remain even today unorganized, underpaid, and almost helpless in the face of employer determination to maintain the miscalled "open shop."

The Utica strike was scarcely over when the Lusk Committee of the New York state legislature "investigated" the strike and pronounced it the work of those "closely allied with the activities of the Communist Party of America which seeks to overthrow the government of the United States by force." "Testimony," said the committee, which had as its counsel the infamous reactionary Archibald Stevenson, "showed the existence of an inside ring of anarchists of the worst type working within the Communist Party . . . and the extreme Socialists in Utica."

The Lusk Committee "investigation" of the Utica strike lasted one part of one day. Some committee members came to the city from Albany, listened to the testimony of a few police officers, gave none of us on the other side any opportunity to testify, and then issued a story with a screaming headline: "Finds Utica a Hotbed of Seditious Effort." There was no attempt to disclose any facts about the illegal deportation of Sidney Hillman and other labor leaders. One "Paul D. Blanchard" was briefly mentioned as a potential teacher of classes in "Socialism, Communism and Bolshevism" but was given no opportunity to testify.

The mood of the Lusk Committee was dramatized by two events of that year. Five elected Socialist assemblymen were expelled from the legislature of New York for "disloyalty" for questioning the policy of the government in World War I, and the Lusk Committee in its final four-volume report declared: "John Haynes Holmes changed the name of his so-called church from Church of the Messiah to Community Church as an outward mark of his change of heart from Christianity to Communism."

So far as I know, I never met a Communist in Utica, either before or during the strike. The Lusk Committee declared that Communist Party headquarters in Utica were close to our union headquarters and that there was close cooperation with the union. I never even knew of the existence of such headquarters.

I felt so guilty about the defeat of our strike and especially about the fact that some faithful strikers lost their jobs that I thought I should share their labor status and face the music. I went around to various mills in Utica and asked for work, any kind of work. The employers looked at me with some astonishment and said no. But I did secure, in a small union shop in the clothing industry, a job as a seam presser, the lowest of the unskilled jobs in clothing manufacture. So, for several months, I was a member of the working class and proudly carried my union card.

Sidney Hillman rescued me from this token membership in the proletariat by making me educational director of the Amalgamated Clothing Workers in Rochester, New York. Julia and I moved there joyously not only because I was given the princely salary of $55 a week but because labor unions, especially the Amalgamated Clothing Workers, were well established in that city, and we were tired of being outlaws. The Amalgamated had just recently organized this quality clothing market and brought into its industrial union thousands of skilled and unskilled workers, mostly Jewish and Italian. They needed to be given a new sense of solidarity and an intellectual background. Hillman thought that mass meetings, classes, and labor literature were needed. Also, I suppose he thought that a middle-class Gentile like me could make some contacts with the middle-class critics of unionism and the editors of newspapers. So I set out to be a kind of public relations contact man with the outside world as well as an educational director. It was work for which I was far better prepared than the straight organization of shop workers.

Julia and I firmly believed that we should continue to live as proletarians, so we searched for a small house in the working-class end of town and finally found it, a one-story cottage with a back yard. To make ends meet we lived in the back three rooms and rented the front three to a Lithuanian factory worker. The cramped quarters made it impossible for us to do much entertaining. I remember only one guest who ate at our table during our four years there. It was Justice Louis D. Brandeis, who dropped in on us one morning for a call with his daughter Susan. We had known them in Boston. They ate lunch on our kitchen table, the only table in the house.

My work in Rochester was both zestful and successful. With an able assistant, Miss Edith Christenson, who became a warm family friend for life, we organized great educational mass meetings every Friday night, staged vaudeville and musical programs to bring the members out to hear distinguished labor leaders, edited a small weekly educational paper, and ultimately conducted a series of classes for workers in the history of trade unionism, public speaking, etc. Every new member of the Amalgamated union was compelled to take some educational work in order to know something about labor objectives.

Hillman, at the time I worked under his leadership in the 1920's, was not yet the finished politician that he became during the administration of Franklin Roosevelt, when FDR's famous phrase "clear it with Sidney" became the symbol of Hillman's political power. He was a good speaker but not a finished speaker in English because he had come from Lithuania when he was twenty and his rather unpleasant accent still persisted. He was astonishingly young for a great labor leader and very attractive physically. He had a kind of cultured suavity about him that was quite ingratiating. It was very difficult for an employer who talked to this man to brand him as dangerous or unreasonable. He had the intelligence to hire first-class economists and statisticians to present the union's case for industrial improvements whenever a dispute threatened.

In 1923 when he visited me briefly in Toynbee Hall, East London, he told me of his personal feelings about Russian and British labor leadership. I had just introduced him to Sidney Webb and other British leaders, and after long conversations he said: "These British labor leaders don't compare with the men I have recently met in Moscow. Those Moscow boys know what they want and they know how to get it. These British labor leaders are living in a dream world."

That comment by Hillman revealed the rather surprising dual viewpoint of the man. In the industrial field he was hard-boiled and practical; in the political field he continued to cherish a romantic admiration for the Russian Revolution. He had interviewed Lenin and he had come away with a permanent sense of awe. In the 1920's his enthusiasm for Russia led him to organize a clothing corporation to build modern scientific clothing factories in Russia in cooperation with the Stalin regime. All of us in the union helped to raise $300,000 for this venture. The scheme collapsed when the Stalin regime became too fearful of American influence and abruptly refunded all the money which had been raised by the American dreamers.

Perhaps Hillman's admiration for the Russian experiment helps to explain his own system of total control over his own union. He organized the controlling board of his union in such a way that his own organizers held the key posts. No anti-Hillman union member had any chance to defy Sidney Hillman on any major issue, and Hillman could be utterly ruthless in handling dissenters. That is one reason why he had a running battle with Norman Thomas over the years, since Thomas personally intervened on several occasions to defend the rights of Amalgamated dissenters. Fortunately, Hillman was both honest and courageous, and he rarely made a mistake in the assessment of his opponents.

Hillman was able to maintain his left-wing position in international politics and at the same time hold the respect of America's clothing capitalists because of his constructive policy concerning the quality and quantity of work in the clothing shops. He scorned the dawdling, go-slow tactics of such A. F. of L. unions as the bricklayers and accepted piecework pay for the whole men's clothing industry, protecting the system of payment-by-results by agreeing to the appointment of an impartial chairman in each labor market to approve the work standards.

I think that the best explanation for Hillman's rather complex radicalism can be found in his own early history. He had never been essentially a proletarian, although he had worked in a Chicago clothing shop for $8 a week during a brief period in his life. Actually he was a middle-class intellectual, son of a merchant in the old country, educated to be a rabbi, a lover of good books, and a left-wing political idealist. Because of his Russian sympathies there were times when he was much too lenient with the Communists.

Happily, in the years I worked for Hillman in Rochester he was broadly tolerant of free speech in labor propaganda. He warmly approved when I succeeded in getting the local central labor council of the A. F. of L. to unite with the Amalgamated in founding a "labor college," really nothing but a series of night classes in which the members of the two fighting branches of organized labor attended sessions together and got a good grounding in labor history. (I taught the economics classes.) He also allowed me to bring in any left-wing or right-wing speaker who seemed able to entertain and instruct the workers. Our speaking list was astonishingly varied, including William Z. Foster,

Elizabeth Gurley Flynn, Scott Nearing, Norman Thomas, Roger Baldwin, A. Philip Randolph, and Jean Longuet, the grandson of Karl Marx. To balance these left-wingers I frequently invited the local Catholic priest, Father Staub.

While working in Rochester I began to speak in many universities and at national conventions of welfare groups as a spokesman for labor. I wrote two pamphlets for the Amalgamated which gained wide circulation, one on "The Open Shop Movement" and the other on "How to Run a Union Meeting," an elementary guide to parliamentary law. I had articles published in *The Outlook, The New Republic, The Nation,* and *The Survey,* including a written debate on labor unions with Samuel Rea, president of the Pennsylvania Railroad. Leaders of the Democratic Party in Rochester asked me to run for Congress, but I declined on the ground that I was still a convinced Socialist.

Through the good offices of Sherwood Eddy of the International YMCA I spent two summer vacations in Europe, one in London and the other in Milan and produced not only some articles on fascism but also a short book, *An Outline of the British Labor Movement,* with an introduction by Arthur Henderson, later British Foreign Secretary. It wasn't much of a book, but Oh what a joy it was to see the name of Paul Blanshard as author on the cover! And Oh what a joy it was to meet in person Bernard Shaw with his pink whiskers and pink shirt and Ramsay Macdonald with his "bell-like, bull-like voice." British labor was then in the stage of heavenly optimism, and how eagerly I sang its praises! I wanted to transfer across the ocean every British Labour dream, omitting all the unpleasant doubts about Labour's preparedness to govern. I became an ardent apostle of an American Labor Party to parallel the British experiment.

In Rochester one night I presided at a great debate on the open shop movement in the city's largest auditorium. The participants were Clarence Darrow and a representative of the National Association of Manufacturers, Noel Sargent. Sargent was a frail young economics professor who recited with no great force the usual arguments against the abuses of trade unionism. He called his non-union plan for industry "the American Plan." Darrow was on his way back to respectability after almost losing his status as a lawyer in a scandal which grew out of the confessions of the Macnamara brothers that they had dynamited the *Los Angeles Times.*

While Sargent was speaking that night—he spoke first —Darrow sat slouched in his chair without taking a single note, apparently quite oblivious to all that was going on. When his turn came he slowly unwound his long legs, walked to the lectern, and one by one repeated almost word for word all the essential points of Sargent's speech, then demolished them so completely that the great audience screamed in delight. It was the finest forensic feat I had ever witnessed.

Afterward Sargent was asked if he would be willing to debate Darrow on this same subject in a series of university forums. Sargent was willing but Darrow was too busy for the assignment. Somebody turned to me and asked me if I would make the tour with Sargent. To my surprise Sargent readily accepted the idea, and a few weeks later we debated before several city clubs and student audiences in the great universities of the Middle West. Sargent seemed to be getting the worst of it, and I wondered why he accepted such punishment. Then, when I got home, clippings about the debates began to come in, and I understood. The stories in many newspapers carried long accounts of Sargent's arguments, then added one sentence at the end: "Paul Blanshard of the Amalgamated Clothing Workers also spoke." The National Association of Manufacturers had so much power in so many newspaper offices that its publicity handouts were accepted as news without alteration.

In those Rochester years Julia had a much harder time than I. I had the satisfaction of public platforms and reasonably successful classes. Julia was almost completely isolated in our little cottage, soon with two boys instead of one, since our second son, Rufus Anderson Blanshard, was born in 1921.

I have said little in this narrative about my two sons and their families because I value their privacy as much as they desire it for themselves. But I must say proudly that they have both grown up to be bold advocates and practitioners of social justice, and their wives and children have joined them gladly in the struggle. In the 1960's Paul, who now runs his own public relations business in Philadelphia, abandoned his work and went with his wife Priscilla—she now holds an important post in the Philadelphia library system—to Nigeria as West African representatives of the Friends Service Committee where they lived with their three children for two years in the slums of Lagos. One of Paul's daughters, after marrying a Quaker conscientious objector, recently spent five days in a Washington jail for demonstrating against the Vietnam war. (Both of my sons, incidentally, served with distinction in combat zones in World War II, so their opposition to war is more than theoretical.)

Rufus, now married to a Radcliffe Phi Beta Kappa, graduated at the head of his class in Swarthmore, secured his Ph.D. at Harvard, and is now a professor of English at the University of Connecticut, where he is serving as head of the local teachers union. After having two blond children of their own, Jane and he have adopted two colored children and embarked on a successful crusade to break down the prevailing prejudice against inter-racial adoption.

I have not tried to influence my sons one way or another in matters of religious commitment, although I suppose that some of the skepticism of both Julia and myself must have rubbed off on them. Paul is quite religious, a devout Quaker, but Rufus is not.

In Rochester, after Rufus was out of diapers, Julia secured the services of a blessed German mother who moved into our front three rooms with her husband and child and took care of our two offspring. Julia went to work in a clothing shop in Rochester, then switched suddenly to the post of society editor on Rochester's leading newspaper, the *Democrat-Chronicle*. Perhaps the editors thought that she, coming from outside all the accepted circles of Rochester society, would be the best one to maintain impartiality in a tensely competitive situation. At any rate, she succeeded brilliantly from the beginning, and her success lasted until her death. She served during the next few years, while we wandered about the world, as a reporter on the *San Diego Sun* and the *Newark Ledger*, ending in the 1930's with several years of service as woman's page editor of the leading Scripps-Howard feature syndicate in New York, the Newspaper Enterprise Association.

6. THE L.I.D. AND NORMAN THOMAS

THOSE UNIVERSITY DEBATES with Noel Sargent of the National Association of Manufacturers were destined to change my whole future. Repercussions of them reached New York, where a national organization known as the League for Industrial Democracy had its central offices.

One day Arthur Gleason of *The Survey,* then a director of the LID, came to Rochester and told me that the LID board wanted me to serve as full-time field secretary and lecturer for the organization, spending nearly all my time traveling in the colleges. The board felt that my experience in the labor movement gave me the chance to get across to students the precise combination of labor and socialist idealism which the LID represented.

This LID was socialist in a broad sense and it had a good reputation in the college community for solid scholarship. Its general outlook was similar to that of the Fabian Society in England and its proclaimed purpose was "education for a new social order based on production for use and not for profit." The two executive directors were Norman Thomas and Harry Laidler. Laidler was the technical scholar of the movement, author of many textbooks about socialism, and Norman Thomas was our shining moral leader.

I accepted the LID offer with considerable relief. In spite of my reasonable success in the labor movement, I had to confess that a so-called intellectual in that movement was made to feel a little like an outsider. Educational work was regarded by the rank and file as something extra, a luxury to be sloughed off if more money was needed for the salary of an additional organizer. I realized that I was a fifth wheel even in so progressive a union as the Amalgamated. The power lay with the men who had come up through the shops.

I was to spend most of the time intermittently from 1924 to 1933 with the LID, leaving for a time to serve as an associate editor of *The Nation,* then as executive director of the City Affairs Committee of New York. I think that my years with the LID were the second most useful of my life. I accord first place to my campaign against Catholic power.

The students and professors of American universities in the 1920's and early 1930's had not yet acquired the exaggerated fear of communism and socialism which characterized the Joe McCarthy era. There was an immense curiosity about the British Labour Party and its rise to power, and I could give the students firsthand glimpses of British tactics. The liberal students of that time were more Wellsian than Marxist, and so was I. In fact I was not a Marxist at all, and if I had been I would not have been able to reach as many thousands of students as I did.

Marx seemed to me too bitter and too fatalistic to serve as the appropriate prophet for a vigorous young nation like the United States. His thesis that the plight of the workers under capitalism was getting steadily worse was contradicted year by year as the physical conditions of labor improved. This improvement, of course, was particularly apparent in America, which was steadily moving toward the highest standard of living in history. Although I sounded as bitter as Marx on occasion, my rather simplistic philosophy was one of steady amelioration through democratic pressure. Relatively, I was a sunny optimist.

Malcolm Cowley, in describing the 1930's as an age of radical faith, has summed up quite well the kind of idealism that inspired us in the LID. We were "not much interested in Marx as a philosopher or Marx as an economist." We "revered him as a prophet calling for a day of judgment and a new heaven on earth." Our faith was "apocalyptic and millennial." We held that man's progress

toward a new social order was to be gradual, not catastrophic. We said appreciative things about certain aspects
of the Soviet Union but flatly rejected a proletarian dictatorship for the United States. Behind all our thinking was
the conviction that the world was moving inevitably toward some kind of socialist dawn. It was all so logical—
and very, very moral.

The technique which the LID followed in placing me
before college students was embarrassingly self-assertive
and very exhausting. Harry Laidler or Norman Thomas
would write ahead to college professors they knew saying
that I was available, sometimes without a fee, to speak to
classes, chapels, or open meetings. A rather handsome
lecture folder would accompany the offer, listing some
pretty up-to-date subjects. Some liberal professor could
usually be located who would want me under such conditions. Why not? A professor might agree with me, or he
might simply welcome the chance to prepare one less lecture himself, or he might want to wake up a sleepy class
scheduled for the first hour after lunch. Perhaps the fact
that I was still technically an ordained minister opened
some doors. One year I spoke at ninety-seven colleges.

When I arrived at a college, traveling usually on a tourist sleeper at the lowest possible rate, I would sometimes
be scheduled for five or six speeches and discussions in a
single day. All my lectures were followed by exhausting
question periods, the best feature of the day. Fortunately,
I had acquired from somewhere the gift of sleeping almost
anywhere when I was tired. I was able to refresh myself
with short naps and keep on talking.

The things I said were not at all profound, far below
the caliber of the addresses of such later advocates of
socialism and economic liberalism as Michael Harrington
and John Kenneth Galbraith but for those days they were
something new because they were firsthand. I had really
seen the inside of a jail as a strike leader and the inside
of the fascist movement in Italy and the inside of the
labor movement in Great Britain. I talked a little about the

theories of socialism, but only briefly. Usually I emphasized immediate remedies such as unemployment insurance, collective bargaining, the union shop, short hours of work, and only ultimately a planned control of economic society under nonprofit standards. I rarely mentioned Karl Marx; I often mentioned and quoted Bernard Shaw and H. G. Wells. I opposed Bernard Shaw's concept of equal incomes because of what H. G. Wells called "the devil of laziness in all of us," but I did often suggest that in a morally planned society the proper income range would begin at $5000 a year and not go above $25,000.

Happily, the LID allowed me to range over a whole variety of controversial subjects even when my words annoyed local patriots. I attacked the compulsory Reserve Officers Training Corps, then universal in land grant colleges under the Morrill Land Grant Act of 1862. In an article in *The Nation* on "Military Glory in the Colleges" I jeered at the whole system of using pretty girls and parades as decoys to bolster up college militarism. "Military propaganda holds the universities in its grip," I said, "by the same devices of rivalry, myth, social ostracism, group repression, and rhythm that made America a conformist's paradise during the war."

In another article in *The Nation* I said:

Campuses are dominated by the swaggering captain of the drill; students who hate militarism and all its appurtenances are forced to go through the motions of killing men. "Now fellahs," said the leader of the bayonet drill at Kansas State Agricultural College one night last spring as he stood in front of a line of rookies, "now, fellahs, remember when you run the bayonet through their guts, grunt a little and look fierce. It is not only what you do that counts but how you feel and look."

I pointed out that the federal law did not make ROTC compulsory for every student; it only obliged a land grant college to *offer* ROTC to its students. (This elementary point was quite unknown in many universities.) It took about forty years for American students to organize an effective movement against ROTC on American campuses, and then the primary force behind the successful movement was the public's disapproval of our policy in Vietnam.

Such attacks on the military establishment naturally aroused the ire of the American Legion, and in several places the legion succeeded in blocking my appearances. It failed in Topeka, Kansas, largely because William Allen White of Emporia published an editorial in his *Gazette* entitled "Abou Ben Blanshard," ridiculing the suggestion that my address under the auspices of the YMCA at Washburn College would start a revolution. After the address the local paper described it as "a calm, dispassionate presentation of certain social theories held by a large group of very respectable economists."

At this period the legion was being fed by a number of rightist organizations which were later to come to full flower in the McCarthy era. They were particularly effective in keeping Norman Thomas and me out of Southern universities. *The Southern Textile Bulletin,* organ of the nonunion forces in Southern cotton mills, published an editorial called "Blanshard and His Buddies" after I had written for *The New Republic* a series of articles on "Labor in Southern Cotton Mills" and had been "lionized" by some economics professors at two North Carolina universities. Said the editorial:

Blanshard is a professional labor union organizer and parasite, who was disloyal to the United States during the World War and who has served two terms in jail. . . . Paul Blanshard secured several jobs as a minister, but always failed to make good as he has no ability except as a prolific writer of muck-raking articles. It would be impossible for him to succeed in any of the usual vocations of life. . . . He rightly belongs in the group of disloyal radicals that our Government shipped to Russia.

Occasionally my own extreme language got me in trouble. I remember when I was speaking as a substitute for Norman Thomas in a debate on economic justice before the American Academy of Political Science in Philadelphia. The other speaker on the panel was Dean Wallace Donham of the Harvard School of Business Administration. It was in the middle of the Depression and I was feeling desperately militant. In outlining what Socialists proposed to do I said:

> We Socialists flatly say that we prefer social revolution to the return of that kind of [capitalist] prosperity. We propose to accomplish that revolution peacefully and gradually if the American upper classes will permit a peaceful transition. . . . If we gained control of the American Government, we would probably begin with a complete revision of the national governmental system. We would do one of two things. We would write an amendment to the Constitution giving the Federal government the right to regulate all private business and to enter into any business which it deemed proper, or we would abolish the Constitution altogether and give the National Congress the power to interpret the people's will. . . . Having once captured the Government and shelved the Supreme Court, we Socialists would nationalize as many large industries as we could chew. . . . We would do it by peaceful democratic means unless Fascists and other reactionaries prevented peaceful change.

I followed this mercurial stuff with a calm advocacy of the British form of parliamentary government for the United States, with an American Labor Party as the democratic instrument of change. But, of course, the qualifying sentences in my speech were omitted from the newspapers and I was made to look like a Communist in social-democratic clothing.

It is quite common in these days of campus riots and sit-ins to denigrate the student generations of the 1920's and 1930's as timid and unprogressive. That is a one-sided judgment. The students were less noisy than the students of the 1960's but there was a great intellectual ferment on the campuses of that period and it helped to produce many of the leaders of the New Deal in Roosevelt's administration. Student liberal organizations frequently helped strikers and demonstrated against militarism. In an article in *The Nation* in 1924 I pointed out:

> Social radicalism is spreading most rapidly in our theological seminaries and girls' colleges, notably in the former. . . . The theological student of today . . . is a humanist using Christianity as an illustration. . . . The novels which held honorable place on the desk of the older student generation have given place to *Babbitt* and *Janet March* and *Gargoyles*. The successor to the young man who went fussing to a girls' seminary once a week now sits out the dances with a bobbed-haired co-ed who discusses quite uncoyly the damnations of monogamy.

That was my side of the story. I saw the college liberalism of the 1920's and 1930's as intellectual salvation. Many professional rightist organizations saw it as Bolshevism and treason. The mood of these organizations was symbolized in the famous directory of dangerous citizens put out by Elizabeth Dilling in 1934. Her book, *The Red Network*, gave me thirty-two lines. This was more than the lines accorded to Robert M. Hutchins, who was considered worthy of only twenty-two lines, or Felix Frankfurter, who was given seventeen lines, or Monsignor John A. Ryan, who was given twenty-nine lines, or La Guardia, who was given only nineteen lines. But many other dangerous radicals were obviously far more dangerous than I was. Paul Douglas and Mrs. Roosevelt received thirty-five lines each; Norman Thomas forty-one lines; and Jane Addams received the longest diatribe of all.

In all the work of the LID, our shining light was Norman Thomas. After working in the same office with him for more than eight years and writing a book with him, I came to feel that he was the noblest human being I had ever known. He was never mean or unfair or petty. He had come over to the LID from *The Nation* in 1922—people were always moving away from *The Nation* because there was no money to pay their salaries—and he became co-director of the organization with Harry Laidler. Mary Fox, later Mrs. John Herling, was the brilliant spark plug and manager of the organization, and with her was a young lady who was later to be my wife for almost thirty years, Mary W. Hillyer. Mary organized lecture circuits for the LID while I did some of the lecturing.

It was natural that Norman and I should be very close. Our backgrounds and our points of view were almost identical, although he was eight years older than I. We were both born in Ohio parsonages, both ordained Protestant ministers who had lost our orthodox faith, both of British extraction, both Phi Beta Kappas, both Socialists who had come to socialism as a humane, rational ideal, not as a fatalistic Marxist dogma. I occasionally talked about religion to Norman and found that he was essentially a secular humanist but he wished to avoid all religious or anti-religious labels because he was the leader of a political party which needed the support of all faiths. He had officially demitted from the Presbyterian ministry for intellectual reasons. When, in the 1950's, I was under heavy attack in the Catholic press, he came to my support very generously by writing several favorable reviews of my books. He paid a heavy price for this in the right-wing Catholic journals.

Occasionally we crossed paths on our lecture tours. We always traveled on the cheapest tourist sleepers or on day coaches to save money for the LID. I would find Norman sitting up on a day coach reading a book or scribbling furiously on a big yellow pad in preparation for his next speech. I never heard him read a speech in his life. He was constantly bringing fresh details into his speeches, based on the latest news items in the press, and his memory was so good that he never needed any written material except for the wording of actual quotations. Every speech he made tended to be new, whereas I tended to follow the pattern of current vaudeville and repeat a speech over and over again if it seemed to be reaching the audience.

Norman was careless about his clothes, often arriving at an important meeting in a rumpled suit and wrinkled shirt, perhaps with a spot of gravy on his vest. He ate prodigious meals and then burned up all the energy his food had created. His capacity for work was almost miraculous. After riding all day on a sooty train he could sit through a long dinner with the comrades, speak to a large audience, follow up the lecture with a difficult question period, then go to some comrade's house for refreshments and discussions which lasted until midnight— and rise early the next morning to do the same thing all over again.

Norman at his best was one of the finest speakers I ever heard, witty, forceful, and inspiring. His great, long head, topped by a thin thatch of white hair, made him look like a biblical prophet. Although his voice was somewhat metallic, it was very powerful and he knew how to mix solemnity with humor. Since he was primarily an intellectual, never a proletarian, his best performances were before intellectual audiences. Before his death in 1968 he had become the most popular college speaker in America, filling the largest college auditoriums with cheering student audiences. It is hard to remember that in the 1920's, when we both rode the college circuit, Norman was often relegated to student audiences of twenty or thirty.

His best speeches were against militarism and war; often his addresses on economic reform were pretty thin and very general. What would he do if he became President? When the students asked him such questions, he was best on foreign policy, weakest in financial areas. This was the weakness of all of us in the Socialist movement. We were lusty and eloquent in attacking the evils of capitalism; our remedies were often rather amateurish. We could console ourselves that nearly all of our immediate demands, such as unemployment insurance, old-age pensions, and minimum wages, were ultimately taken over as sensible reforms by a "capitalist" society. Actually our capitalist society was being transformed before our eyes into a partially controlled combination of private and public enterprise, and the transformation was, to some extent, due to the pressure that liberals as well as socialists were exerting in behalf of more humane standards in the distribution of wealth.

Unhappily Norman was not nearly as effective before working-class audiences as he was before college audiences, and sometimes he drove himself so hard that he was too tired to make a good speech at an evening mass meeting. One night in Detroit during one of his six Socialist campaigns for the presidency, I watched with horror while nearly one-third of the working-class audience stirred restlessly, then strolled out. Norman was talking over their heads. At that moment he needed some of the simplistic approach of Eugene Debs and he did not have it. Debs was a locomotive fireman; Norman was a Princeton valedictorian. That is one reason why in six campaigns for the presidency Norman never received as high a proportion of the American vote as Debs received in 1920.

In his personal relations with his associates Norman was the very model of generosity and modesty. He had a small office next to mine with a secondhand $10 rolltop desk. He took from the LID the same salary that I received, $100 a week. Fortunately for him, he was freed from the worst financial anxieties by his marriage. His wife Violet, a charming and devoted helpmate, was a Stewart and had inherited enough of a fortune from that family to provide Norman with a $10,000-a-year cushion against destitution.

Norman, because of his moral influence, was largely responsible for a great influx of young Protestant clergymen to the socialist movement in the 1920's and 1930's. He spoke frequently to great audiences in churches and seminaries. Both of us stressed the superior moral appeal of socialism, not its materialistic undertones. In a rather impudent article I wrote in *The Christian Century* in 1932, I asked: "But isn't socialism materialistic and anti-moral?" and I answered:

Nonsense! Socialists talk about bread and clothes and shelter because these things are the preliminary essentials to a moral life, and they are sick of the preachers who ignore that obvious fact. . . . How about the church under socialism? I don't know. The Socialist Party has nothing to say for or against any man's religion, but I think that the only churches capable of surviving in a socialist society would be those with a modern scientific viewpoint. The church's survival depends largely on whether the ministry has the courage to rise to the moral level of socialism.

The only period in my life when I was alienated from Norman Thomas was that period of the 1930's and 1940's during which he spoke on the same platform with Charles Lindbergh and members of the America First Committee against American entrance into World War II. During that period Norman was always careful to explain to his great audiences that he was not a member of America First and that he adhered to the platform of the Socialist-led Keep America Out of War Congress, of which he was the chairman. (Mary Hillyer was its executive director.)

As Hitler's villainies became more intolerable and his imperialist intentions more clear, thousands of Norman's friends, especially the Jewish people of New York, deserted him. The Socialist Party in New York split wide open, with leading Jewish members going over to the Social Democratic Federation. But Norman never lost his moral poise or castigated those former friends who regarded him as a traitor. Many years later he did acknowledge that he might have been wrong. "In my old age," he said, "looking back on my life, I can admit various mistakes, but I regret no major decisions except possibly my opposition to American entry into World War II."

My strenuous years with the LID were made even more strenuous by my work with the Socialist Party and the La Follette progressive movement of 1924. We Socialists were often accused of doctrinaire squabbling and childish political separatism because we would not cooperate officially with the older political parties. At the same time the Communists were accusing us of selling out to the capitalist machines and betraying the working class. The Communists worked inside many Socialist locals, disrupting them systematically by their program of direct action. We tried to say temperate things about them and we went out of our way to praise anything we could find to praise in the Soviet Union, but their abuse continued. I remember debating the Communist leader Earl Browder at Cornell on socialism and communism during the so-called United Front days, and even then his denunciations of me and my brand of democratic socialism were fantastically unreal. I was an agent of "capitalist imperialism." With such opposition on the left and with the inevitable internal recriminations that usually afflict any defeated political movement, it was not pleasant to be a Socialist in the 1920's and 1930's.

When in 1924 the dull, reactionary Coolidge and the Wall Street lawyer John W. Davis were nominated for the presidency on the old party tickets, we Socialists decided to make the break from socialist separatism and support for President Senator Robert M. La Follette of Wisconsin on an independent Progressive ticket. He was not a socialist, but he was a brave fighter for almost all of the immediate demands of the socialist movement, and his bristly pompadour had become a political symbol of indignant righteousness. His platform called for the government ownership of railroads and water power. The Farmer Labor Party and the A. F. of L. went along with us in supporting him.

By this time Julia and I, growing tired of the long dreary winters in Rochester, had united with our two best friends, Edith Christenson, union organizer, and Spencer Williams,

Utica and Rochester journalist, in a wild trek to the Pacific Coast, where we lived for a year in San Diego's sunshine. We crossed the continent in Edith Christenson's Model T Ford, bumping along over great stretches of unpaved road and frequently alighting to fix an expiring tire.

It was from San Diego that I was commandeered for work in the La Follette campaign. La Follette himself, very temperamental and touchy, had refused to schedule a single campaign speech west of Kansas City although the West Coast was the most fertile field for his political evangelism. (In the 1924 election he ran far ahead of Davis in that area.) He was very effective in personal appearances but his radio personality—radio was just becoming important in politics—was not pleasing. His rather vociferous oratorical style came over the air with the effect of ranting. Nevertheless, in spite of all the difficulties, we thought we had an excellent chance under his leadership of launching a new progressive third party, and the Socialists worked very hard to attain that goal.

Because of the lack of money I was the only out-of-state campaign speaker in several western states, and I was a pathetic substitute for La Follette himself. I remember an awful moment in Reno, Nevada, when a great crowd of cattlemen and farmers had filled the city's largest theater to hear a rousing speech and suddenly, about ten minutes from the end, my voice almost disappeared. I had worn it down to a hoarse whisper and the peroration could be heard only in the front two rows.

On our side in that campaign we stressed the Teapot Dome scandals and tried to pin some of the responsibility on Coolidge because it was his party that had given us Harding, Daugherty, and Fall. This was somewhat unfair to Coolidge, who had no direct connection with the scandals. Our best campaign speaker was a man who had been active in exposing Teapot Dome, our candidate for Vice-President, Senator Burton K. Wheeler. In view of his later very conservative record it is hard to remember how progressive he seemed in 1924. When Coolidge refused to debate on Teapot Dome or to discuss its implications, Wheeler responded by putting an empty chair on each platform when he made a campaign speech, wagging his finger at the absent "Coolidge" very effectively and reciting all the unpleasant facts for the empty chair to "hear."

Our anti-Coolidge aspersions were unsuccessful, largely because, with the exception of the Scripps chain, the newspapers of the country were virtually unanimous in their bitter opposition. Coolidge blandly ignored us and continued to talk about the national prosperity. He announced mournfully that "When more and more people are thrown out of work, unemployment results." That seemed to be the limit of his economic perspicacity. Why not keep cool with Coolidge? The spirit of that question did more to defeat us than all the propaganda. The official anti-radical propaganda was turned loose on us in great quantities in the closing weeks of the campaign. I think that if the election had been held on October 1, La Follette would have carried six or seven states. There was considerable Catholic resentment against the Democratic Party because it was believed that Al Smith's religion had been the primary cause of his defeat in the 1924 Democratic convention. We hoped to secure many Catholic backlash votes.

Then one of the greatest smear attacks in the history of American politics began. The Republicans spent more than $4 million in the attack while we were spending $221,000. They flooded the newspapers and certain picked magazines with articles declaring that La Follette was a Red, supported by a motley collection of pro-Red conspirators who wanted to take over American society and Sovietize it. It was said that Russian money was behind La Follette. Many west coast employers notified their employees that if La Follette should be elected their factories would close down. According to the *Saturday Evening Post*, La Follette was the candidate of "the Reds, the Pinks, the Blues, and the Yellows." Joseph P. Kennedy warned his fellow Catholics that the election of La Follette would destroy their church. When 213 college professors came out for La

Follette, they were pilloried by the *Cincinnati Enquirer* with a demand that they be discharged as unfit to teach American youth.

The campaign of economic terror paid off. Prosperity and Americanism were vindicated in the Coolidge landslide. Although La Follette polled five times the vote ever polled by a Socialist candidate, he carried in the end only one state, his home state of Wisconsin. It was a crushing blow for him and for the whole movement toward a progressive third party. The labor unions soon deserted the sinking ship and we Socialists were left with no appreciable gain for our own party.

7. CHINA AND RUSSIA IN REVOLUTION

ONE OF THE GREAT BENISONS of my seasonal work with the LID was that long summers were available for travel and writing. Travel was favored if it could produce college and lyceum lectures for consumption the following winter, bringing in fees for the organization. I was free to travel almost anywhere at my own expense if I could live on my salary checks, which arrived each week during the year.

One of my ambitions for years had been to see communism at work—also Western imperialism, as it was confronted by "the yellow peril." There were two places in the world where I could see these things, Russia and China. Why not go there? Julia suggested that we try to work out a plan to go together. Julia was willing to leave her San Diego newspaper job briefly for such a venture, and she found that her bosses were willing. But what of the children?

Paul Jr. was six and had just started school in San Diego; Rufus was only four. A blessed solution to that problem was found when my Aunt Annie, who was then living on her farm in Irvington, Alabama, with a summer cottage in Bay View, Michigan, volunteered to take the boys and give them loving care. We shipped them off to Bay View with our German housekeeper, Tante Adele, and started our own long journey westward. By this time we had expanded our plan to a world tour. It was just as sensible to circle the globe on such a journey as it was to come back to California. We firmly intended to come back to California but we never did because the lure of New York captured us both.

So, in 1925, four of us, old friends and Socialist adventurers, undertook the long journey, Julia and I, Edith Christenson, and Spencer Williams, who was then working on the *San Diego Union*. (Spencer, then a liberal journalist working on a conservative newspaper, was destined later to live many years in Russia, finally becoming a full-time propagandist against the Soviets.)

We were all young and healthy and full of romantic illusions. We saw no serious obstacle in the fact that our total budget allowed only $1000 each for our five-month trek. We actually managed the world tour on that amount, and out of it I produced a lecture, "Around the World Steerage," which was quite popular in colleges and forums. Also I produced several articles for *The Nation, The World Tomorrow*, and the Sunday magazine of *The New York Times*.

I hate to think of the physical chances we took on that five-month trek, the chances of dysentery, smallpox, typhus, yellow fever, and malaria. We slept on the floors of freight trains in rural China, wedged in between sweating coolies, tossed restlessly on straw mattresses among the bedbugs of the Trans-Siberian railway, and lay on the mats of Japanese hotels where the stench of open sewers came up from below. We finished those five months still hale and hearty, with only a few agonizing intervals of dysentery. Ultimately, two years later in 1927, I returned to the Orient alone, and I witnessed some of the most exciting events of the Chinese revolution.

In that first oriental journey in 1925 we were lucky enough to land in China at one of the most critical moments in its history. A great revolt against foreign extraterritorial concessions had broken out in Shanghai, spearheaded by a student strike. Nationalist fervor was combined with Communist plotting and the fiery exuberance of youth. The "white imperialists" were the enemy, and we were whites, but we soon made it apparent that our sympathies were with the Chinese. *The Nation* had long been a champion of Chinese rights, and I carried credentials from *The Nation*. In any case, Americans, although their gunboats had been anchored in the Yangtze for many years, were not quite so villainous in Chinese eyes as the European powers which had built their great extra-territorial concessions in Shanghai and Hong Kong. At that time Great Britain was the No. 1 villain, and Japan was No. 2.

I interviewed the student strike leaders in Shanghai and sent back their statements to *The Nation*. I also interviewed a few Chinese and foreign businessmen. My reporting was distinctly partisan. The student leader of the Shanghai strike, a soft-voiced young man with a long white gown and thick-lensed glasses, told me earnestly: "This strike of the Chinese people is not Bolshevik, not anti-Christian, and not anti-foreign. It is anti-imperialist. It is a human movement for human rights. It is directed chiefly against Great Britain and Japan because they are the worst offenders."

He was telling part of the truth. His strike movement was shot through and through with Communist influence and there were anti-foreign and anti-white undertones in the campaign. Why shouldn't there be? The whole history of China's relationship with the West had been a history of military humiliation and racial discrimination. The beak-nosed white man, backed by his gunboats and followed by his missionaries, had come into the Orient as a self-righteous conqueror, carving out of the nation many of its choicest areas, areas where foreign troops and police dominated the scene and mercilessly shot down any Chinese who challenged their rule.

Shanghai was the star exhibit in this network of foreign concessions. It was rich and prosperous—for the foreign whites. It provided a startling contrast between the poverty of the poor (Chinese) and the riches of the rich (European). From the point of view of Chinese patriots, Shanghai was a structure of arrogance based on racial humiliation, sanctified by Christian hypocrisy. The Chinese rebellion which I witnessed in 1925 and 1927 was a war of color as well as of class. The two could not be separated. In the middle of the 1925 strike I saw British ladies in black silk gowns, carrying black-bound prayer books, walking slowly across the park on their way to the Anglican cathedral where they prayed for the health of King George V. They were serenely oblivious to the issues that lay behind the strike. Their chief concern was that they might be thwarted in their common practice of hiring a good Chinese servant girl for $10 a month. On their way to the cathedral they passed a sign at the entrance to a park which read "Chinese and dogs not admitted."

After I saw that sign, the dispatches I sent back to America were more than ordinarily one-sided. I wondered what the reaction of Americans would have been if China had captured part of New York City and erected a sign: "Americans and dogs not admitted." I cabled to the United States urgent appeals to send money to aid the strikers, and for years afterward those telegrams, having fallen into the hands of the various anti-Red professionals in Washington, were used in the *Congressional Record* and elsewhere to brand me as a "Communist."

The Chinese revolution had already become, to some extent, anti-Christian simply because the enemy was nominally Christian. The leftists wanted to abolish all Christmas celebrations, close down all Christian schools, and keep every Christian student out of all nationalist enterprises. The student rebels favored this anti-Christian program in spite of the fact that their patron saint, Dr. Sun Yat-sen, had once attended a missionary school and for a time had been a devout Christian. (Sun had died just before our 1925 arrival.)

In Shanghai the four of us stayed during the student strike at the compound of the American-controlled China Inland Mission, where good meals were served cheap and the mosquitoes did not devour anyone who kept his bednets closed at night. At the long tables in the dining room, Georgia fundamentalists, attired in white duck, ate their quite elegant food while Chinese boys in the balconies kept them cool by pulling back and forth gigantic punkah fans tied to the ceiling. For the time being the missionaries had nothing to do but pray, read the Bible, and talk about the Chinese corruption which had produced the great strike. Most of them were absurdly undereducated products of southern American Bible seminaries, the last persons in the world who should have been trusted to act as ambassadors of western culture to one of the oldest civilizations in the world. One of them summed up his social outlook to me by saying: "What these people need is character. They lie and cheat and steal until the Lord Jesus Christ comes into their hearts. Have I any program for social reform in China? I do not mix in politics. I am a minister of Christ."

In practice, these missionaries were ministers of the white race living so far above the level of the Chinese workers that the relationship between them and their "rice Christians" was a relationship of master and servant. Although the missionaries were making very little headway in China, they were sending back to America the usual rainbow-tinted versions of their success, alleging that millions of the Chinese people were "hungrily calling for Christ" and that a little more American money might make the difference between a heathen nation and a Christian commonwealth. Actually it was costing these missionaries far more to win a Chinese convert to Christianity than the conversion of a Georgia cracker would have cost at home. The British missionaries were spending at least $800 to secure each Chinese convert, and the American missionaries were spending much more. In one district the Americans had to hire, on the average, four salaried workers to acquire one Chinese convert. Later on, when the Communist forces captured mainland China, ninety percent of the alleged three million Chinese Christians faded away.

Usually I did not bother to argue with any of these missionaries about religion, but once in Hankow in 1927, during my second stay in China, I could not keep quiet.

I was staying at the mission compound of a Georgia Baptist missionary who, while ministering to a small congregation of rice Christians, was making a good extra living by boarding foreigners who came up the Yangtze. (I never saw his congregation and I think it was largely mythical.) Discovering my clerical past, he launched into an exposition of his religious philosophy. The future of man, he said, is all made clear in the Bible. The Bible told us what would happen to the world.

He took down his Bible, turned to an obscure and ambiguous verse in Daniel, and read it aloud to me. This, he said, was the voice of God saying that the world would come to an end in 1936. That gave us nine years to repent. He, the missionary, would do his best during those nine years to save a few souls for the Judgment Day. The time was late and persons like myself should heed the warning.

Having nothing else to do for several hours, I launched into a detailed discussion of this missionary's prophecies, basing my points on biblical higher criticism. I found that, like most fundamentalists, he knew practically nothing about the real origins of the books of the Bible, assuming that the whole amalgam was produced by God himself and transmitted to man by some infallible, magic mechanism. He did not even know what languages had been used in the writing of the Bible, assuming that the original of the King James version of the New Testament had been written in a language that Jesus actually spoke.

I thought then that my exposition was a waste of time. My missionary seemed stubbornly determined to cling to his established belief. But ten years later I discovered him in California entirely cured of his earlier fundamentalism and preaching a modernized social-service gospel. Perhaps one factor in his changed outlook was that the nine fateful years had already passed and the earth was still serenely moving around the sun.

The great northward drive of the Kuomintang, led by Chiang Kai-shek, had begun in 1926, and by the time I returned to China in 1927 the Wuhan-Hankow complex had been captured from the warlords. But then the revolutionary movement split in two. Chiang took the more conservative section to start a new government in Nanking, and the leftist sympathizers set up their own regime in Hankow under the nominal leadership of a smooth politician, Wang Ching-wei. That Hankow regime was one of the strangest conglomerations of patriots and expatriates in all history. Its foreign secretary, Eugene Chen, a native of Trinidad, could not even speak Chinese well. The dominant figure in the regime was a man who held no office, Mikhail Borodin.

I talked with Borodin a number of times through the good offices of that red-haired beauty of the revolution Rayna Prohme, who was immortalized by Vincent Sheehan as a kind of mystic, revolutionary saint in his best-selling *Personal History*. The other notable lady who was with us in Hankow at that time was Anna Louise Strong, apple-cheeked apostle of Stalin who later became an equally starry-eyed disciple of Mao Tse-tung. She told no lies—well, hardly any—but she could omit more significant truths in her dispatches than any other correspondent I met. I had known her in New York when she wrote effective and emotional working-class "poetry" for the Socialist *New York Call*. She piloted me around Hankow with all the naïve enthusiasm of an adolescent. When she died in Peking in 1970 at the age of eighty-four, the American press rightly described her career as one of the most bizarre in history.

Borodin, then a vigorous and swarthy man of forty-three with a heavy black mustache, talked to me with amazing frankness. He was a man of magnetic presence with a deep, vibrant voice, and he spoke in colloquial Chicago English, which was natural enough because he had lived in the United States for eleven years and had once been a Chicago schoolteacher. Starting life with the name of Mikhail Grusenberg, he had fled to the United States to save his life after he had been assigned by Lenin to a dangerous mission in Riga. Returning to Russia after the Bolshevik Revolution, he moved up gradually in the

Soviet hierarchy until he became the chief Russian representative in the Orient and the ranking adviser to Sun Yat-sen in Canton. There he helped to shape the early stages of Kuomintang development along Soviet lines.

The Chinese, he told me, were not ready for communism. This was obvious enough, but it was rather startling for the leading Communist in the Orient to admit it so frankly. The Moscow bureaucracy at home did not entirely agree with him; it was split wide open over the theory of its coming world revolution. Stalin, for the moment, seemed to be on Borodin's side. Stalin had published his theory of "socialism in one country" in the fall of 1924.

Borodin failed in China because the force of Chinese nationalism was far stronger than the force of Russian communism. But his masters at home did not welcome failure even when it was excusable and inevitable. Borodin was forced out of Hankow on the very day I left the city in 1927. He fled overland to Russia with Madame Sun Yat-sen and the children of Eugene Chen, then retired to a minor post in Moscow, where he never regained government favor. Finally he was sent to a Soviet concentration camp in one of the Stalin purges and died there in 1953. It took the regime eleven years to restore him to national honor on the eightieth anniversary of his birth in 1964.

I saw a kind of sardonic parallel between Borodin and the American Christian missionaries I met in China. They were both answerable to doctrinaire mission boards at home which were more interested in demonstrating their own wisdom and power than they were in adjusting their campaigns to Chinese realities. Stalin was an unrealistic fundamentalist of the left; the missionaries from the other Georgia were unrealistic fundamentalists of the right. Both required some public success in China to vindicate their own particular types of cultural imperialism. The Communists later captured most of China because, in the last analysis, their communism was more realistic than bourgeois Christianity. It emphasized hunger, exploitation, and redemption in *this* world.

The Communists, with all their fearful cruelties, did accomplish several useful things early in the Chinese revolution. They helped to destroy the ancient family system of authority which enslaved the young to the oldest member of each family grouping. The Kuomintang had talked about a new marriage and family system which might free the women and the young people of the nation; the Communists went beyond talk, abolished the practice of child brides, and exempted the younger generation from the worst forms of family tyranny. It is not surprising that the new women of China played so prominent a part in the Communist movement.

When I finally came to interview Chiang Kai-shek in Nanking, I was rather startled by the contrast between the man before me and the image of the man as it had been presented to me by the left-wingers in Hankow. He certainly did not look or talk like a dictator. He was soft-spoken, modest in language, and seemingly quite idealistic. In his simple tunic he looked even younger than his forty-one years. It was hard to reconcile this man with the fiendish and reactionary butcher of the Hankow legend. He told me nothing new but the things that he did tell me seemed sincere. I came away from the interview saying to myself, "Will a white man ever understand these Chinese?"

This is no apology for the Chiang Kai-shek who later became a right-wing tyrant and puppet of American military interests. But the evolution of Chiang Kai-shek underscores the fact that power corrupts, especially when it is bought power, bought by mercenary interests. Chiang began as an honest patriot inspired by a great vision, the vision of his master, Sun Yat-sen. He still had some of that visionary idealism when I saw him. Later on, after disillusionment and defeat, we bought him as damaged goods and used him as a symbol of a phantom Chinese democracy.

As a result of my two trips to the Orient during the Chinese revolution I arrived at one firm conviction about the future. No race of beak-nosed white men, Russian,

American, or Western European, will ever rule the yellow peoples. The quicker the West can squelch its unrealistic and imperialist-minded militarists and get out of the Orient the better. After centuries of humiliation, the seven hundred million people of China and the many other non-white peoples of Asia are coming into their own. The particular label we attach to their defiance is "communism." There is certainly plenty of communism, Leninist and indigenous, in the Orient but the thing that will defeat us and all other white adventurers, in Vietnam and elsewhere, is national and racial pride. These yellow men are fighting for their home continent and their own race, and no aggregation of white men will ever be able to take the Orient away from them again.

My reaction to Russia in 1925 was more equivocal. Like nearly all the socialists and near-socialists of the period I wanted fearfully to find something good in the Soviet Union. Remember, I said to myself, this is a new society, the first of its kind in the history of man. We should not demand the essentials of a democratic society so early in the game. Give it the benefit of every doubt.

In my anxiety to be fair I was like most of the correspondents in Moscow at that time. Louis Fischer and Walter Duranty both held back a little when it came to complete realism. My old friend and boss Albert Rhys Williams, who helped to pilot us around Moscow, was turning out tracts that were definitely pro-Soviet. Even Bertrand Russell, after he had gone to Russia, reported in a private letter that he loathed the Bolsheviks because "no vestige of freedom remains," but he added, "Yet I think it is the right government for Russia at this moment."

When we four intrepid travelers wanted to reach Russia from China in 1925, there was no way to get there in comfort. The student strike had spread inland from Shanghai, and much of central China was in a state of wild disorder. The four of us were packed with several hundred other customers into a boxcar and slowly dragged toward the north. There was barely room for us to sit down on the floor, but everybody was cheerful and very kind to the white strangers, perhaps because it was rumored that we were on the Chinese side in "the troubles."

Finally reaching Mukden, we caught the famous Trans-Siberian train for Moscow. Eight days for $85 each! That was without meals, but we lived well by buying roasted chickens, black bread, and fruit from the pink-cheeked young peasant women who came down to the train at its frequent stops. Inside our train we slept on four board shelves in an open, crowded coach. Each section had on each side a lower wooden seat, the back of which folded up to make a second bed, and a special top shelf for the third sleeper.

The word "sleeper" is a euphemism. There was no privacy and no silence, no place to take off one's clothes or take a quick bath. After eight days without change of clothing one's body felt crawling even if it was not crawling. And there *was* some crawling. We had all rented for fifty cents each straw ticks or mattresses to soften the hard boards a little and they had all been used before, with resultant predatory life.

My first—and also my last—impression of the Soviet Union of 1925 was one of appalling poverty. At every big station along the Trans-Siberian route great masses of peasants with huge bundles on their backs lay on the cement floors waiting to get on board the train. I was told that many of them had waited for weeks. When a train arrived, they would make a wild scramble for the few available seats, and then drop back before the attacks of the police. No one seemed to look on such things with any special horror or impatience.

In Moscow itself, the picture was a little better, but not much. Although the city was a beehive of industrial and commercial activity, great gangs of ragged youths, looking like scarecrows, ran through the streets, especially in early morning and at night, menacing anybody with a handbag or a purse. And the contrast between the poor and the privileged seemed to be as great as it was in the United States. In this case, of course, the privileged were not the capitalists but the Communist officials. In great limousines these Communist bureaucrats dashed through the narrow streets at reckless speed, oblivious to hapless pedestrians.

I had enough doubts about the validity of the Bolshevik policies to stay away from any formal writing about the economic and political power structure. The one subject I did feel qualified to write about was the shifting moral situation, the revolution in sex and family standards. This subject fascinated me, and it was wide open. The Russian authorities seemed to have no objection to investigation and ventilation in this area. In fact, the government seemed to want some sort of publicity by friendly journalists because a worldwide scandal had been created by the so-called nationalization of women. In America and in Europe the Russian leaders were being pictured as defilers of women and destroyers of the home because of their new code of sexual and family liberty.

Although I soon discovered that there was no such thing as the nationalization of women, I found that there was a sensational story in the rapidly changing sex standards of Moscow as promoted and encouraged by the government. Russia had become the first great country in the world to attempt a quick change in "bourgeois" sex and family life by official action. The new laws constituted a good story in themselves, and the reaction of the young people constituted another striking story.

The wild rumors about the nationalization of women had originally sprung from the new legal policies about marriage, divorce, and abortion adopted in the fall of 1917. New statutes had rescinded the family law of czarist Russia and instituted a regime of almost complete personal freedom in matters of sex. Lenin himself was not personally responsible for this new line of thinking since he was a rather prudish individual, not much concerned with matters of sex. His associates were not prudish. Some of them, particularly the famous woman diplomat Alexandra

Kolontay, preached against the "enslavement" of women and against monogamy itself. If people cared to live together without marriage, they were perfectly free to do so without social stigma. The new philosophy was connected in propaganda with the anti-God movement of this, the first officially atheist regime in history. In official denunciations, Greek Orthodox religion and bourgeois sexual conventions were joined together as absurd relics of superstition.

The thing that impressed me most about the new sexual code of the revolution was the utter frankness with which the young people discussed serious sexual issues. They were developing some of the same kind of frankness about sex which appeared in the United States in the late 1960's, but there was at that time less exhibitionism about it. They seemed to take it all very easily and naturally. Gossip was taboo. Moscow had no gossip papers or scandal magazines and the private life of even the most famous personalities was never discussed publicly. There were probably plenty of sex crimes but they were not discussed in the newspapers. This general policy in handling sex matters was to continue clear through the regime of Khrushchev, although general sex standards were by that time destined to become very much more conventional.

One day I attended an outdoor meeting of six hundred young Communists in Moscow which had been called to discuss sex, abortion, and family standards. Their ages ranged from eighteen to twenty-five. The meeting lasted five hours, and almost everybody stayed to the end. All the speakers favored the right of abortion in licensed hospitals —that right had been established by law in 1920—but there was much detailed discussion and a sharp difference of opinion as to the order of preference for the patients applying for abortion. The government had set an order of preference and the young people examined it soberly. They agreed with the government's order of precedence. First came women out of work, then women with many living children and no husband, then other classes of women.

The one thing in all the propaganda for a new sexual society that was most surprising to me was that birth control was almost never mentioned. Although it was not definitely condemned, its importance was downgraded. A struggle was going on inside the Kremlin about this anti–birth control policy and one result of the struggle was that official policy wavered from year to year. In 1925, when I was there, birth control was a "bourgeois remedy"; later on it became an instrument of working-class emancipation. (In 1950, when I was in Rome for the Holy Year, the Communists had returned to an anti–birth control position, and I watched with amazement while leading Italian Communists quietly helped the Vatican in its campaign against contraception.)

The most startling feature of Moscow's sexual code in 1925 was easy divorce. When both parties agreed to a termination and signed a government application blank asking for divorce, there was not even a space on the blank for "grounds for divorce." Even adultery was not considered significant when couples agreed to disagree. The important thing was that the marriage had failed and that at least one party found its continuation undesirable. This "aggrieved" party could go to the nearest registry office even without telling the other party, secure the divorce for about seventy-five cents, and allow the other party to receive notification by mail. The proceedings in the registry office might take fifteen minutes.

This was the simple procedure if no children were involved. The process was much more complicated if there were children to support. Then arrangements had to be agreed upon (or superimposed) for alimony, and alimony was not a matter for the registry office but for the courts. If there was some father's or mother's income, then each child was entitled to a proportionate share determined by a court.

With such easy divorce it might have been expected that Moscow would have a divorce rate much higher than the divorce rate in the United States. Officially it did not. The Moscow rate was lower than the rate in Cleveland,

and the official Russian rate is still lower than that of the United States.

The great "sexual revolution" in Russia lasted until about 1936. Then Stalin and his associates swung full circle in the direction of what they had once called bourgeois marital standards. The stability of the family became a Communist virtue. The divorce process became more deliberate and much more expensive. Husbands and wives who wanted a divorce were compelled to appear personally and explain. Virginity before marriage was even restored to some of its former glory. The one liberal policy that survived the counter-reformation was easy abortion; that was permitted to continue.

Perhaps the most important permanent improvement in Soviet marriage law was formalized in 1944, the provision that no specific grounds for divorce had to be asserted by either husband or wife. It was enough that they both agreed after due deliberation that the marriage was a failure. Judges were allowed to use wide discretion in deciding whether the reasons for termination were acceptable. This has always seemed to me the most civilized approach to the whole divorce problem, much more civilized and decent than the knockout adversary approach of the American system which often condemns both the combatants and the children to unspeakable public humiliation.

Nominally, religious freedom had been established in the Soviet Union in 1918, but neither religious freedom nor the separation of church and state existed in fact. The Russian Orthodox Church was regarded as the most contemptible and slavish servant of the czarist regime and its priests were treated accordingly. Although Stalin had once matriculated at an Orthodox seminary, he retained no affection for Orthodoxy, nor did Lenin, who equated Christianity and capitalism. The Orthodox Church was disestablished in 1918, its schools were closed and all its great landholdings were taken away.

8. *THE NATION*—AND SEX

I HAVE MENTIONED *The Nation* SEVERAL TIMES. I considered it my magazine in a special sense not only because I had contributed a number of articles to it from many parts of the world but because it was in those days the magazine par excellence of the radical intellectuals. It had a unique standing in the 1920's and 1930's, and it already had a very long and distinguished record as a courageous critical weekly.

I was therefore delighted when in 1926 I was invited to work on the editorial staff of *The Nation* during the summer months while the college work of the LID was in abeyance. Probably my old friend Lewis Gannett was primarily responsible for the opportunity. We had known each other in Maverick Church in East Boston and in Rochester, where his father had served for many years as minister of the Unitarian church. Altogether I was to work for *The Nation* on and off, mostly off, from 1926 to 1929, finally achieving the status of associate editor.

The editorial work was supremely exciting. I had always wanted to write for a living and here was a spot where I could write what I believed. I sat in my small office at 20 Vesey Street, right opposite St. Paul's Episcopal graveyard, and polished each paragraph concerning world events with the loving care of a diamond cutter. I knew that I was always the last man on the totem pole and that made me all the more anxious to contribute something of value to its pages.

The Nation, under its owner and editor Oswald Garrison Villard, had become a kind of journalistic corridor through which passed in quick succession many of the most successful writers and political liberals of the time. The reason for the quick passage was usually financial. The magazine almost never earned any net profit for its owner —it lost $100,000 during the first year of Villard's ownership—and Villard was constantly dropping writers when he felt that he could not afford to keep them on the payroll any longer. His stable of notables included at one time or another all the Van Dorens (Carl, Mark, Irita, and Dorothy), Ernest Gruening, Norman Thomas, Heywood Broun, Ludwig Lewisohn, Max Lerner, I. F. Stone, Charles Angoff, Robert Bendiner, James Wechsler, Raymond Gram Swing, John Macy, Henry Hazlitt, George Soule, and a side stable of contributing editors who were not supposed to do any actual writing—H. L. Mencken, Anatole France, Robert Herrick, and John A. Hobson. During my period on *The Nation* the routine editorial work was done by Freda Kirchwey, later to become managing editor and then owner of the magazine; Dorothy Van Doren, Mark's wife; Arthur Warner, who did the whimsical column "The Drifter"; Joseph Wood Krutch, who covered drama; and Lewis Gannett.

Gannett was the best all-round journalist I had ever known, incredibly swift and accurate in his writing, competent in several languages, and expert in several fields of learning. His specialty then was foreign affairs. He was the logical man to succeed Villard when The Boss—we all called him The Boss—began to slough off his responsibilities, but for some reason Villard did not promote him to the editorship rapidly enough and Lewis, bitterly disappointed, resigned and went to the New York *Herald Tribune,* where he became nationally famous as the daily book columnist, an astonishing proof of his versatility.

Villard was a rather strange person to be editor of a liberal journal. Son of a railroad millionaire, he had inherited a considerable fortune from his father, including ownership of the old New York *Evening Post.* He sold the *Post* and bought *The Nation.* He came by his liberal outlook by family tradition. He was the grandson of William Lloyd Garrison. He was a genteel person whose gentility came in for a great deal of good-natured ribbing at our weekly editorial conferences, over which he presided. We Young Turks did not think much of him as an editor, and I am afraid we showed it a little too plainly.

Generally we suggested assigning the most important editorials to other persons. We were more socialistic than he was and much more bohemian. Heywood Broun—our columnist when I was there—once remarked that *The Nation* "suffers chiefly from the fact that it is edited by gentlemen. . . . Clearly it is his [Villard's] intention to be both radical and respectable." We thought that *The Nation* needed some of the brusque nonrespectability of Mencken, without Mencken's tolerance for fascism, and we all tried to create a nonrespectable image by writing with a considerable amount of daring and innuendo. One of the most joyous occasions during my period on Vesey Street was a blacklist party called to celebrate the fact that *The Nation* had been blacklisted as unpatriotic by the DAR.

There was one area in which Villard was very good, war and militarism. He had specialized in disarmament and imperialism and wrote about them with great authority, even acquiring some influence in high places in Washington. He was perennially excited about American military aggression in Latin America and his continuing attacks on the Yankee invasion of Nicaragua in 1926 and the long occupation of Haiti did a great deal to force our armies out of those countries. At the end of his career, after he had surrendered ownership of *The Nation,* he continued to be so violently opposed to all war, even the American war against Hitler, that he published his "Valedictory" in *The Nation,* repudiating the pro-government policy of Freda Kirchwey as a prostitution of the ideals of the magazine. At his funeral in 1950, *The Nation* was not mentioned.

The Nation in my day was a very much more important influence in national affairs than it is today. Its decline in influence, I think, is largely due to the rise of new kinds of competition. *Time, Newsweek,* and the great television networks now spend millions of dollars to explore every nook and cranny in the political and economic world, and there are very few absolutely new stories to be dredged up. *The Nation* of the 1920's and 1930's frequently scooped all other journals with important inside muckraking stories from Washington and elsewhere, stories which the journals of larger circulation and more conservative bent were unwilling to publish. At that time also *The Nation*'s chief rival, *The New Republic,* was relatively weak, its circulation was less than half that of *The Nation,* and it was not until it moved to Washington that it clearly passed *The Nation* in the race for readers.

A critical political weekly like *The Nation* found it very easy to function effectively in the era of Harding-Coolidge-Hoover. What inviting targets they were! A political cartoonist always finds it easier to lampoon the enemy than to prettify a friend. We wrote our jocularly poisoned paragraphs about the "reactionaries" with a great deal of gusto —and considerable truth—because there was much to expose that needed exposing and there were few journals willing to speak as frankly. Our editorial style was sharp, with a suggestion of a jeer. We were much sharper and more derisive than *The New Republic.* From all over the country bright young journalists sent in articles which had been rejected as too hot for publication by standard journals and, after careful scanning and inquiry, we often published them.

I was assigned for a time to be the first reader of these articles, which meant that every unsolicited article passed through my hands. I had the fearful responsibility of sending it up higher for possible approval or returning it with one of those dreadful rejection slips. At first this rejection process inspired me with all the horror that a decent man feels in drowning an unwanted kitten. But gradually I became accustomed to the exercise of editorial cruelty and before I was finished I accepted the role of executioner with complete confidence in my infallibility. I remember now that I sent back several articles on China by a young lady, then unknown, named Pearl Buck. They were not, I said, in *The Nation* style. It was true that *The Nation* did not carry fiction and Pearl Buck's talent lay in fiction. *The*

Nation wanted quick, sharp reporting with an emphasis on the muckraking approach, leaving rumination on world policy to the editorial columns.

It was often my job to put the magazine to bed at the printer's, shaving the sacred thought of each writer in order to fit the divine words into the appropriate number of ems. In the process I had to correct the spelling of Joe Krutch. Although he was a full professor of English at Columbia, he was the worst speller on the staff; otherwise we all considered him our Great Brain. He became perhaps the most distinguished drama critic of his generation, although he made the egregious error of declaring when talking films first captured the country in 1927 and 1928 that they had no substantial future.

In addition to my reading and revising duties I wrote a great many editorial paragraphs and articles on labor and economic conditions. This was natural enough because I was the only person on the staff who had ever been in the labor movement. My approach to these issues might be described as socialistic-simplistic. I underscored the obvious facts of social injustice and usually laid all unpleasant responsibility at the door of the employers or the reactionary government.

After I had circled through the South and seen for myself a number of the great protest textile strikes that were then disturbing the region, I wrote an article from Greenville, South Carolina, entitled "How to Live on 46 Cents a Day." I described how a typical couple, whose name I disguised, survived by working in a Southern textile mill of those days. They both worked. He received $12.85 a week, she got $9.95. She got up at 4 A.M. to start breakfast for five children, the oldest of whom was nine. For beans, sweet potatoes, fatback, and sometimes pie they spent about $16 a week. There was no sink, only a faucet with running water on the back porch. The children went through the third grade, then entered the mill at the age of nine. She made all the children's clothes; he half-soled their shoes. This was simple stuff for a sophisticated New York audience, but it needed expression and documentation. Even New York liberals needed to be reminded of the way in which their society, the richest society in the history of the world, at that moment intoxicated with Wall Street fever, was neglecting its poor.

In view of the tremendous splash caused by my articles in *The Nation* on the Catholic Church in the 1940's, it is interesting to note that the editors had taken a specifically anti-Catholic line on many aspects of church policy long before I appeared on the scene. It was more than an anti-Catholic line; it was an anti-Christian line, almost an anti-religious line. We Young Turks on *The Nation* thrived on free thought, sexual liberalism, and Fabian socialism, a blend which might be described as the spiritual wine of the period. H. L. Mencken never attended an editorial conference but his name was carried on the masthead as a contributing editor for many years and his attitude toward Christian orthodoxy was popular at *The Nation*. In a 1929 review that Mencken wrote of *The Twilight of Christianity* by Harry Elmer Barnes, he said "I believe that, on the whole, religion is a curse to the human race, even when it is relatively mild and decent." I had not yet gone that far in my iconoclasm.

When the Vatican-Mussolini Concordat of 1929 was signed, a *Nation* article proclaimed: "The agreement between the Pope and Mussolini, which is in effect an alliance between the Papacy and Fascism, shows once more that the Catholic Church never changes and that, if from time to time there seems to be a certain liberal tendency at Rome, it never lasts and the Papacy returns inevitably to a reactionary policy." "The Catholic Church," the article concluded, "cannot be reconciled with modern civilization."

It was something of a shock when, one day, Joe Krutch confessed to me that he was an atheist. In spite of my heresies, I was still enough attached to spiritual symbols to feel that the complete renunciation of God was a bit extreme. Heywood Broun, who had just moved to *The Nation* after a row with Roy Howard over a column on Sacco and Vanzetti, seemed to hold a view of Christianity which approximated my own view. In a broadside attack

on both Catholics and Christianity in 1929, he proclaimed:
"At the present time any liberal or radical movement in
America must be anti-clerical. Freedom in America cannot
be won unless there is a great diminution in the power of
organized religion all along the line." Criticizing the Catholic Church for its policies on birth control and divorce, he
described himself as "a mild sort of Unitarian," and said:

> I cannot conceive of liberty in a land which worships a
> jealous God. . . . If it were possible to wipe out dogmatic
> religion by pressing a button I would hold my finger upon that
> bell with all the fidelity of a small boy who blocked the ocean
> from sneaking through on Holland. . . . In a clear defiance of
> the Constitution, the fiction has been set up that this is a
> Christian country. . . . The pursuit of happiness belongs to us,
> but we must climb around or on the church to get it.

This was written by a man who, only a few years later,
was to become a convert to the Catholic Church. His conversion was, to me, inexplicable. I had known him quite
well and I had thought of him as about the last person in
the world to make the leap to Catholicism. It seemed possible that his amazing decision was the work of his new
wife, who was a Catholic. But this, apparently, was not
true.

My own comments on religion in *The Nation*, when I
was allowed to discuss religion, were quite frank. I attacked the Salvation Army as a "quack doctor" in the field
of welfare. In reviewing *The Ethics of Jesus* by the liberal
Union Seminary professor Harry Ward, I proclaimed, "Golf
and intelligence are two important reasons why millionaires do not go to church." I criticized Harry Ward for
trying to bring his advanced economic thinking within
the narrow confines of the thing called Christianity. I
asked:

> Is it necessary for a professor in a theological seminary to
> pretend that a sound economic morality must come from
> Jesus? Anyone who reads the Gospels with an impartial eye

will discover that Jesus' teaching concerning economic values was confused, fragmentary, and quite inapplicable to a world of tickers, billionaires, and communists. What Ward really means by "the ethic of Jesus" is the ethic of Harry F. Ward, and I don't see why he should be so modest about saying so.

I was allowed to produce an editorial on "Saintly Profiteering" in which I pointed out how unfair it was to allow churches and synagogues to reap tremendous profits by selling downtown land and moving uptown. I pointed out that the Madison Avenue Methodist Church of New York had made $650,000 by moving around the corner and selling its old site for an apartment house and that Temple Emanu-El, with one of the richest congregations in the country, had realized a clear million by selling its land at the corner of 43rd Street and Fifth Avenue and moving twenty-three blocks up the avenue. I concluded that the taxation of churches might not be an ecclesiastical disaster.

Occasionally we strayed over from politics and economics into religious conflict with science, and here we were all on the side of science. I wrote one paragraph on this subject in 1928 when some fundamentalists in Arkansas were trying to impose their anti-science on the public schools. I think it fairly epitomizes the debonair, slightly sneering condescension of *The Nation* intellectuals toward orthodox faith:

Although *The Nation*'s astronomical expert is not in the office as this paragraph is written, we venture to estimate that the center of the universe is 258,532,712,000,000,000 miles from Arkansas. Professor Harlow Shapley and his associates of the Harvard Observatory have at last located in the constellation of Sagittarius the elusive spot which is supposed to be the magnetic focus of our system of stars. We, it seems, are near the edge of things, but nobody knows just where the jumping off place is located. Beyond our universe may be other universes—no comfort for the monists can be found anywhere. There is something incalculably cold-blooded in these astronomers who can toss off lightly a statement that we are a few quadrillion miles away from that Bosom of Omnipotence where our forefathers thought we were. No wonder our Arkansas kinsmen are afraid of these men. While they are measuring the distance between the stars, their brethren in the field of physics have learned to use light waves so accurately in measuring an object that the measurements are subject to an error of not more than three one-millionths of an inch. Some day they may be able to measure the mind of a fundamentalist.

The Nation was far from being anti-Catholic in the invidious sense of that term. Although it was staunchly anti-clerical, it fought hard against the anti-Catholic bigotry which played such a conspicuous part in the Al Smith–Hoover campaign of 1928 and in the Democratic convention battle of 1924. In October before the 1928 election *The Nation* carried an editorial, "The Protestant Menace," declaring: "No we are not alarmed by the Catholic peril in the United States." And it added:

If there is a church menace in this country it is a Protestant rather than a Catholic menace, simply because the tradition of this country is Protestant and the bulk of the population is Protestant. The danger of religious oppression always comes from the majority church. Catholics, despite a different attitude in countries predominantly Catholic, have in this country loyally supported the Constitutional principle of separation of church and state, well knowing that the unofficial state church of this country was Protestant.

It is a little startling to realize that *The Nation* was almost correct in saying that the Catholic Church supported the principle of the separation of church and state. The struggle for birth control had not yet reached national proportions and at that time the hierarchy chose not to assert its demands for tax grants for its schools. (Bishop Hughes of New York had made such demands in 1840 and had been repulsed with so much bitterness that the Catholic bishops withheld similar demands until the 1940's.)

In the liberal circles of the 1920's most non-Catholics agreed with Mencken that the Protestant "wowsers" were more menacing than the Catholic priests. Accordingly, the shortcomings of Catholic policy were rarely discussed in intellectual journals. It was considered bad form to mention the dictatorship of the Pope, and use of the word "papist" was confined to extreme right-wing Protestant journals. Al Smith, though he was a loyal son of the church and had once introduced a bill in Albany giving financial grants to Catholic schools, was not known as a militant Catholic. When he was asked whether he accepted the encyclicals of the Popes as a guide for his political conduct, he burst out, "What in hell is an en-kyklical?"

As we moved nearer to the election of 1928, the political split in *The Nation*'s editorial board became more embarrassing. We were against Hoover, of course, and I was allowed to blister the Scripps-Howard chain for supporting him, but most of the board, including Freda Kirchwey and myself, decided to support Norman Thomas. I liked and respected Smith, but I was still the incorrigible idealist, and in addition I was still a dues-paying member of the Socialist Party. Villard supported Smith, but he was a very genial man about our disagreement, and during the campaign Norman was given friendly billing in both editorials and articles. The election, of course, was a disaster for Norman as well as for Al Smith. Norman polled only 300,000 votes in the whole country, and even Victor Berger, the Socialist Congressman from Milwaukee, was defeated.

The Nation of those days was very "advanced" in matters of sex, and its circulation was based partly on the desire of the younger generation to break through puritan barriers. A sexual revolution had begun and *The Nation* was one of the few journals ready to discuss it frankly. The new attitudes dated from the war, when the flapper emerged on the scene with higher hemlines and silk instead of cotton hose. It was admitted that men had always wanted women; now women, dangling cigarettes from the corners of their mouths even on the street corners, began to admit openly that they wanted men. Some even went so far as to admit that they wanted men outside of marriage. In most of our editorials and articles on sex the institution of marriage was on the defensive. We did not officially advocate free love but we came very close to it.

In 1929, as part of a series of articles on modern marriage, Charles Wood wrote a piece on "What Is Happening to Marriage?" in which he concluded:

It would not surprise me, then, if this turned out to be an age of specialization, in which women when they want children will look for the best fathers for them which they biologically can find, that those who want companions will look for companionable souls, and that those who want love will seek for first-class lovers instead of trying to make a romantic lord and master out of some henpecked breadwinner who must be home regularly on the 5:15.

Editorially we did not go that far. We stuck to such standard liberal theses as the contention that divorce should be obtainable by mutual consent after a due delay for reconciliation, and, of course, we were always harping on the necessity for birth control. One of the most successfully sardonic among us in writing about marriage was Joe Krutch. In his book *More Lives Than One,* written much later, he comments about *The Nation* and his attitude on family problems: "That the institution of marriage could survive more than one generation of frankness and honesty I gravely doubt." In that autobiography he commented about "the gay crusaders" on *The Nation* of the 1920's: "We were all Liberals but even more conspicuously Libertarians or Libertines—in the Eighteenth Century sense of the term, as well as, frequently at least, in the modern sense also." He, like the rest of us in the 1920's, advocated complete frankness in marital relationship. "Husbands and wives," he said, "had the right, almost the duty, to seek 'experience' where they could find it, provided only their partner was kept informed—preferably in detail." In his later judgment Krutch added, "Nothing could have worked worse." In his sixties he advocated a marriage code under which husbands and wives should keep their adulteries (if any) secret from each other.

Neither Julia nor I accepted that last judgment of Joe Krutch. After our children were born, we became utterly typical samples of the sexual revolution of the 1920's, unashamed and joyous in our defiance of orthodox sexual taboos, and we could never say that "nothing worked worse." On the whole, for us, it worked well. We told each other everything and our marriage still endured.

How extraordinarily ordinary that paragraph of my sexual confessions sounds when it is written in the 1970's! Julia and I never did anything in the way of amatory adventure which would not be accepted by today's younger generation as routine. The world has caught up with us— or gone down the moral drain with us. Probably we were more basically conventional than most members of the present generation. In spite of dalliance we firmly adhered to the idea of responsible parenthood, and we conceded that monogamy was the natural form of marriage. We believed in marriage and we believed that people should stay married unless there was complete incompatibility.

I cannot say that my own sexual life outside of marriage was altogether sensible or inspiring or even civilized. The male animal when sexually aroused is not naturally a kindly animal. There is something very cruel in the selfish masculine impulse to woo the desired female with breathless ardor, take her, then discard her. In this instinctive process I occasionally was guilty of inflicting deep wounds without being entirely conscious of my perfidy.

One reason for dissatisfaction in sexual matters during this period was the accursed condom, which was then considered necessary for the prevention of conception.

After the condom came the pill—and blessed be the pill! Perhaps some future historian will hail it as our century's greatest contribution to happiness—and also to the dissolution of Christian monogamy.

The year 1929 was a year of doom for many of us, at *The Nation* and elsewhere. In Wall Street, a few blocks away, men jumped out of windows when the October crash came. *The Nation* had already plummeted in circulation after the excitement of the 1928 campaign, and Villard began to lose more money than ever. He suddenly decided to bring back as managing editor a man who had previously held that post, Henry Raymond Mussey of Wellesley. Lewis Gannett went over to the *Herald Tribune,* and I felt unprotected. I was not surprised therefore when Villard finally informed me that he could no longer afford to keep me, but our parting was very amicable and I had the most pleasant relations with him for many years afterward.

I could always go back to the LID for college lecturing— and I did go back within a year—but I was resolved to try free-lance writing for a while, and the two women in my family made it possible. Julia, bless her, kept me alive for a time by working as a reporter on the *Newark Ledger,* and my Aunt Annie kept the boys on her Alabama farm for a time where, in spite of poor schools, they had a wonderful outdoor life.

I, presumptuously imitating Heywood Broun, developed a syndicated newspaper column called "A Number of Things," but it did not sell well. My style was not suited to whimsy and I lacked both the money and the experience to start a political muckraking column from Washington. For one summer I was blessed with a writing fellowship at Yaddo, a kind of charitable colony for artists and writers in upstate New York financed by George Foster Peabody, where a number of big literary and musical names appeared, including Winthrop Sargeant of *The New Yorker* and a young composer, Aaron Copland, who then pronounced his name to rhyme with top-land. His clanging dissonances completely baffled me. I produced a "book" called *Racketeering High and Low*, which was accepted by a big New York publisher but never published because the libel lawyers refused to clear it. Within two years every anti-corporate charge I had made against the conglomerates of those days had been verified by judicial action, but then it was too late for publication.

Although Julia was at the peak of her journalistic career in those days, I began to notice occasional rather mystifying signs of strain. She had moved over to New York from Newark and had become the woman's page editor of the Newspaper Enterprise Association, the Scripps-Howard feature syndicate. The NEA sent her to Russia to do a feature series on the Soviet Union, especially from the woman's point of view. On the way she stopped in a German nudist colony and did an uproariously funny piece on her own embarrassments among the nude customers where, of course, she had to adopt their costume. In Moscow she saw all the usual public relations officials, including many of our old friends, and came back to do a series which, in retrospect, seems rather naïve. It omitted almost all the ominous features of Soviet policy. But she was unable to finish the series herself, and I, tucked away in a secluded room in the New Yorker Hotel, had to finish it for her. The result was a breezy and interesting but partisan performance which did not reflect the real attitude of either of us toward the Soviet Union. The series, however, was widely used throughout the United States. Its superficial character was revealed when Stalin, a little while later, began his famous purges.

I could not understand why Julia, usually so competent and vibrant, seemed suddenly paralyzed as she faced the task of finishing those articles on Russia. I was soon to know why. One day the telephone in my office rang and a friend of Julia's asked to talk to me. Julia had been complaining for several days of sharp pains in her abdomen and that morning she had gone to a specialist for an examination. I was worried but not much worried. She looked well and cheerful. I thought that it was appendicitis and I knew that appendicitis was easy to cope with. The friend said on the telephone: "I just wanted to tell you that Julia's doctor says she has an obstruction in the intestines and she needs to be operated on immediately. Probably it isn't serious, a tumor or something, but you ought to know. She has gone home."

Somehow I had never thought of physical disaster coming first to Julia. I rushed home to find her cheerful but very, very ill. Fortunately we were able to get immediately the most famous surgeon in New York, but when he had operated upon her the news was tragic. She had intestinal cancer in an advanced stage. A large section of her bowel had to be removed, along with her sexual organs. She almost died on the twelfth day after her operation.

To tell or not to tell, that was the question. I do not know the answer yet. We deceived Julia for a few months after the operation, fixing up some phony explanation for the interruption of her monthly periods. I finally told her. She had hysterics the next day but not in my presence.

Those were frightful years, the two years between Julia's first major operation and her death in the spring of 1934. I had thought before Julia died that I could calmly and judiciously face the problem of death and euthanasia. Neither one of us believed in immortality and we had often confided to each other our belief that in cases of incurable cancer a patient should have the right to speed up the termination. I think that Julia would have taken sleeping pills if she had not felt that that kind of an exit from life would have hurt my standing in the community. In the last months her pain was ineffably horrible. She gradually faded away into a frail, broken shadow, dizzy with drugs. But I found that even in these circumstances I could not bear to hasten her going. About two days before the end, she suddenly stopped breathing while I was watching her. I could have stood there and done nothing. Instead, the thought of my Julia going on out of my reach suddenly overwhelmed me. I caught her frail body and shook it until she was aroused and began to breathe again. She did not die for another forty-eight hours.

9. TARGET: JIMMY WALKER'S TAMMANY

IN THE EARLY 1930's I was suddenly and by pure chance transformed from a Fabian socialist agitator into a New York civic reformer. The transformation was not as bizarre as it might seem. Norman Thomas had become a great civic force in the life of New York City and he inspired me to try out my reform ideas in the New York environment. Two other individuals influenced me to commit myself, James Joseph Walker, the playboy mayor of New York who represented for me all that was loathsome in civic life, and Fiorello La Guardia, the peppery little Italian Congressman who, after a spectacular career in Washington, was destined to become the greatest mayor in the city's history.

Up to that time I had been interested in civic reform only as a rather conventional Socialist who held that the economic system was primarily responsible not only for poverty and injustice but for municipal corruption as well. In general, we Socialists were on the side of the angels in matters of civic rule. We wanted clean government and we had great faith in the cleansing power of democracy but we tended to look down our noses at those good-government leaders who concentrated entirely on good government. We wanted the whole economic and political system transformed, and we never for a moment allowed anybody to forget it.

In New York City the Socialist Party had come to occupy a special position because of two things, the great personal prestige of Norman Thomas, who had become a kind of civic conscience for the middle class, and the presence of a very influential backlog of European-born Jewish workers who had brought sophisticated socialism with them. Thousands of nonsocialists in New York were willing to cross party lines on election day and vote for Norman Thomas because they trusted him personally in spite of his socialism. When he ran for mayor against Jimmy Walker in 1929, with the endorsement of the prestigious Citizens Union, he polled 175,000 votes. When he ran for alderman on the Lower East Side, I served as his campaign manager and for the first time became familiar with the lower world of the city's politics. Norman was soundly defeated by an opponent whose only claim to fame and fortune was summed up in his campaign slogan: "I got the lights on Second Avenue."

During Norman's various campaigns, many nonpartisan committees were formed to support him, numbering many of the most notable independents in the city. Out of these nonpartisan groups we formed a new civic committee and called it the City Affairs Committee. John Haynes Holmes of the Community Church was chosen as chairman. Rabbi Stephen S. Wise was chief vice-chairman along with three other vice-chairmen—Norman Thomas, Professor John Dewey, and Bishop Francis J. McConnell of the Methodist Church. I was chosen executive director and had a "brain trust" of two very brilliant young men who were later to go with me into the La Guardia administration—Henry J. Rosner, who was destined to serve as chief financial expert for New York City's welfare system, and E. Michael White, a Harvard Law School graduate who was to become much later assistant superintendent of the Massachusetts General Hospital. Our office manager was a charming and swiftly competent young lady who had been a journalist on the *Tampa Times* and the Richmond *Times-Dispatch*, Beatrice Mayer, then married to a New York medical student. She was the most versatile genius who ever worked for me, and she kept the committee alive by handling both finances and publicity while I was away on long speaking trips. Thirty-five years later, after the death of our spouses, we married.

Our committee quickly developed a rather amazing influence in the city's newspaper offices partly because the city was ready for a clean-up after years of dismal corruption and partly because we enlisted many leading citizens as members and officers. Morris Ernst, Heywood Broun, Walter Frank, and Joseph McGoldrick were on our executive board. Louis Waldman, well-known labor lawyer, served as our volunteer counsel in many important cases. McGoldrick, then a Columbia professor, was destined to be city controller under La Guardia.

Holmes and Wise were the ideal front men for a moral crusade. They were fearless, eloquent, and theatrical. Between them they could fill any hall in the city for a mass meeting of protest. I have never heard a more dramatic speaking voice than that of Stephen Wise. Holmes was even more theatrical; he actually wrote an anti-war play later which scored a moderate success on Broadway. He had opposed the government in World War I, suffered much public abuse, and survived. At that time Holmes and Wise were great admirers of Norman Thomas but Wise was later to turn against him because of Norman's opposition to our entrance into World War II.

I doubt that any civic reform group in American history ever produced more decibels of noise per dollar of expenditure. For some time I drew only $30 a week from the committee and eked out a living wage from the LID, one reason why we had our offices on the same floor as the LID. In our biggest year, 1932, our total payroll was less than $10,000. After our various financial mailings, asking for citizens' contributions to save the committee, Beatrice Mayer would often come in early to open the envelopes breathlessly and tell us whether we would have full salaries that week.

Our primary target was Tammany, and by Tammany we meant the entire system of corrupt and incompetent government by district leaders. Jimmy Walker, as mayor, was the front man for that system but he was only the top of the iceberg. He presided over the visible government of the city, which centered in the board of estimate, with several citywide officials and five borough presidents, but everybody knew that behind this visible government was the government of the district leaders, Democratic and Republican, who decided which front men would sit behind the horse-shoe desk in the classic old chamber in City Hall. The existence of the board of estimate with its regular open meetings gave us a magnificent opportunity to advertise the corruption in the total system. Many a time Norman Thomas, representing the Socialist Party, and I, representing the City Affairs Committee, attacked the system's leaders so fiercely that we were threatened or expelled from the chamber. Once, I remember, when we were both appearing in opposition to a "corrupt" bus franchise, the police threw me out of the chamber bodily because I called the members of the board "diamonds, very rough diamonds," whereupon one of them shouted, apropos of my Utica jail experience, "You Communist, you jailbird!"

At that time the corruption in the Tammany system was not as crude as it had been during the Tweed era, when votes were bought almost openly. Tammany leaders, under attack, had developed what came to be known as honest graft. They rarely violated a statute because that was unnecessary; they developed equally lucrative techniques for accomplishing the same purpose. As George Washington Plunkitt, who had once operated a bootblack stand in front of the New York County Court House, said: "There's an honest graft, and I'm an example of how it works. I might sum up the whole thing by sayin': 'I seen my opportunities and I took 'em.'"

The "opportunities" were partly in the field of municipal employment and partly in such auxiliary services as insurance, law, and building contracts. A skillful district leader could quite easily skim off the financial cream for himself and reward the appropriate contractors and city employees without being caught in any legal trap. Joseph McGoldrick estimated that, in the years just before our City Affairs Committee began, the district leaders of the city were averaging a gross of about $100,000 each, and the Seabury investigation seemed to prove that McGoldrick's estimate was modest. The leaders themselves and their families and friends were appointed to sinecures on the city payroll where they performed a minimum of service for the city and a maximum of service for Tammany. All appointees who gained access to the city's payroll in such a manner were expected to kick back to the party a substantial contribution, always legal and rarely publicized, but carefully noted by the district leaders, who penalized any ungenerous underling.

The lower courts of the city were particularly corrupt in this regard. A Tammany mayor appointed magistrates and other lower court judges on recommendation of the leaders, and the usual payoff to the machine for a $10,000 job— that was the prevailing salary of magistrates—was $10,000 or one year's pay, contributed over a period of years. This particular part of the judicial racket was operated on a two-party basis. Democratic and Republican leaders met in quiet sessions and agreed to split the number of judges, the Democrats getting the lion's share because the Republican Party was relatively weak. The higher court judges, also nominated by the machines, were expected to contribute heavily to party coffers, sometimes as much as $50,000 for a high appointment, discreetly passed on to the right parties in unmarked bills.

The system was more than a system of corruption; it was also a system of clubhouse dictatorship at election time. Each precinct captain in a district could normally rely on the support of about six hundred officeholders who, if they were not beholden to him directly, were usually anxious to curry favor with him. There were some 106 district leaders on the city payroll in 1932, nearly all in positions exempt from civil service examinations. At election time these district leaders and their underlings habitually resorted to illegal means to capture their districts, and at this point they often secured the cooperation of the police.

Here is one incident which was quite typical of Tammany election methods in those days. As a watcher at the polls in a Tammany district in the Lower East Side, I watched while a woman consulted with precinct leaders, then voted twice in a voting machine. I shouted to two police officers: "Arrest that woman. I will testify that she voted twice." The police captain turned on me and threatened: "If you make any more trouble around here, I will arrest you." I continued to protest, whereupon the police gave me "the bum's rush" out to the street. They did not arrest me because that would have given me a day in court. Fortunately, many other witnesses could testify to irregularities in that precinct on that day, and the woman offender, thoroughly frightened by some astute questioning from the staff of Thomas E. Dewey—Dewey was just then on the way up as a young federal prosecutor—confessed. Four election inspectors were found guilty and one of the Tammany henchmen went to prison for several years.

We were fortunate in having as our major target James Joseph Walker, universally and correctly known as the playboy mayor of New York. It suited our purposes to promote and emphasize this description of Walker, and almost daily he gave us ammunition. Frequently he stayed up most of the night at theater parties and then came in two or three hours late to the all-important meetings of the board of estimate, where he tried to handle an agenda which he had not even scanned. He took seven vacations in his first two years in office, totaling 143 days. He was far happier with his theatrical friends than he was with his political pals, and I think he always cherished a secret ambition to make good in the world of music and the theater. He had, in fact, started life as a vaudeville gag man and pianist and when he was a very young man had written at least one fairly successful song—"Will You Love Me in December as You Did in May?"—a piece that seemed all too appropriate many years later when he was leaving his wife for the actress Betty Compton.

Many of New York's voters enjoyed the doings of this

debonair young man and wished that they could have such a good time. They read about his joyous parties with envy and some admiration. Even when he lost $2000 in one night at a baccarat table in Cannes, France, and the *Daily News* headed its editorial, "Come on Home, Jimmy," most of the voters laughed. Their Jimmy was a happy man, always generous to his friends, and as yet nobody had caught him in anything illegal. Even when he was finally caught by Seabury, it is not certain that the populace would have rejected him at the polls if he had been able to win another party nomination. On the night after his dramatic exposure by Seabury in May 1932, he spoke to eighteen thousand cheering admirers at Madison Square Garden, attacking the "vindictiveness" of his enemies and their "political jealousy."

As the scandals in New York City politics mounted, Governor Franklin Roosevelt in Albany was in a tight squeeze. The revelations indicated the need of a thorough investigation of the whole Tammany structure of favoritism and graft, reaching into the bank accounts of the district leaders, their tame judges, and their police associates. But Roosevelt desperately needed the support of Tammany to secure the Democratic nomination for the presidency in the summer of 1932. So he stalled, deploring the partisan nature of some of the criticism of Walker's regime and refusing for a long time to order a general inquiry. His hand was forced by the Appellate Division of the Supreme Court, which chose Samuel Seabury to investigate the magistrates' courts of Manhattan and the Bronx, and out of this limited inquiry and its resultant scandals came the general inquiry which finally led to Walker's downfall. Our small but effectively noisy City Affairs Committee helped to keep the pot boiling by filing with the appropriate officials many sets of charges against the various malefactors of suspicious wealth who were exposed by Samuel Seabury and by our own investigations.

The man, Samuel Seabury, who challenged Tammany in the great inquiry of the early 1930's, was not a popular politician. (Herbert Mitgang of *The New York Times* has written an admirable life of him.) He was rather aloof, august, imposingly respectable, looking down from his white-headed dignity through pince-nez eyeglasses. Before he began his inquiries into city government he had already become one of the highest priced appeal lawyers in the city, wealthy and secure in his legal eminence. Descended from an Episcopal bishop of the same name, he represented the old Protestant aristocracy, which was rapidly fading away in the New York area. Becoming a city judge at the age of twenty-eight, he had served as a member of the state's highest court and when he was only forty-one years old had presided at the trial of Herman Rosenthal, who was convicted of the murder of the police lieutenant Charles Becker.

What most New Yorkers did not remember about Samuel Seabury was that his early political record was almost as liberal as that of Norman Thomas. He had supported Henry George on a single-tax platform for mayor of New York in 1897 and served as president of the Manhattan Single Tax Club. He once ran for a minor judgeship on the ticket of the Independent Labor Party.

As Seabury exposed various Tammany officials, usually through the device of the subpoenaed bank account, we in the City Affairs Committee tried to popularize everything that he discovered and distribute the material to the public. Our vice-chairman, Professor John Dewey, produced—I wrote most of it—a pamphlet called "New York and the Seabury Investigation," which, with tongue in cheek, we offered as a "textbook" in municipal corruption to the New York City public schools. We asked: Why should not the children know the truth about the way the city was ruled? We used the techniques of ridicule rather freely. The stout boss of Brooklyn, John H. McCooey, was pictured sitting on a milking stool milking a cow whose rear end appeared in the foreground of the picture and underneath was the inscription: "A jolly family man from Brooklyn who loves milking. He is John H. McCooey, Democratic boss, father of a rising young Supreme Court judge, and brother of an associate superintendent of schools." The picture made an instant hit and was used nationally by *Time* and other publications.

We secured a picture of the Democratic boss of Queens, John Theofel, looking like the Democratic boss of Queens, trying to shield his face from photographers just after he had come out from a grilling by Judge Seabury. Next to that picture we printed part of Theofel's own testimony describing the way in which district leaders chose New York's judges, allotting a certain number of judges to each of the two dominant political parties without much consideration of fitness. One Democratic-Republican deal had given a Supreme Court judgeship to a thirty-one-year-old son of Boss McCooey. In our "textbook" we moralized:

Why are party workers—precinct captains, district leaders, county bosses—willing to give so freely of their time without pay? The answer is that their work is not without pay. . . . The great majority of professional politicians are in politics for what they can get out of it. Little bosses do favors for big bosses because they expect favors in return. Big bosses do favors for little bosses for the same reason, and these favors are at the expense of the citizen and taxpayer. As Boss Croker testified in 1889 in answer to the question: "Then you are working for your own pocket, are you not?" "All the time, the same as you."

E. L. Godkin of *The Nation* once said, "The three things a Tammany leader most dreaded were, in the ascending order of repulsiveness, the penitentiary, honest industry and biography." Seabury specialized in what might be called sardonic biography, and we in the City Affairs Committee assiduously circulated the biography, with appropriate trimmings. Seabury's first big coup in sardonic biography came when he examined Sheriff Thomas M. Farley of New York County, who was simultaneously leader of the fourteenth district of Manhattan, a man who had come up through the Tammany system by serving successively as alderman, deputy county clerk, and county clerk. Before a packed hearing chamber Seabury asked him to explain bank deposits of $360,000 in seven years on an explainable income of $90,000. He stuttered and stammered and then admitted the existence in his home of a tin box, a "wonderful tin box" from which he seemed to draw endless riches without seriously impairing the original supply. "Kind of a magic box," said Seabury. "It was a wonderful box," replied Farley. "A wonderful box," said Seabury. "What did you have to do—rub the lock with a little gold and open it to find more money?" Instantly the leaders of Tammany became "the Tin Box Brigade," and the appellation was worth a hundred books of statistics in the anti-Tammany crusade.

Roosevelt, in the face of the ridicule, decided that he would have to act. He removed Sheriff Farley but carefully preserved his own standing with Tammany by appointing to the post another district leader recommended by John F. Curry. In the eyes of Tammany Farley was not a disgraced person even after his "tin box" testimony. He was the guest of honor at three great banquets at three of New York's leading hotels and the banquets were attended by many of New York's leading capitalists and churchmen. When Farley died he was given a huge funeral at St. Patrick's Cathedral.

Even before the major Seabury charges against Mayor Walker, Holmes and Wise and the other members of the City Affairs Committee board had decided to marshal all the evidence against Walker which had been produced up to the spring of 1931 and file charges against him with Governor Roosevelt, asking his removal. Unhappily I had to be in California for the LID when this move was made and had no part in it. The committee had sent several other charges against other officials to Roosevelt in an attempt to smoke him out and force him into an open break with Tammany. Then in March 1931 the committee formally asked for Walker's removal.

The committee in making such preliminary charges was open to the criticism that it was acting prematurely for the sake of publicity but it should be remembered that up to the time of its charges against Walker no *general* inquiry had been ordered by Roosevelt into New York City affairs. There was danger that after all the turmoil and hubbub the investigations would be confined to little pockets in the whole corrupt system. Seabury apparently welcomed the Holmes-Wise cooperation, for he was gunning for the Democratic nomination for the presidency himself and he had no serious objection to embarrassing Roosevelt through two distinguished New York divines.

Roosevelt allowed Walker to answer the Holmes-Wise charges with superficial generalizations and then dismissed them without permitting a rebuttal. Whereupon Holmes and Wise blistered him with high-toned clerical rhetoric, and he blistered them by declaring, "If they would serve their God as they seek to serve themselves the people of New York would be the gainers." On the whole I think that Roosevelt came out second best in the exchange.

In the New York newspapers Roosevelt was pictured as an evasive politician. The *World-Telegram*, discribing him as an "irritable autocrat who has all along been trying to keep Tammany votes," said, "His capacity for sustained rage against critics contrasts strangely with his cautious approach to the evils they would reform." Although the Holmes-Wise charges were pretty thin legally, they were very strong morally and they served a useful purpose. Within a week after they were filed, the New York state legislature put through a resolution calling for a general inquiry into New York City affairs, with Seabury as chief counsel.

Seabury, working against tremendous obstacles, finally produced in May 1932 at public hearings the information that led to Walker's downfall. On the day Walker took the witness stand before Seabury, a circus atmosphere prevailed. Outside the chamber a huge crowd of admirers cheered him. Upon entering the hall he waved his gray fedora and held up his hands in the style of a victorious prizefighter. Several women rushed to throw roses in his path. During a recess he came out, posed for the newsreels, and heard the newsboys shouting, "Jimmy wins the first round by a K.O."

Inside the chamber several Tammany members of the state investigating committee used every means short of a riot to block Seabury's questioning. Seabury, standing calm and firm like a judicial iceberg, proceeded to take Walker to pieces. The mayor, garbed in a natty blue ensemble, started his testimony with cheerful confidence, parrying the Seabury thrusts with great aplomb. His composure lasted for several hours; then he began to wilt as Seabury uncovered the facts about mysterious credit manipulations.

Walker, being a lawyer, had been clever enough not to build up large unexplainable bank accounts, but he had failed to cover up all traces of his credit arrangements and stock transactions. A minor clerk in one of the great New York banks had tipped off the Seabury investigators to look for letters of credit, and in tracing down one letter of credit enough unexplained graft was disclosed to ruin the playboy mayor. The chief scandal centered around a bus franchise involving the Equitable Coach Company, a franchise which Norman and I had repeatedly attacked before the Board of Estimate. Seabury showed that on or about the day on which Walker had signed away the city's streets to this fly-by-night bus concern—it did not own a single bus—Walker had received from one of the promoters of the company a letter of credit for $10,000. The inference was overwhelming that the $10,000 was part of a slush fund. Another Walker "benefactor" had opened a joint brokerage account in the mayor's name from which Walker received $246,000 without investing a penny of his own money.

Seabury finally located Walker's own tin box but he could never prove that it was actually a tin box containing embezzled funds. He proved that a $3000-a-year bookkeeper named Russell T. Sherwood, an employee in Walker's law office, had deposited nearly a million dollars in brokerage and stock accounts, about $700,000 of it in cash, and then had fled to Mexico as soon as Seabury had uncovered the unsavory trail. Seabury, thwarted in his pursuit of final proof, could only make public the suspicious figures and call Sherwood and Walker "the Gold Dust Twins." When confronted with the facts about Sherwood's deposits, Walker cracked back: "I hope he proves it is mine. I will try to collect it."

In spite of these disclosures, Walker attempted to brazen it out. He rightly claimed that he had never been convicted of a crime and that he had not enjoyed the privilege of cross-examining his accusers. He could also claim, for a time at least, that he was the most popular mayor New York City had ever had. Had he not beaten La Guardia by more than 2 to 1 in 1929? And was he not the victim of a Red plot? He utilized to the full the Catholic anti-Communist syndrome, declaring to a Holy Name Fire Department breakfast after the Holmes-Wise charges that the whole thing was "Communistic propaganda" and that he would protect every decent public servant from such attacks. Holmes and Wise, he said, were men whose "work is the salvation of souls who use their power to wreck and destroy others." (The other featured speaker at that fire department communion breakfast was Father Charles E. Coughlin of Detroit, who declared that Holmes "dare not have his name scrutinized.")

When Seabury finally summarized the charges against Walker and sent them to Albany in June 1932 at a time when they would cause the utmost possible embarrassment to the governor before the Democratic presidential convention, Roosevelt acted with great adroitness. He summoned Walker to answer the charges but did not call him into public hearings until he, Roosevelt, had been nominated for President. Then, with the national audience in mind, Roosevelt questioned Walker with skill. The absurdities in Walker's alibis became all too evident.

On September 1 Walker resigned with one terse sentence: "I hereby resign as mayor of the City of New York, the same to take effect immediately." Because of that resignation millions of people in the United States looked upon Roosevelt as the great White Knight who had been chiefly responsible for cleaning up New York. Norman Thomas and I, in a joint public analysis of Roosevelt and his conduct in the Walker case, pointed out that "the White Knight of Albany took his civic conscience out of mothballs only after he had dawdled and dodged his way to the Democratic nomination with the help of Tammany."

Much later Dr. Thomas Darlington, grand sachem of Tammany Hall, told Norman the inside story of how Walker was actually forced to resign. It was not Roosevelt at Albany who tipped the scales against him but "The Power House" in New York, meaning the Roman Catholic Church, whose leaders, after the scandals associating his name with Betty Compton, passed along the word to the district leaders that it was time for Walker to step down in favor of "a good family man." Al Smith was the man who brought the bad news to the district leaders at a meeting in the Plaza Hotel one night during the Roosevelt hearings. "You must resign for the good of the party," Smith told Walker. Walker looked around at the ring of cold faces and knew that he was finished.

Walker had met Betty Compton, a beautiful young Catholic divorcée, during his first year as mayor when he went backstage at the Imperial Theater where she was playing a minor part in a production starring Gertrude Lawrence and Victor Moore. He was forty-six and she was twenty-three. Walker fell madly in love with her, moved away from his wife to live in a hotel, and finally gave Betty money so openly that the liaison started a wave of gossip throughout the city. In the Walker hearings before Roosevelt, Betty's name was protected by a gentleman's agreement—she was described simply as "the person"—but after his resignation, when he dashed off to Paris immediately to live with her, there was no further need of concealment. Walker and his wife were divorced, he married Betty. The new marriage went on the rocks, Betty married another man and died of cancer at the age of forty.

Jimmy Walker's fate seemed so tragic that a great many

New Yorkers felt sorry for him. La Guardia himself seemed to share that sympathy, as his later conduct revealed. I remember sitting next to La Guardia one night in 1937 when he was mayor. The City Hall reporters were giving the annual dinner and variety show. Jim Farley came over and said in a low voice to Fiorello, "Jimmy Walker is here and he would like to come over to shake hands but he wants to be sure that you would welcome the gesture." La Guardia hesitated a moment, then said, "Sure, send him over." So in a moment La Guardia was shaking hands with his old rival while the cameras clicked, and I was smiling as genially as I could—rather stiffly.

Those of us in the City Affairs Committee soon changed our attitude toward Roosevelt after he became President. Wise and Holmes made peace with him, after Wise had made a special call upon him at the White House, because they were devoted champions of the New Deal. I followed suit later. When, in 1933, I had come to the conclusion that FDR should be supported by all of us because of the possibilities in the New Deal, I sat down while crossing the ocean and wrote him a note telling him of my changed attitude but stressing the fact that I still believed in a reformed social structure. He sent me a most cordial note in which he said: "There is no doubt in my mind that although many changes are involved, we are headed towards a new form of social structure. I take it that local, city, and county political methods will be the last to fall in line. Pressures against these current, local methods must be one of our next undertakings." I suppose that is the nearest that FDR ever came to a halfway apology for the fact that he had been so slow in reforming "city and county political methods." He added, "I do hope that you will run down to see me some day after you get back." I never did. At that particular time I was more interested in clean-up politics in New York.

There were so many things around New York to clean up in the early 1930's that it was a very exciting place for a reformer. Norman and I together produced a book called

What's the Matter with New York, which Macmillan published in 1932. In it we tried to pull together all the facts and arguments for simultaneous reform of city government and an unjust social system. I had to write about eighty percent of it because Norman was too busy with other things. It received good reviews but it never sold well. It did produce this story in *The New Yorker* about an incident in Macy's:

Mr. Paul Blanshard, head of the City Affairs Committee and co-author with Norman Thomas of *What's the Matter with New York*, paused in his civic research the other day to conduct a slight personal investigation. He went into a bookstore and picked up a copy of *What's the Matter*. "How's this book selling?" he inquired of a salesgirl, trying to appear casually interested. "Very well," she replied, smiling wisely. "You're Mr. Blanshard, aren't you?" Mr. Blanshard was both pleased and surprised. "Yes. But how did you know me?" he demanded. "Well," said the lady simply, "you aren't Norman Thomas."

The summer of 1933 was a season of particular agony for me for a number of reasons. I knew that Julia's end was near, and by the end of the summer I knew that she knew it. But she held up bravely and kept on working at top speed. When she was sent by her newspaper syndicate to the big Paris fashion openings that summer, I decided to go along to accomplish several purposes of my own. Charles W. Berry, the city's controller, had announced that he was going to tour Europe—at the taxpayers' expense—to study Europe's "municipal methods." It looked like the usual junket. With the blessing of the City Affairs Committee I decided to satirize Berry's project. I traveled all through Europe in the approximate path of the Berry party and, by going third class, I spent $499 while Berry was spending $3000 in tax money. The *Times* ran a triple headline: "Blanshard Tours Europe for $499 . . . Saw More than Berry."

I really did see a great deal more than Berry that

summer because I was concentrating on European methods of reducing funeral costs, and the municipal funeral authorities in Paris, Berlin, Vienna, Dresden, and other cities welcomed my inquiries. They were proud of their accomplishments in cutting down funeral costs to a small fraction of the American average. They had established a democracy in death by selling three grades of funeral, all priced very reasonably, through their city-owned funeral parlors. My findings fitted into my own studies on the subject very neatly. I had published an article in the *Reader's Digest* on "The High Cost of Dying" after undertaking a rather dramatic experiment in the field. In a prison investigation I had noticed the plain pine boxes used by the city for burying its pauper dead. I persuaded the man who made these boxes to make a child's coffin for me in the same style. Then I covered it with velvet and put on brass handles at a total cost of $19 and took it around the country for a lecture tour on funeral extravagance. Later the City Affairs Committee published a small pamphlet on the subject advocating municipal funeral establishments for the United States. I still believe that this type of publicly owned establishment would be the best device for breaking the back of the casket trust and for undermining the foolish vanity of funeral display.

That summer of 1933 was also agonizing for another reason. I finally left the Socialist Party to become an independent progressive, and I handled my exit very clumsily. While serving as floor leader of the so-called militants— Heywood Broun was my assistant in that venture—at the 1932 Milwaukee convention of the party, I had been elected to the executive committee of the Second (Socialist) International after a hot race in which I won out over the famous novelist and editor of the *Jewish Daily Forward*, Abraham Cahan. I had planned to attend a session of the executive committee of this International in Europe, and when I suddenly decided to drop out of the movement after it was too late for the party to choose a substitute, it looked like inexcusable treason to my old friends. And when, a few months later, I went into office with La Guardia in New York, I was widely condemned by my old comrades as a traitor who had sold out to conservative power. Several of my friends, including my future wife Mary Hillyer, would hardly speak to me.

Actually my departure from the Socialist Party had nothing to do with La Guardia. At the time of my decision I had never met him and he was not even nominated for mayor. I think that the determining cause for that decision was the shock of what I saw in Germany. I watched a great demonstration of Hitler youth in Berlin and heard the wildly fanatical orations of Nazi leaders. I watched long lines of Hitler youth trying to stand rigidly at attention like hypnotized robots, many of them fainting in the heat. I saw the anti-Jewish placards and heard of the decree already issued by Hitler dismissing Jews from all government services and the universities. I suffered a case of delayed realism conquering academic theory.

Somehow my theoretical Fabian socialism, even my Socialist Party socialism, seemed too feeble an instrument for dealing with such a threat as Hitler. I felt that American national power was the only answer, and I came to feel that Socialist Party power was too fragile for the emergency. After all, with an excellent candidate even in the middle of a depression in 1932, the party could not elect a single Congressman or poll more than two percent of the national vote.

My old comrades did not take my defection graciously but I noticed that within two or three years my most severe critics followed my example and either joined the New Deal in Washington or joined the La Guardia administration. Most of them tacitly accepted the New Deal as a kind of surrogate for their socialism.

10. LA GUARDIA: MERCURIAL GALAHAD

IT WAS VERY ODD that until the fall of 1933 I had never met the man who was to dominate my life for the next four years, Fiorello La Guardia. Once he and I had been scheduled as the featured speakers at a May Day mass meeting on the Lower East Side and I, wanting to get to bed, had arrived early, made my speech, and left the hall just as he was entering it. Probably he would never have appointed me to any public office if he had heard my speech that night. I was feeling desperately angry about the neglect of the unemployed and I indulged in one of the most revolutionary diatribes of my life.

Fiorello La Guardia was nominally a Republican, but his presence in that party was wholly accidental. He was far to the left of the Republican Party in almost every area of local and national policy and expressed his true convictions in 1924 when he bolted the party and supported La Follette against Coolidge and Davis. Once in New York City, being denied nomination on all old-party tickets, he ran for Congress on the Socialist Party line and was elected. He explained that he was not a Socialist—and this was certainly true—but he was not a Republican either in anything but name. Emotionally and intellectually he belonged in the progressive wing of the Democratic Party, but he refused to be a Democrat in New York City politics because he had a genuine and abiding hatred for Tammany Hall. He tried to help the Democratic Party nationally in 1936 by cooperating with Jim Farley in founding the American Labor Party, a contrivance designed to permit non-Democrats to vote for Roosevelt without seeming to endorse Tammany.

La Guardia had had a checkered career, both professionally and politically. Born in the Lower East Side of New York City in 1882, with an agnostic Italian father and a nonreligious Jewish mother, he had come up through a boyhood of poverty and condescension. He was "the little Wop," short, nonathletic, and without social standing. His father was an itinerant bandmaster in the United States army, moving from camp to camp while trying to support a family on the pay of an enlisted man. Fiorello spent his formative years in Prescott, Arizona, and then, without going to college, he secured a post at the age of nineteen as an American consular agent in Budapest, trading on his knowledge of many foreign languages. He spoke, in addition to English and Italian, a smattering of Serbo-Croatian, Hungarian, Yiddish, and German. Returning to the United States, he became an interpreter for immigrants at Ellis Island and, after taking a special examination, he was allowed to enter New York University Law School to study law at night. Opening a tiny private law office in New York, he practiced for five years quite unsuccessfully, then entered politics and secured a post as a deputy in the state attorney general's office. Then he became the first Italian-American Congressman in Washington, representing a district which was largely Italian. Entering the war as a flier, he was hailed as a war hero and in 1919 was elected for a short term as head of New York's board of aldermen, the second highest post in the city. Then, after all this conspicuous public service, and seven terms as Congressman, he was defeated for re-election. In 1933 he was reduced to the status of a foot-loose unemployed ex-politician. That year of disaster turned out to be his year of opportunity. He became the triumphant Corsican of New York's reform movement.

Judging from my experience with La Guardia, his early hardships had left deep scars upon him. Although he had a brilliantly retentive mind, he had never won social and intellectual recognition. He was the underdog throughout his boyhood, the "little Wop," outside the establishment. It was natural that he should conceive of himself as the representative of the little people, the disinherited, getting revenge on the rich and the snobbish. Being a failure at the law, he had an almost psychopathic loathing for lawyers. The profession had turned him down; now he would turn the profession down. He very rarely consented to talk over any civic problem with any attorney representing any interest. When I would suggest that he might see a certain attorney who represented somebody involved in one of my investigations, he would bark: "Throw him out. I don't want to see any lawyers." (He even applied this rule against me later when, as a lawyer, I tried to see him for a client.)

From his father's career and his own experience in army camps he inherited two affirmative things, a love of music and a commitment to military discipline. Listening to good music was almost his only form of relaxation. Inflicting military discipline on his subordinates was his idea of efficiency. He was the brusque Napoleon, and his physique was startlingly similar to that of his idol. When he opened his law office in 1910, paying $15 a month in rent, he put a bust of Napoleon Bonaparte on his desk. His favorite title for himself was "Major," the title which he had richly earned as a flier in World War I, and all of us called him Major always. All of us except Robert Moses, who was a law unto himself.

With all his deficiencies in education, La Guardia was a very intelligent man, with a shrewd, penetrating, and retentive mind. Somehow also, in spite of a rather shrill, high speaking voice, he had developed into a very effective orator. He was a master of the arts of pause, emphasis, and gesture. He knew how to begin a speech slowly and informally, then to build up to a roaring climax in which he would burst out in rapid-fire eloquence. He rarely used notes and he rarely forgot any important point. He could also tell a good joke with perfect timing, but never a dirty joke. He had a definite mind-block against sex, an ingrained Puritanism, and his attitude regarding marital irregularities was wholly conventional. His sexual philosophy came into the open in the famous Bertrand Russell case in 1940 when the English philosopher was dropped from the roster of the faculty of New York City College because of right-wing criticism of his *Marriage and Morals*. La Guardia, then mayor, made no effort to save Russell from the wolves, and the budget line for Russell's salary was expunged.

The first time I met La Guardia was at his newly opened campaign headquarters when, largely through the influence of Judge Seabury and Adolf Berle, he had already been nominated for mayor on the Republican and Fusion tickets. Paul Kern, one of his closest associates, telephoned me one day to say that the Major would like to speak to me. Kern, a young lawyer then serving as a specialist in the drafting of legislation at Columbia University, was already the Major's most important Man Friday. A former student of Adolf Berle at Columbia, he knew all about my work at the City Affairs Committee and he had heard that the leaders of the committee were ready to support La Guardia for mayor.

When I entered the big bare room at 1501 Broadway, I saw at the other end of the room a short, swarthy stoutish man sitting at his desk with a white apron around his neck, his face covered with lather while a barber was shaving him gingerly. The Little Flower—the English for "Fiorello"—was shouting orders through the foam to several subordinates and trying to dictate a letter to a stenographer at the same time.

When he spied me with Paul Kern, he beckoned me over, shook hands cordially and, when the shaving was finished, entered into an eager conversation. He had read a lot of my stuff from the City Affairs Committee. Was it true that I was ready to support him in the mayoralty race? Yes, emphatically. The campaign desperately needed a research director to pull together all the pertinent data about Tammany, issue a campaign handbook, and supply the speakers with foolproof material for their speeches. Would

I come up to headquarters as director of research for the campaign? Nothing was said about money. I said yes, if the officers of the City Affairs Committee were willing to release me and pay my salary for the period. Since the officers of the committee were more than glad to have me at the center of the campaign, I moved to La Guardia's headquarters almost immediately and soon acquired many top-flight assistants. I edited the campaign handbook and was happy to see that the Major used almost everything we produced without question and without disaster.

Working close to La Guardia was like working in the vicinity of a charged wire. He absorbed ideas almost instantly and he had an immense knowledge of the city and "the club-house bums" he was fighting. He worked with tremendous energy and devotion but he had not learned to assign responsibility to others for organizing the details of a campaign. He would issue orders in one direction and a subordinate, not knowing of the higher orders, would issue orders in a contrary direction. There were amazing gaps in the discipline of his campaign. Henry Pringle, Pulitzer Prize biographer of Theodore Roosevelt and William Howard Taft, had been asked as a volunteer to contribute a biography of La Guardia for campaign purposes. At considerable sacrifice of time and effort he wrote an excellent short biography and sent it in to La Guardia. Then he waited for many weeks to hear what had happened. He thought that it had been rejected as unsatisfactory. But one day he decided to find out for himself. He telephoned La Guardia and asked the Major whether he had had time to read his feeble effort. "Why, didn't you know?" said the Major. "We have already printed a million copies and it is being distributed now to campaign headquarters."

On our side, the campaign was easy not only because of La Guardia's colorful personality and the support of the great newspapers but also because he produced the most specific pledges of reform—and later carried them out to the best of his ability. He declared himself against a general wage cut for the hard-working civil service employees but he promised many cuts in the pay of the big politicians. In our *Fusion Handbook* we proclaimed: "Our city government costs every New York family of four $328 a year! But see what you get for your money!" Marshaling the Seabury accusations against Tammany leaders, we reprinted a statement La Guardia had made when he ran for mayor in 1929: "There is hardly a Tammany politician, with the exception of Alfred E. Smith, who can risk an examination of his private bank accounts."

La Guardia in 1933 dramatized Tammany exploitation with very specific figures. The sinecure chauffeurs of the board of aldermen were getting $2530; he said he would cut them to $2400. The president of the board of aldermen was getting $20,000; he promised to trim him to $15,000. As soon as he became mayor he cut his own salary by $10,000 and he simultaneously cut the salaries of nearly all of us in his cabinet from $15,000 to $10,000.

Although religious scandal played only a small part in the campaign, religious and ethnic loyalties played a very substantial part. In order to appeal to certain minorities and all localities the Fusion and Republican forces felt compelled to produce a "balanced" ticket. For citywide offices there was La Guardia from Manhattan, an Italian Protestant. For president of the board of aldermen there was Bernard Deutsch, an able lawyer from the Bronx who had been very active in the American Jewish Congress. For comptroller there was an unknown Catholic banker from Queens, W. Arthur Cunningham. It was taken for granted that bloc voting and bloc prejudice had to be respected. The Fusion movement relied heavily on the ethnic pride of more than 1 million New Yorkers of Italian descent who had never had an Italian mayor.

And, in the end, bloc prejudice and political inertia almost defeated La Guardia. He became a minority mayor by virtue of his split opposition. He won with nearly 900,000 votes but he could not claim a majority even after all the exposures of the Seabury years. Joseph McKee, supported by Boss Ed Flynn of the Bronx, polled about

600,000 votes, and Tammany's O'Brien came third with a few less. If the Democratic forces had been united, La Guardia might never have become mayor.

Long before he was sworn in as mayor, La Guardia had asked me to become head of the city's Department of Investigation and Accounts, and I had gladly accepted because it was the one important job in the administration that I wanted. Unfortunately, the post was then called Commissioner of Accounts rather than Commissioner of Investigation, the revised title. The old title was always an annoyance to me because my task was really the investigation of all city-oriented graft and incompetence, and routine accounting checks constituted only a small part of the operations of the department. The post was the hottest job in the administration and the commissioner was rightly called "the eyes and ears of the mayor." The post had, for a number of years in the early days, been one of the most important in the city's government. John Purroy Mitchell had held it before becoming a reform mayor, and so had Raymond Fosdick.

My new job could be called the most exciting in the city with the exception of Dewey's post as district attorney of New York County. The law gave me the power to examine any person having relations with the city government and to subpoena any bank account of any city or county official. Although I had no power to prosecute anybody, I had a continuous exposure power and I used it to the limit for the entire four years of the first La Guardia administration. With 150 lawyers, accountants, and assistants on my staff I roamed over a corrupt city with the gusto of a hunter. I took with me into the department not only my old associates of the City Affairs Committee, Henry J. Rosner, E. Michael White, and Beatrice Mayer, but two other close friends, Will Maslow, who later became executive director of the American Jewish Congress, and Louis Yavner, who later was appointed Commissioner of Investigation by La Guardia. As the department's special counsel

and deputy commissioner the mayor appointed Irving Ben
Cooper, who was later to be a federal judge.

When I accepted the office, La Guardia had promised
me that no major finding of any report I gave him would
be suppressed, and he kept that pledge faithfully. This was
a tremendous change in policy, for Walker and other
Tammany mayors had steadily degraded the office by
pigeonholing any reports that showed up defects and mal-
feasance in city offices under their control.

I suppose that the first six months of my first year with
La Guardia were the most exciting months of my life. I
had moved down to a big office on Lafayette Street, about
a block from City Hall, and every few hours would come a
peremptory call from the mayor's office asking me to come
over and run down some scandal which had excited the
mayor. Probably I spent more hours with him in those
months than any other commissioner. With every scan-
dalous complaint that came in, he was as excitable as a
little boy with a new toy, taking seriously many complaints
which were obviously exaggerated or ill informed. Even
anonymous letters often gained his attention. He would
pounce on them greedily, toss them to me, and say: "Now
get on to that. Put your men on to that."

At that time he had his office on the north side of the
beautiful old City Hall, and he would sit behind a big
mahogany desk in that office, swinging his short legs above
the floor like a swarthy Buddha and reaching his fingers
every few moments to one of the six buzzers he used to call
his office slaves. When he was in good humor—about half
the time—there was something cherubic about him and his
enthusiasms. He inspired everyone about him to participate
in his great crusade. In ordering us about, he had absolutely no compunction about our possible discomfort.
Sometimes he would call me in the middle of the night
about some new hot tip he had received and order me to
get my men on the job before anyone could cover up.

One time he called me at 4 A.M. to order me to get my
inspectors to several city hospitals to check some maggoty

and short-weight meat which, according to an anonymous letter, was being delivered without proper inspection. That time the tip was good; our inspectors got to the hospitals before dawn, waited until the meat was delivered, then pounced on the drivers and exposed the whole unsavory racket. Once the mayor got a message to me while I was playing golf on Staten Island on a Saturday afternoon, ordering me to have my entire staff of 150 "stand by" during the whole weekend for a potential raid. By the time I had brought in a few inspectors to the office, La Guardia had already cooled down and canceled the complete mobilization.

At La Guardia's suggestion, we established in our office a citizens' complaint bureau, which had some of the broad functions later developed in European countries under the title ombudsman. More than two thousand complaints about city, county, and borough governments poured into our office in the first three months, many via the mayor's office. Some of them were invaluable hot tips, often written anonymously on unidentifiable paper, by civil service workers within the Tammany system who had been waiting vainly for years to tell somebody about the graft they saw all around them. By May of that first year, I had twenty-one important inquiries going simultaneously.

The most important graft we exposed was the "honest graft" of the spoils system. There were 834 positions in the county offices exempt from civil service examinations, and almost all these posts were held by ward politicians who knew very little about their "work" but managed to draw substantial pay checks from the city treasury by coming in on pay day. That had been the general procedure in my own department when it had been controlled by Walker; there were not even desks, chairs, or telephones in the offices for most of the exempt political employees at the top of the department payroll. They simply strolled in at the appropriate hour, received their unearned increment, and strolled out again. In the civil division of the New York County sheriff's office the average exempt deputy sheriff handled less than three papers a month on which any work was demanded; in Brooklyn it was four papers a month. In the Bronx ninety percent of all the employees in the sheriff's office were members of the county committees of their respective parties, charging to the city's taxpayers the cost of their service to their parties.

There was nothing clearly criminal in this kind of spoils system, so we usually resorted to gentle ridicule in exposing the little people in the system, making no attempt to secure criminal action. One civil service worker whom we designated as Clerk X told us frankly how the spoils system worked in the sheriff's office in Kings County:

A. I claim, and I believe, that the office could be run at this time with 12 deputies and assistants. . . .

Q. How many deputies are there now?

A. 20.

Q. How many assistants are there?

A. Also 20.

Q. So that you could save 8 deputies and 8 assistants?

A. As I said before, when those 4 deputies and 4 assistant deputies were appointed in 1930 I told McCooey they weren't needed, and then there must have been a deal there, because 4 of them are Republicans and 4 are Democrats. . . .

Q. This Miss Wright [Minnie Wright, secretary] does she do any typing?

A. No.

Q. Does she know anything about bookkeeping, do you know?

A. Well, candidly, no. She is a housewife, a wonderful woman.

Q. What is she, a political appointee?

A. Oh yes. They all are.

Q. What is she, an election captain? A district captain?

A. Oh no, she is a co-leader. . . .

Q. Does she do any real work there?

A. I wouldn't call it "real work." It is just copying work . . . in conjunction with the accountant she keeps certain records. She copies from my books and papers and the general cash

book, and I am afraid to balance them because I would
never be able to get a balance out of them. She does the best
she can.

In our campaign against Tammany phrases such as "She
is a housewife, a wonderful woman," and "She does the
best she can" were more valuable than a statistical chart
showing the amount of waste in city government.

One of our prize exhibits was a Brooklyn politician,
Hymie Schorenstein, commissioner of records of Kings
County who was widely believed to be illiterate. I examined
him on this issue:

Q. Can you read anything?
A. A little.
Q. Can you spell your own name?
A. Certainly.
Q. How do you spell it?
A. H-s-t-c-t-e-i-n.
Q. Did you sign this check? [Handing the witness a check for
$2000]
A. Yes.
Q. That is your own signature?
A. Yes.
Q. You wrote that?
A. Yes.
Q. Can you read these letters? [Showing witness a check and
indicating the signature]
A. No. [He had learned to draw his signature as a child draws
a picture.]
Q. Can you read what it says on the red line? [Handing the
check to the witness and pointing to figure $2000]
A. No.
Q. What are the functions of the office of commissioner of
records?
A. I am there every day and see that the work is conducted and
see the books are overhauled and see all the work is done
there. . . .

Q. Do you keep records in your office?
A. Everything is kept in records in the office.
Q. What records do you keep?
A. Whatever the work is done there.
Q. What records are kept in your office?
A. That is taken up with the chief clerk. He conducts the work in keeping the records of everything.

Hymie was not quite so unknowing as he sounded. Although he could not read and write, he had helped to work out a clever scheme for milking a bus corporation for the benefit of himself and two other insiders, and he was not forced to return his ill-gotten gains until exposure by our office.

We found that the city was strewn with unexplained bank accounts of Tammany politicians but that a mere unexplained bank account was not enough to convict a man, especially when the courts were dominated by the same political machines that provided the politicians with sinecures. Before Robert Moses came in as park commissioner and staged a swift and magnificent cleanup, the city's five park departments had been honeycombed with "honest graft." The Brooklyn park commissioner, James J. Browne, and his wife, had banked over a million dollars at a time when his salary totals during the years of service were less than $100,000, and they could give no credible explanation of the surplus amounts.

Altogether during the first three years of our inquiries, ninety-four public officials resigned or were removed under fire as a result of our investigations, and 119 private citizens were prosecuted and penalized by the appropriate prosecuting agencies. Criminal indictments were returned against twenty-eight public officials and twenty of these were convicted, while eighty-six independent citizens were indicted and seventy-five of these were convicted.

Occasionally my inquiries touched the underworld and almost overlapped some of the investigations made by Dewey. Our investigation of the policy or numbers racket attracted a great deal of attention, although I am not sure it did any permanent good. This numbers racket was the Wall Street of the poor, especially of the Negroes in Harlem. It was illegal but it was carried on with the utmost sangfroid in cooperation with paid policemen, paid lawyers, and paid judges. The annual take of the racket was estimated even in those days at $100 million.

The operating scheme of the numbers racket was quite simple. A purchaser of a numbers ticket could, if he chose, get into the game by buying at a neighborhood cigar store a ticket that cost only a few cents. He usually bet on some uncontrolled digits such as the last two numbers in the bank balance of the Federal Reserve System. The chances of winning were astronomically against the purchaser, but the game was rigged so that a great many people won small amounts, and a few, very few, won handsome prizes. The intricate network of racketeers was so arranged that very few collectors—the men who collected the money from small cigar stores and groceries— knew anybody above them in the racket hierarchy except one man, to whom they paid their collections. The collector was at the bottom and above him came the brass man, the controller, the banker, and at the top the famous gangster Dutch Schultz, who collected the ultimate gravy. (After amassing millions through his control of the beer racket in Harlem and the Bronx, Schultz was murdered by his own crowd because he insisted on a plan to kill Thomas E. Dewey and his advisers recognized the folly of such a scheme. Ultimately Dewey proved that Dutch Schultz's chief political protector was the famous Tammany leader Jimmy Hines, and Hines went to Sing Sing.)

Associated with Schultz and his hierarchy were a number of bail bondsmen who suddenly cropped up at the courts to bail out any offender belonging to the ring. A few little people paid fines, which were promptly refunded by the hierarchy. The lawyers were also paid by the hierarchy. The bail bond racket operated so carelessly that the same property was often used over and over again for underwriting bail bonds simultaneously. We uncovered one house that was being used eighteen times concurrently. Under Tammany the district attorneys were so notoriously lax that anyone who shared his spoils in the approved manner—approved by Dutch Schultz—could count on "beating the rap."

La Guardia himself was almost a fanatic in his opposition to gambling of any sort. In his boyhood he had seen how gambling professionals mulcted the soldiers at army bases in Arizona. His own mother had frequently bought policy slips, and never won. I have never seen him express more hatred for any human being than for "the King of the Bookies," a gambler named Frank Erickson, who was said to operate a $12-million-a-year gambling business in Manhattan behind the screen of a florist shop. La Guardia called him a "tinhorn punk" and ordered me to go after him. (Erickson was finally convicted of tax evasion.)

Someone told La Guardia shortly after his election that he had the optional power to sit as a magistrate in the lower courts and commit gamblers to jail. He promptly appeared one day without warning at a Manhattan court and sentenced a slot-machine operator to jail. The headlines and photographs went all over the United States. Next week he did the same thing in Brooklyn. He followed up these gestures with a grand slot-machine smashing spree, breaking up some captured slot machines with a sledge hammer before the cameras. His primary target was the slot-machine boss of New York, Frank Costello.

About fifty little people were convicted as a result of our numbers inquiry, and Dutch Schultz's lawyer was ultimately disbarred. But I could not avoid raising the question of whether it was worthwhile to spend time on the gambling rackets of the little people in the enforcement of a law which seemed impossible to enforce. In 1968 I picked up a copy of *The New York Times* and read a story headed "15 Indicted in Policy Racket" which used exactly the same kind of ammunition in describing the numbers racket that I had used in 1935. In 1970 a New York police inspector estimated that ten thousand employees of organized crime in New York City operated a policy (numbers) racket with a gross annual take of $250 million. The police, he said, raided twenty or thirty policy banks a year, but their operators were all back in business the next day.

The real question for civic reformers to face in analyzing the gambling problem is whether the outlawing of gambling leads to more evil than to good. I have always loathed gambling, but I am inclined to feel now that it would be better to have legalized state-operated gambling than the undercover type of operation which does so much to corrupt the police and the courts. Also there is a problem of class discrimination and moral inconsistency in our present policy. The biggest gambling racket in the history of man is operated openly in a place called Wall Street. As Samuel Untermyer indicated in the Pujo inquiry, eighty-nine percent of the transactions on the New York Stock Exchange are in the nature of gambling. Granted that successful gambling on Wall Street involves a little intelligence, whereas the numbers racket requires none, still the sin—if there is any sin involved—is different only in degree.

11. "THE EYES AND EARS OF THE MAYOR"

AFTER JULIA'S DEATH, I sold our Queens house at a loss, moved to Brooklyn, and did something which my friends, including the mayor, thought foolish and belittling. At the age of forty-two I entered Brooklyn Law School at night as a freshman. I felt desperately the need of legal training for my work with the city and I also wanted a profession to return to after my city service. When the papers got hold of the story and played it up, I had to stick it out until I graduated, although the double schedule by day and night almost killed me. I finally managed to graduate after three years and I was lucky enough to pass the bar examination on my first try.

Living in a Brooklyn hotel I was, with all my daytime excitement, fearfully lonely. The boys went south to stay with Annie. My life seemed empty. I wanted a woman to share in all this, and also to re-establish a home for myself and the boys. I found her finally very close to home. She was Mary Wilder Hillyer, who had worked with me for years in the LID under the general direction of Norman Thomas.

Mary was then a sturdy, handsome, athletic woman of thirty-three, ten years my junior, a militant Socialist who had braved the goons of Southern reaction in a sharecroppers' strike in Arkansas when male union organizers had been afraid to enter the region. Coming from a conventional middle-class home in Topeka, Kansas, she had traveled a course to socialism quite similar to my own. She had served the YWCA as an industrial secretary and had gradually come to feel that religion was futile without a reorganized industrial society. She had left her post in the YWCA to become an undercover stitcher on neckties in a Philadelphia nonunion shop where she organized the workers and won a strike for higher wages. Then she had become a full-time organizer for the Amalgamated Clothing Workers and the International Ladies Garment Workers Union, successfully leading a great strike of shirt-workers in Troy.

Mary was very unlike Julia in many ways, more imperious, more conventional in sex matters, more aggressive in radical activities. She was an excellent sportswoman, having been a star in tennis and hockey. She was also an excellent public speaker, possessing a voice of an unusual silvery fiber. Over the years she appeared effectively on many national radio and television programs, often with Norman Thomas in his opposition to war. After our marriage in 1935 by Mayor La Guardia, she startled the clerks in Wall Street by making a speech in favor of their unionization, standing in front of the United States Treasury Building while the news cameras clicked. A little later she appeared in Flint, Michigan, as one of the leaders of the sit-down strike in the auto industry. She had been a close friend of the Reuther brothers for years, and she had also become a close friend of Heywood Broun when he came to her assistance while she was leading a great strike of dressmakers in New York City. Several times Heywood, looking, as Alexander Woollcott put it, like an unmade bed, marched at the head of her picket line for a block or two, then climbed into a waiting taxi to "rest my feet."

Mary and I set up housekeeping in Brooklyn Heights and I continued my breakneck double role of commissioner by day and law student by night. Mary also continued her work with the LID. Paul Jr. and Rufus spent their summers with us and their winters in an excellent Quaker institution, George School in Pennsylvania.

This may be the place to say that, in spite of many departures from fidelity, I have been the most fortunate of husbands because all three of the women whom I married were marvels of intellectual and physical courage. All three were professionals of high intelligence. They never flinched under attacks from reactionary politicians, the Catholic hierarchy, or the Communists. All three were Socialists, faithful to the moral goals of a new social order. They never asked me to shade my principles or curb my pen in favor of financial security, although they, particularly Julia, had to bear a considerable burden of poverty because of my left-wing dreams.

My twenty-nine years of marriage to Mary proved to be much more stormy than my nineteen years with Julia, and once or twice we came very near to splitting up. The most serious break came not because of anything sexual—by that time I had relapsed into monogamy—but because of our deep ideological differences about military preparation for World War II. Mary was a militant pacifist, or perhaps I should say that she was a militant opponent of war with guns. When I insisted on going to a Citizens' Military Training Camp in Plattsburgh, New York, shortly before the United States entered the war, she said that she did not want a man around the house who surrendered his soul to militarism. I took her at her word, checked out from our Brooklyn home, and checked in to a Manhattan hotel. Two days later her cheery voice came over the telephone asking me to forget everything and come back. I accepted with great alacrity.

Toward the end of the first La Guardia administration relations between the mayor and myself became steadily worse. I no longer spent so many hours in his office and sometimes he neglected me for weeks. I was no longer his white-haired boy. The reason for the new coolness escaped me, since the work in my office seemed successful.

That phrase "white-haired boy" needs special emphasis in understanding La Guardia. There was something singularly parental about him. Children fascinated him. When he saw a child at City Hall, his face would light up. His affection for children won national attention when, during a New York newspaper strike, he read the Dick Tracy comics over the air in a manner that brought delight to millions of children. Never having mature children of his own—his only child by his first wife had died in infancy—he had adopted two children on whom he lavished affection.

Somehow he got the impression that I was very young and that I occupied toward him the position of son toward father. As long as he regarded me as a youngster, I was the beneficiary of his parental impulses. Actually I was only ten years his junior, with a pretty determined code of conduct of my own, resolved that under no circumstances would I be a mere creature in his administration. Even before his election I had seen him abuse some of his associates with amazing cruelty, and I resolved that I would build my own reputation regardless of the personal risks. I suppose I got more publicity during the first two years of the La Guardia regime than any other commissioner, and I never retreated a single inch in order to play down any revelation of corruption for the sake of political adjustments. And it should be said for the record that La Guardia never asked me to compromise. In such things he was both honest and fearless.

But he was also a wretched administrator of great emotional instability, extremely suspicious of almost everybody, a man who played the part of a "loner," having many acquaintances and almost no intimate friends. One physician who knew him well said that he was "definitely psychotic" at intervals, and I could believe this. Charles Garrett of Rutgers, who has written the best book about La Guardia, *The La Guardia Years*, says that the mayor had an "almost psychopathic inability to take criticism of any kind." When, shortly before World War II, Roosevelt appointed him head of the Office of Civilian Defense and wanted to appoint him secretary of war, the counter-attack on the mayor's temperament assumed national proportions. According to Joseph Lash in his 1971 masterpiece *Eleanor and Franklin*, Judge Samuel Rosenman told the

President that Fiorello was a "mad genius"; Ickes said that the mayor "would not work with the team but would run all over the field with the ball;" and the director of the budget told the President that the OCD under La Guardia could not get and hold good people because of his "careless habit of firing people without much concern."

His moods varied so markedly from day to day that the legend of his "black days" spread through the city. Whenever I planned to report to him on a major investigation, I would call Betty Cohen, his secretary, on the City Hall telephone and ask, "How are things for a report today?" She would pause a moment and say, "Fine," or "The weather tomorrow might be better." In spite of these precautions I would sometimes come over to City Hall on the wrong day and see the work of months dissipated in a stormy moment because the mayor was in a black mood, unwilling to tackle a problem on which my lawyers and examiners had worked for months.

One of these occasions, oddly enough, involved the Catholic Church; it was the only occasion I can recall when the church became an issue in one of our reform programs. Louis Yavner had taken up the study of municipal funeral establishments where I had left off several years before, with my $19 casket, and had worked out with me a sound plan for a municipal funeral establishment in New York. The scheme fitted well into La Guardia's social predilections, and I thought he would accept it eagerly. But I arrived with that plan on a black morning and it was brushed off arbitrarily.

I kept coming back with it and finally discovered that the mayor was worried about the reaction of the Catholic Church. He had some basis for apprehension on this score. Catholicism is very jealous of the "holy ground" in its denominational cemeteries, and Cardinal Cushing, in opposing the idea of city cemeteries, had charged that Catholics were about "to be buried in great nonsectarian, nonreligious, nonprofit, nonpersonal, nonsensical, national, Socialist cemeteries." La Guardia himself was definitely anti-clerical and his father had been a free thinker, but he had a wholesome respect for Catholic political power.

I pointed out again and again to the mayor that our plan had taken full account of possible Catholic objections and that we provided for completely separate burial and ceremonial facilities by denominations, Protestant, Catholic, and Jewish. I begged the mayor to take it up directly with "The Power House" of the Church to get approval for the plan, but he stalled and stalled. Finally I took my political life in my hands, called up the office of Cardinal Hayes, and asked for an appointment without even mentioning authorization by the mayor. The appointment was made immediately and when I drove up to 50th Street I was ushered into a bare room where, under a powerful floodlight, sat Cardinal Hayes in full scarlet regalia looking like a medieval emperor.

Hayes was cordial but obviously worried. I had hardly started talking about my municipal funeral plan when I saw a look of relief come over his face. He had evidently thought that the only thing which could justify a personal visit from the mayor's chief graft investigator was the discovery of some high Catholic sinner, and like all good Catholics he hated scandal. When he realized that the young ex-Socialist before him—I had once caustically attacked him for his part in jailing Margaret Sanger—had not come to propose anything more unpleasant than a plan for cheaper funerals, he completely relaxed and we discussed the whole concept frankly. When I had finished, he said he saw no objection whatever to the concept so long as the Catholic funeral and burial facilities were kept separate. When I told La Guardia of my interview, he was amazed at my temerity but, I think, rather pleased that nothing worse had developed. However, he never did anything about my funeral plan.

La Guardia treated many of his commissioners with far more cruelty than he ever treated me. Often we commissioners joked with each other about the number of times the mayor had "fired" us, then allowed us to stay without any word of apology for his outbursts.

I wonder if there is a word in the vocabulary of psychology to describe those who tend to turn on the associates who are closest to them? The men who were closest to La Guardia suffered the most, and at the end of his three terms almost none of them remained with him in City Hall. Paul Kern, Lawrence Dunham, Stanley Howe, and Lester Stone were closest to him in his first term, and their sufferings were terrible to witness. Kern, who was the closest of all, was made a civil service commissioner and ended up his relationship with La Guardia in a grand public row in which he was fired after accusing the mayor— probably correctly—of softness in dealing with Boss Ed Flynn of the Bronx. La Guardia often treated Newbold Morris, later city council president, like a juvenile delinquent, and for months he would not even see his commissioner of welfare, William Hodson, but insisted on dealing with a deputy commissioner in the department. Langdon Post, an excellent commissioner of housing, left the administration in disgust. Paul Windels, corporation counsel and the mayor's chief legal adviser, stuck it out through the first term, then resigned to become counsel to a giant corporation. He told me once that the mayor had boycotted him for two months after a minor quarrel over policy.

The only one of his commissioners who ever defied the mayor openly was Robert Moses. Moses, serving as both parks commissioner and a member of several operating transit authorities, had two advantages, he was an important Republican who might have denied the mayor renomination on the Republican ticket, and he was independently wealthy. To see these two men square off against each other in the mayor's office, as I frequently did, was like having a reserved seat at a cock fight. Moses dared the mayor to fire him, and La Guardia swallowed his pride and took it. Moses knew that in many of his tantrums the mayor was acting, but he, Moses, was just as good an actor as the mayor. I never knew Moses to be defeated in a colloquy.

Most of La Guardia's tantrums never reached the newspapers in a form to do him any harm. He was the brisk

and courageous reformer—at least in the journals which
supported his administration—and they rightly praised
him for having the most honest and competent administration in the city's history. But after his re-election in 1937
the *World-Telegram*, the mayor's most ardent supporter,
came out in the open with a rebuke headed "Time to Climb
Down." It said:

So many seasoned officials of superior ability are getting out
of the city service now. . . . Mayor La Guardia must remember
that New York City in re-electing him also was voting for a
continuance of the independent services of such first-class
team-mates as Commissioners Moses, Blanshard, Forbes,
Goldwater, Valentine and others, of Corporation Counsel
Windels and former Comptroller McGoldrick. When the mayor
makes public service unbearable for some of his ablest
associates and puts on a personal vaudeville act in the midst
of important business he is doing neither himself nor the city
any good.

By this time the mayor had stopped attending meetings
of the board of estimate and assigned his duties there to
subordinates. His manners became more and more Na-
poleonic. I think some of his difficulty was plain over-
work. He did not know how to spare himself. He would
begin his day quite early in the morning by dictating a
stream of letters into a recording machine while he was
being driven downtown in his big Chrysler Imperial. Then,
storming into his office in his ten-gallon black hat, he
would start shouting orders and continue the process all
day, often working right through the lunch hour while
wolfing a sandwich. At the end of a long afternoon he
would often make two or more public speeches at banquets
and public meetings, reaching home about midnight.

No constitution could stand such punishment for long.
Perhaps some of his psychic difficulties had a physical
basis. When he died at the age of sixty-four it was discovered that he had been suffering from cancer of the spleen,

and this disease often takes many years to reach a climax. Samuel Johnson once remarked that "every animal revenges his pain upon those who happen to be near, without any nice examination of the cause."

I have spoken of La Guardia's administrative incompetence. I should speak of my own. I did not have an executive mind and I hated administrative responsibility. I could never screw up the nerve to fire anybody and I hated even to admonish any of my staff for inferior work. (I left most of these things to Beatrice Mayer and the civil service workers.) Mrs. Mayer, especially, as secretary of the department, relieved me of the heavy burden of administration, supervised many investigations in the early stages, and served as a deputy commissioner without portfolio. I continued to operate as a muckraking journalist. This emphasis was good for the opening months of an anti-Tammany cleanup; it was not so appropriate for the aftermath. And I was not even a lawyer. Most of the municipal experts of that period believed that long legal experience should be required for the post I occupied.

Although the mayor never unconditionally fired me, my relations with him finally degenerated to the firing stage when he suggested that I be transferred out of investigation to become chairman of the civil service commission. I rightly regarded the proposed move as a vote of no-confidence, although he later said I could stay if I wanted to. I said I would prefer to step out entirely at the end of his first administration. My digestive ills had become worse, and Mary insisted that I would die in harness if I tried to stay four more years under Fiorello. Probably she was right.

When I stepped out after four years, it is probable that many of my friends thought that my departure was due to the very heavy attacks upon me by Tammany in the mayoralty campaign of 1937, when La Guardia won re-election for the first time. It is true that during that campaign the Tammany candidate, an egregious Red-baiter and judge named Jeremiah Mahoney, singled me out as a major target for scurrilous attacks, including some very fraudulent character assassination. Getting hold of the leaflet I had issued from jail in 1919, "An Injunction Against the Capitalist Class of Utica," he sandwiched my horrible picture into a montage with Communist pictures which I had never before seen and published the rigged libel in the newspapers of largest New York circulation. He combined this attack with the "revelation" that I had allowed Communist propagandists to remain on my investigating staff. The only truth in this latter charge was that the federal government had assigned about forty WPA workers to my office for routine work and that I had not fired them for being Communists so long as they made no attempt to propagate communism on city time.

Mahoney's attack on La Guardia and me in that 1937 campaign was a classic of McCarthyism. In a hysterical radio address, Mahoney made me the chief target of his phony campaign:

Standing high over all the varied departments and agencies of the city of New York is the figure of Paul Blanshard—the most powerful and the most despotic single factor in the city. The irony of it is that this self-avowed Red is the man La Guardia appointed to investigate Red domination of Home Relief. . . .

Blanshard set the pattern in Utica—La Guardia follows it slavishly in New York.

Blanshard is against the Police—La Guardia is against the Police.

Blanshard pats on the back the outfit that riots against the Police—La Guardia refuses to permit the Police to defend either themselves or property against attack.

Blanshard and his crew lead—La Guardia follows.

Every street disorder, every smashing of windows, every bombing of theaters, every act of vandalism against food and meat shops, every overturning of taxicabs, every howling, parading, screaming mob have been incited by the Communists who follow the political leadership of Blanshard and La Guardia. . . .

Blanshard doesn't want property protected. Blanshard says he wants America to follow the example of Russia. He wants a revolution.

La Guardia himself told me to pay no attention to such accusations; he had been called a Communist so often that the accusation was old hat, and, as far as he was concerned, the Mahoney attack was too silly to answer. But—and this had something to do with my stepping out of political life at that particular juncture—the Mahoney attack made me realize that I could never win high elective office in a city with a large conservative population. For many voters the mere fact of having been an official Socialist was almost as bad as being a Communist. As an ex-Socialist and jailbird who had once proclaimed that no capitalist nation was worth dying for, I was probably doomed politically.

This pessimistic feeling about my political future was confirmed when the character committee of the Appellate Division of the New York Supreme Court held up my admission to the bar for several months because of charges by right-wing organizations that in the Utica strike I had attacked the government of the United States in language not suitable for a member of the bar. The chairman of the character committee was a right-wing Catholic. I was finally admitted only because I contended—and rightly—that the evidence against me all came from an employee of the textile manufacturers in the strike.

La Guardia defeated Mahoney easily in 1937 but this was the high-water mark of his power. He was a brilliant lone-wolf Congressman but he was utterly unable to build a political organization capable of governing the city. I am not sure how much he wanted to pass on his power to a successor; he certainly did everything imaginable to alienate his political supporters. He treated the Fusion Party leaders with cruel contempt and often refused to see any of them. He wisely refused to run for a fourth term because at that moment not a single political party in the city except the left-wing Labor Party was willing to support him for re-election. A drab Democratic politician, William O'Dwyer, almost defeated him in 1941, and finally succeeded him in 1945. La Guardia became for a time director general of UNRRA, a post for which he had no special qualifications; later he tried a newspaper column more successfully but his productive habits did not fit into a routine. Before he died in 1947, he complained bitterly that the world had forgotten him.

The complaint was wholly unjustified. Fiorello La Guardia will always be remembered in American history as a unique phenomenon. His talents were as extraordinary as his faults. Although my work with him was full of tension and agony, I retained more affection for him than for any other person except Norman Thomas. Our relationship was a kind of love-hate relationship with the love predominating. Occasionally, even today, I will wake up in the night with the taste of a pleasant dream on the edge of my consciousness. La Guardia, the parental, warmhearted, impish La Guardia, will be sitting behind his big mahogany desk in City Hall with his feet swinging above the floor, reading one of my reports. He will skim through it quickly, then, with his big horn-rimmed glasses pushed up on his forehead he will say: "Good boy, Paul. *That's* a real report. Go to it!" Then the force of my pleasure will wake me up.

Are cleanup campaigns in city government worth the effort? My six years of labor in civic vineyards left me with a great many doubts in my mind concerning the place of the intellectual in municipal reform. My Socialist friends thought that I had diverted my energies to something less than worthwhile, fighting for bourgeois civic virtue rather than for class justice. But my faith in industrial democracy was grounded in a faith in political democracy, and I never saw any necessary conflict between civic reform and basic economic reconstruction. Nor did I agree with Lincoln Steffens that nearly all civic corruption was derived from the shortcomings of capitalism. Graft, I noted, existed in

Moscow, with the payments in official favoritism rather than in cash, and this could be just as dishonorable as any corruption under capitalism. I was old-fashioned enough to see no substitute for personal integrity under any social system.

I granted that the exposures of the Seabury–La Guardia era would be only temporary. The rascals would return, and they did return in great numbers even in the regime of John Lindsay. In fact the exposures of the Lindsay period rivaled those of the Tammany period, including revelations of a grafting commissioner and regular pay-offs to water inspectors, firemen, and the police. This did not prove that a department of investigation is ever use-less. On the contrary it proved that eternal investigation, independent and fearless investigation, is the *sine qua non* of efficient government. A permanent civic watchdog with an accounting and legal staff is as necessary in our American cities as a police force is.

The question of the worthwhileness of graft investigations goes deeper than the issue of honest investigators. While I tend to agree with Montaigne that changing the forms of government is not usually worthwhile so long as democratic choices are kept open, I do not think that this reasoning applies to the present form of American cities. Local government is absurdly distorted and limited by out-of-date geographical boundaries. We have created monsters which cannot be governed efficiently. New York City, especially, is a conglomerate which exists like an octopus with its legs cut off; no government of the city can solve the regional problems without regional jurisdiction, and such regional jurisdiction can come only if the whole organization of states, counties, and cities is revolutionized.

The Center for the Study of Democratic Institutions in Santa Barbara, sparked by my old friend Rexford Tugwell, has produced a suggestion that seems to me to constitute a genuine prophecy: Let the United States reorganize all our nonfederal jurisdictions into a new set of regional authorities with power over all local situations. This would save the taxpayers many billions and it would attract to regional government those men of distinction who now scorn the boards of aldermen and the city councils. It might take fifty years or more for this new arrangement to become corrupt. Then somebody could come forward with a new plan for guaranteeing civic virtue, and that plan might last for fifty years before it was discredited by man's eternal self-interest.

Meanwhile, city government suffers from the prevailing conviction of first-rate men that it is not worthy of their commitment. A wisecrack by Senator Eugene McCarthy in 1969 is all too true of municipal politics: "Being in politics is like being a football coach. You have to be smart enough to understand the game and dumb enough to think it's important."

12. FAILURE AT THE BAR

MY FIRST FOUR YEARS after the La Guardia experience were, for the most part, years of disastrous failure. I tried to be a poet and novelist and failed. I tried to be a successful New York lawyer and failed. I tried to be a specialist in crime prevention and scored only a very moderate success. Then the war came and put me temporarily into a rather bizarre and exciting career on the fringes of American diplomacy.

My first dream in those years, as always, was to support myself as a free-lance writer and I might have done it successfully if I had stuck to my forte, economic and political muckraking. After I resigned from the La Guardia administration, several publishers had written to me and asked for books. They assumed that I would write as a civic reformer, exposing the underworld of New York politics as I had explored it. But at that particular moment I wanted to try my hand at something more ambitious and creative. So I tried something completely beyond my range of talent, fiction and poetry. I worked in this difficult field for two years, actually producing much in the way of quantity but very little in the way of quality. In poetry I believed in rhythm and rhyme à la Tennyson and I detested the prevailing cult of unintelligibility. The literary public had already moved on from Tennyson to T. S. Eliot, and anything I had to say seemed like Mr. Prufrock's "thousand lost golf balls." In attempting fiction, I found that I had little gift for observation or dialogue. The other day I looked through the remains of those two delusion-filled years and threw the bundle in the fireplace.

But Mary and I had a rather gay and exciting time in the years of my literary miscarriages. After Annie's death in 1935 I had inherited her small farm located in Alabama near the Mississippi border. Moving down there in 1938, we had a joyous time renovating the old farmhouse and relaxing under the bamboo trees. One winter we climbed into our open car with our small dog Scotty and cruised down to Mexico where, because the American dollar was then riding high, we were able to support ourselves in luxury for $1 a day each, living near Lake Patzcuaro in Michoacán. The $1 bought us a furnished cottage near a hotel and three meals a day. Later the same payment bought the lease of a large furnished house with a Communist gardener thrown in, plus the privilege of playing tennis on the court belonging to ex-President Cárdenas.

Then, giving up my creative dreams for a while, we went on a freighter from Mobile to London. I secured a desk in the British Museum not far from the one once occupied by Karl Marx and started a book on religion. It was mostly against religion, and I enjoyed this brief and unfulfilled excursion into religious muckraking very much. When the boys came over for a time during their summer vacations, we had a fine holiday together in London, and eventually went for a brief stay in France. But it was August 1939. Our world collapsed around us in a few weeks. After a few dreadful nights in air-raid shelters in Paris, we sailed home through German submarines under the protection of the American flag.

Landing in New York, I found a small niche in the big Broadway law office of my old friend Arthur Garfield Hays, one of the foremost civil liberties lawyers in the country. I had met him in a debate once when he was supporting Al Smith and I was supporting Norman Thomas, and we liked each other. Later, he had successfully handled a lawsuit for me against Gerhard Dahl of the Brooklyn Bus Corporation.

Hays was the soul of kindness to me throughout my stay in his office, throwing clients to me whenever he could do it justifiably, but I soon discovered two unpleasant facts. My Socialist reputation and my rather stormy career in local politics had not endeared me to any business clients, and the Hays office, in spite of Hays' great reputation as a liberal, had almost no trade union clients. I did not know much about the workings of business since no one in the Blanshard family had ever made money in business. One added factor was that in the years before the war the profession in New York was overcrowded. Many good lawyers were literally starving.

Mary and I survived that two-year period largely because she found new employment and helped to support me. Actually my earnings would have supported a young unmarried lawyer but for a man of forty-seven who had achieved some local prominence the result seemed catastrophic. I was convinced that I was a total failure and I was never so depressed in my life. For the only time in my life I contemplated suicide.

It would have cheered me up a little if I had known how many beginning lawyers of some intelligence had suffered even worse torture. Lenin failed as a practicing lawyer, and FDR would have failed if he had not had family support. Clarence Darrow, when he started practice in Chicago after several years of experience elsewhere, earned a total of $30 in the first two months and averaged $50 to $60 a month in the first year. Perhaps I should add that eventually I did secure a reasonable income and much satisfaction out of the law by serving in Washington for several years as an advisory counsel in church-state matters.

In the Hays office I met many exciting clients. One of the most exciting—I served him in a minor tax case—was the world's greatest theatrical genius and publicity hound, Billy Rose. He was the most unimpressive millionaire I had ever met, a "pint-sized Barnum," but he had an amazing variety of real talents. Starting out at eighteen as a speed stenographer, he had discovered that he could write popular songs, among them "I Wonder Who's Kissing

Her Now." He had also discovered that songwriters were among the most exploited of human beings. Conferring one night with three other songwriters, he had decided that what the profession needed was a good lawyer. He and his friends waked up Art Hays in the middle of the night and poured their troubles into his friendly ears. They had come to the right man; Hays was a genius at contract law and he worked out with them a contract which became the basis of the organization known later as the American Guild of Authors and Composers, netting millions of dollars of earned income to American songwriters.

Art Hays handled some of Billy's divorces—there were five Rose brides, beginning with Fannie Brice—but I had nothing to do with that end of the business. Both the Hays office and Billy Rose reached the front pages of the newspapers after Hays and Billy had died when Billy's will left a large part of his $50 million estate not to his sisters but to the Billy Rose Foundation, destined ultimately for Israel. There was an immense and noisy quarrel over the estate partly because the bereaved sisters wanted to express their bereavement with a $125,000 mausoleum for Billy, and this seemed a trifle excessive to the then surviving partners of the Hays law firm. Eventually there was a compromise and the pint-sized Barnum was entombed in an ornate mausoleum in Westchester with stained-glass windows containing a map of Israel and a representation of the elephant Jumbo to commemorate one of Billy's most successful musical comedies.

Some of my other clients were almost as interesting, particularly those civil liberties clients who had no money even for court costs. One client of this type was a young man named Matson, head of the Workers Defense League of Hoboken, who had decided to sue the city for $10,000 in damages because he and his wife had been manhandled by the city police while Matson was making a speech in a public park. The case came up to trial before a machine-made judge named Thomas Brown in Jersey City, then dominated politically by Boss Hague. The local lawyers asked me to serve as the trial lawyer and, since I was a New York attorney, I had to get special permission from the judge to serve in New Jersey.

When I stood up in the courtroom to ask permission to appear officially, the judge glared at me angrily and shouted, "Do you believe in God?" I was momentarily flabbergasted. Finally I said, "Why, Your Honor, that question is entirely irrelevant." The judge came down from his bench, his face flushed with anger and, waving a finger at me, he said: "To my mind it is very relevant whether or not a lawyer believes in God. In New Jersey a lawyer who does not believe in God does not practice and a man who does not believe in God should not be allowed to hold public office. It is clear to me that you do not believe in God."

I had to make a split-second decision then and I think it was the wrong decision, although I had some excuse for it. If I had backed out of the case at that point in defense of a constitutional principle I would have left my client high and dry since the other lawyers were not prepared to go to trial. I muttered something to the effect that I did believe in God—a very doubtful assertion—and Judge Brown accepted the statement, although he glared with fury when I persisted in mocking him by asking each prospective juror, "Do you believe in lynching?" We lost the case, and I have never ceased to regret my hasty answer.

How eloquent are the after-event speeches that one never delivers! I should have said with smooth aplomb: "Your Honor, I am not wholly unprepared to answer your question since my great grandfather was a clergyman, my grandfather was a clergyman, my father was a clergyman, and I am myself an ordained Congregational clergyman in good standing. But it is constitutionally wrong under both Article VI and the First Amendment for a court to make any distinction between believers and unbelievers in respect to civil rights." About twenty years later in the case of *Torcaso* v. *Watkins* the Supreme Court of the United States sanctified that very principle by declaring that neither the state nor the federal government "can constitutionally force a person to profess a belief or disbelief in any religion . . . nor impose requirements which aid all religions as against nonbelievers."

My years in the Hays law office were exciting for me politically. I re-entered New York politics by becoming vice-chairman of the American Labor Party and chairman of its crusading committee, organized to clean out the Communists from the party. This was an odd and thoroughly unpleasant role for me to play since I had always been so permissive in my attitude toward individual Communists and toward the Soviet Union. But this was the period of the Hitler-Stalin pact, before Germany had invaded Russia and when the United States was not as yet a military ally of the Soviet Union. At that moment in history it seemed to me that the Communists represented everything that was contemptible. On the national front their strategy was dedicated to the destruction of the Roosevelt administration because they felt that Roosevelt might bring the United States into the struggle on the Allied side.

At the local level in New York their tactics were crudely uncivilized. In the various branch meetings of the American Labor Party they would often hold up all important business until late at night by various types of filibusters, then put over their program on the small remnants of the remaining audience by strong-arm methods. In this way they captured the organization in New York County and, using the title of "The Progressive Committee to Rebuild the American Labor Party," they spread outward from Manhattan. We struck back with a committee of our own, of which I was chairman, and we called it "The Liberal and Labor Committee to Save the American Labor Party." The New York newspapers, being overwhelmingly sympathetic, gave us tremendous headlines.

I was appalled by the vilification I received during that campaign. The Communists directed at me the same kind of abuse they had formerly directed against Wall Street and J. P. Morgan. I was suddenly a middle-class stooge and a traitor to the working class. In the *Daily Worker* John Haynes Holmes, who supported us, was "the new red-baiting head of the American Civil Liberties Union," and Freda Kirchwey was "the pro-war editor-in-chief of the war-mongering liberal magazine, *The Nation*." I replied with the same kind of unsubtle mudslinging, and the *Times* gave me generous headlines: "Blanshard Scores Left Wing," and "Sweeping Victory Seen by Blanshard."

I was a little ashamed of the new notoriety, but I kept on talking, smearing the Communists as assiduously as they smeared me. "The greatest menace which confronts democracy today," I said in a special letter to 150,000 enrolled Labor Party members, "is the worldwide movement of nazism and fascism. But week after week the Communist *Daily Worker* and the opposition's tabloid newspaper, *The Citizen,* cannot find time or space to attack the bestial treatment of Catholics, Protestants, Jews, liberals, and trade unionists in the countries now dominated by Hitler."

If this was striking below the belt, it was politics, and in one sense the Communists deserved every word of it. They had practiced treachery at one of the most critical moments in history. "The Communists," I said, "have debased the coinage of social idealism until today no one in the labor movement with any sense trusts them." The American Communists revealed themselves as Russian puppets a few months later when they suddenly reversed all their American propaganda and praised Roosevelt to the skies because he had started to aid the Soviet Union against Germany after the Hitler invasion of Russia in June 1941.

We defeated the Communists temporarily in the American Labor Party in 1940 and I was elected chairman of the party's state convention over Vito Marcantonio after a bitter floor battle, but the Communists finally captured the party, partly because at that particular time both Sidney Hillman and La Guardia were unwilling to roll up their sleeves and fight back for our side. I was especially horrified by La Guardia's timidity in the crisis, although we supported him ardently for re-election and I introduced him in the most flattering terms at a great Labor Party mass meeting. As for the Communists, they kept the American Labor Party as a satellite party only long enough to endorse Henry Wallace for President in 1948, and then they jettisoned it. Our wing of the party formed a new Liberal Party in 1944 which held the balance of power in New York in several important elections, including the 1969 re-election victory of Mayor John Lindsay.

After my dismal experience in Hays' law office I took a new post in 1941 for a time as executive director of a rather famous but decrepit old organization, the New York Society for the Prevention of Crime. My transfer to this post was effected through the help of my old friend and La Guardia colleague, Austin MacCormick, former commissioner of corrections under Fiorello.

The society was a period piece from the nineteenth century. It had once been headed by New York's most famous clerical muckraker, Dr. Charles H. Parkhurst of the Madison Square Presbyterian Church, and its members at one time had included J. P. Morgan, Peter Cooper, and a host of other leading Protestants. Parkhurst, a bewhiskered Calvinist, approached the whole problem of New York crime from a narrowly puritanical point of view, declaring that he was fighting "a corrupt world, and Christianity is the antiseptic that is to be rubbed into it in order to arrest the process of its decay." Disguised as a sporting figure in loud clothes, he had gone "down into the disgusting depths of this Tammany-debauched town" and found it "rotten with the rottenness that is unspeakable and indescribable." Nevertheless he described it in lurid terms, specializing in police corruption, vice, and gambling. At this distance he looks like a sentimental old fool, but he had his uses. He helped to produce the important Lexow inquiry into New York political corruption, and that served as a model for the Seabury inquiry later. However, after a few sensational years his organization had fallen into silence and decay.

Austin MacCormick revived it with a new and more scientific outlook and enlisted as directors many prominent New Yorkers including Walter Thayer, later publisher of the *Herald Tribune*, J. Edward Lumbard, who became a distinguished federal judge, and Benjamin Day, former commissioner of immigration. I started off with high hopes partly because I acquired, first as a volunteer and then as an associate and successor, one of the best men I ever knew, Edwin J. Lukas, who later became counsel for the American Jewish Committee. Lukas and I reasoned that the place to begin our studies of the vast cesspool of New York crime was in the area of the treatment of juvenile offenders. We conceded that, under the existing system, most of the older criminals in prisons were beyond hope. We investigated the handling of juvenile offenders by the terribly understaffed probation departments of the courts and published several pamphlets calling for more probation officers and better psychiatric care. We found many seriously handicapped juvenile offenders who desperately needed psychiatric care and who never got it. Many years later, one of the juvenile offenders who suffered from neglect was Lee Harvey Oswald, diagnosed at the age of thirteen in 1953 as slightly schizophrenic, but never followed up.

We seemed to be on the way to a successful revival of this old society when we organized a national monthly news feature service on crime prevention and secured as volunteer producing consultants a dozen of the most notable crime experts in the country. But the first issue of our new feature service was scheduled to appear a few days before Pearl Harbor. Our promised newspaper space never materialized because every available inch was needed for war news. Presently I resigned to go into federal service.

This brief incursion into the field of crime prevention was almost as dismal for me as my law-office experience because I emerged with no faith in any solutions for the crime problem. I felt that we had to have some punishment for offenders but I saw almost no rehabilitation anywhere in the prison system. Our prisons were training schools for homosexuality, theft, and violence. I felt that social conditions were largely responsible for the appalling situation but I saw no hope of substantial reduction in crime until there was also a great reform in the handling of young offenders. And as the American guns began to boom all over the world no one wanted to think about long-term solutions for apparently insoluble problems.

Before I went into war service I did help to organize a distinguished Citizens' Committee on Harlem which was about half white and half black, and as the chairman of its subcommittee on delinquency I published in a sociological journal some conclusions that might well have been written in the 1960's and 1970's. I found out that there were proportionately five times more Negro juvenile delinquents in New York than white delinquents, and I put the blame squarely upon "the poverty, crowding, and underprivilege of the Negro community." Sometimes, I said:

I feel like climbing on a soap box and shouting the old message of Bernard Shaw that poverty is the greatest crime in the world, that it is the root crime of all other crimes. . . . When we get behind the superficial facts about delinquency we are met with an appalling series of acts of discrimination against the whole Negro population. . . . We must look to our own hearts to find the explanation for much of the Negro crime problem.

13. THE STATE DEPARTMENT

PEARL HARBOR and the war. This time the mood of left-wing America was strikingly different from the mood in 1917 when Woodrow Wilson took us into World War I. Then the Wilson program had been widely challenged as unnecessarily aggressive. Now the Japanese assault at Pearl Harbor united the country. Almost all conscientious Americans felt obliged to support the government. Even if Roosevelt had been tricky and evasive in moving us toward war while using the phrases of peace—and I think he was both tricky and evasive—he was the leader of the nation and, on the whole, the nation was right. So the unpleasant facts about Roosevelt were swept under the rug, and it was not until much later that his extra-legal acts were exposed.

In September 1940, he had usurped the power of the Senate in the famous over-age destroyer deal with Britain in which he gave the British fifty destroyers in "return" for potential American bases in the Caribbean and elsewhere, when those bases were just as valuable to Britain as to us. He committed American forces to the defense of Greenland and Iceland and ordered American vessels to shoot German ships on sight in the western Atlantic. He bypassed his ambassador in London, John G. Winant, and bargained directly with the British government, often giving that government secret favors.

But all these things were outbalanced by the villainy of Hitler. In the landslide vote in Congress for a declaration of war against Japan there was only one dissenting voice. When Germany and Italy declared war on the United States, there was no place for an anti-war liberal to go without seeming to favor fascism. The Communists, of course, were all for war and a second front now that Hitler had broken with Stalin and invaded Russia.

I began some modest war service almost immediately by serving as one member of a three-man enemy alien control board in New York, sitting with Nicholas Kelley, chief counsel for the Chrysler Corporation, and Herman B. Baruch, former ambassador to the Netherlands and brother of Bernard Baruch. Our task was to decide after short hearings whether Japanese and Italian citizens marooned in the United States should be interned or released. I soon moved down to Washington where, with the aid of Walter Thayer, I was appointed to a post in the War Shipping Administration in which I handled certain dealings with foreign consuls in the field of manpower. Then I accepted a transfer to the State Department as a sort of research quasi-diplomat on the staff of the American section of the Caribbean Commission, an international body set up by Britain and the United States to promote welfare and democracy in the colonies of the Caribbean area owned by Britain, the Netherlands, France, and—to the extent that Puerto Rico and the Virgin Islands were American dependencies—the United States. My title in the foreign service was senior economic analyst and there must have been considerable doubt in some quarters that I qualified under any one of my three titles. My actual task was fairly important. I was the first roving researcher assigned to the British, French, and Dutch colonies in the Caribbean and my launching pad was Jamaica, the largest and most interesting of the British islands.

The colonial Caribbean had a special and ominous importance for our government at that particular moment. Hitler had overrun France and the Netherlands. If he should conquer Britain also, he might demand possession of all the British, French, and Dutch colonies in the Caribbean. In that case Roosevelt and Hull were determined that the United States should establish an American protectorate over these territories, granting them democratic institutions. (Puerto Rico already had been granted some self-government.)

Congress, in 1940, had united with Latin American governments in passing a resolution saying that the United States would not recognize any transfer of territory in this hemisphere from one European power to another. Before our entrance into the war, this bold assertion of American authority presented some difficulties. Was the dummy regime at Vichy the real government of France? After the German capture of Paris, the Vichy regime had taken over Martinique and Guadeloupe, and for almost a year we had reluctantly recognized Vichy's Admiral Robert as a legitimate ruler of these islands. Robert actually ruled the French Caribbean for about three years while American cruisers and planes bottled up his ships and his surplus French gold, until we finally delivered the gold—about $286 million worth—to the free French under De Gaulle. Meanwhile our government established seven protective air bases in the British islands and in British Guiana in order to defend both the colonies themselves and the Panama Canal. For the time being, the Caribbean became an American lake.

I was brought into the State Department for my research task through Adolf Berle, then assistant secretary of state. By good fortune, my immediate superior was a first-class liberal millionaire, Charles W. Taussig, president of the American Molasses Company and a member of Roosevelt's original brain trust. Taussig was more than willing to have me do what I wanted to do, quietly prepare a huge "secret" study of the native leaders and the social conditions in this troubled area, designed partly to answer the question: Who would rule these territories if the predominantly black peoples were given the right of self-government? I worked during most of my four years in the department on this study, roving over the colonial islands and the mainland colonies in South America and producing a large "secret" Black Book which was partially incorporated after the war in a book of mine, published by Macmillan, which I called *Democracy and Empire in the Caribbean*.

In those days, before air travel had become popular, the colonial Caribbean was a relatively unknown area.

Very few American tourists had discovered its charms and probably the majority of Americans did not even know that some 6 million people, overwhelmingly black or brown, were living in America's back yard without self-government while the Allies were proclaiming the attainment of democracy as the central aim of the war. Britain had the most important chain of Caribbean colonies, running in a great arc from the Bahamas to Jamaica to Barbados to the Windward and Leeward isles to Trinidad, and finally to the mainland possessions of British Guiana and British Honduras. The Dutch had Curaçao and Aruba with the great refineries which refined Venezuelan oil; farther north, the tiny islands of Saba, St. Eustasius, and the southern half of St. Martin; and, on the South American shoulder, the prize territory of Surinam, rich in bauxite. The principal French possessions were Martinique and Guadeloupe, with French Guiana on the South American shoulder. The United States had the Virgin Islands, purchased from Denmark in 1917 for $25 million, and Puerto Rico, which we held in embarrassed distaste, not really wanting it. We had "liberated" it in the frenzy of the Spanish-American War and now we were giving the Puerto Rican people complete freedom to vote themselves out of "the American empire," hoping that they would accept the invitation.

The European powers in the area had not gone that far. (This was before India and Nigeria had been granted independence by Britain.) They were still acting as if their Caribbean possessions were permanent parts of permanent empires. And their imperialism was white imperialism. All the territories except Puerto Rico were overwhelmingly black or brown, occupied by the descendants of slaves and indentured Indian servants who were still ruled by white men.

In describing my Black Book as "secret," I put quotations around the word. After four years of experience in the State Department I had reached the conclusion that classified documents rarely contained anything that was not known to competent journalists. The "security" involved in the classification system was a farce. I remember my own experience in gathering extra material for my Black Book from department files. Those files were then located on an upper floor of the old Navy building next to the White House, supervised by earnest young men and women who usually had some speech defect which made them unsuitable for direct dealings with the public. After securing the required credentials to gain access to the place, I strolled over and worked there for six weeks. No one ever asked me for any identification or credentials, although nobody in the room knew me personally. If I had been an enterprising spy, I could have walked out of that room with material for a dozen stories for German and Japanese papers showing the inadequacy and hypocrisy of Allied colonial rule in America's back yard.

Of course I was an anomaly in the foreign service of the State Department at that time. Few blacks or Socialists or even liberals found their way into the service. Our consuls assigned to the colonial Caribbean were, for the most part, decent, utterly conventional school-tie boys either on the way up in their early years or on the way down after careers of less than immortal distinction. Both the British and the American governments considered the colonial Caribbean a kind of dumping ground for the second-rate officials. Among such officials, Mary and I were sports in the biological sense. Wherever we went we tended to gravitate toward the black radicals in the region. In Jamaica, where we lived most of the time, we invited black revolutionary leaders to drink midnight cocktails on our porch. I suppose that I was the only foreign service officer in local history to attend black labor mass meetings in person. The army, the navy, and the FBI all had "intelligence" men in the area who got their information about black labor from the white planters and politicians, then passed on "the facts" to their department headquarters in Washington. There was no coordination in our quadruple "intelligence" services, and not much intelligence. I remember one high-ranking American intelligence officer on the island telling me: "All the reds are dangerous. There is practically no difference between Roger Baldwin and Leon Trotsky."

Neither the British nor the American higher-ups were altogether happy about my record and tactics, although my immediate superior, Charles Taussig, was always fair and sympathetic. Once a local conservative consular officer discovered that I was the Paul Blanshard described as a Socialist leader by Upton Sinclair in one of his novels. Thereafter I was attacked on the floor of Congress by a Georgia Congressman, presumably using material from the FBI, garnered from my speeches in the Utica strike.

After the scandal was spread on the pages of the *Congressional Record* I was brought back to Washington to explain to G. Howland Shaw, then head of State Department personnel. I winced a little when I heard that he was a devout Catholic, but I found him utterly sympathetic and reasonable, and I walked out of his office completely cleared. I suppose that one reason for my exoneration was that those *New York Times* headlines about my leadership of the non-Communist committee in the American Labor Party were still available. But the governor of Jamaica did insist that I leave the island during one election because I had demonstrated too much sympathy for Norman Manley, the distinguished Socialist barrister and Rhodes scholar who was running for prime minister against a cousin, a bizarre ex-waiter and moneylender, Alexander Bustamante. Bustamante, head of the Bustamante Industrial Labor Union and one of the most eloquent shysters I ever knew, was elected. Ultimately he became Sir Alexander Bustamante and his party ruled Jamaica for many years. Manley, however, became prime minister for a time and in 1972 his son, Michael Manley, became the island's political chieftain.

Bustamante's rise to power graphically illustrates the dangers of applying a simple formula, "let the people rule," to a population that has never been trained to rule itself. For centuries the Dutch and the British white rulers had treated the black majority as if they were children. In the British islands only about five percent of the people had been allowed to vote, and this handpicked minority had obediently put white leaders in power. In Jamaica about half of the children did not attend school and the existing schools were appalling. In the Dutch possessions the percentage of voters was negligible—only two percent in Surinam when I first arrived there. So, when the blacks, with the insistent support of the Roosevelt administration, were given full franchise in the British islands, it is not surprising that they did two foolish things. They ousted virtually all local whites, no matter how kindly and intelligent, from elective office, and they frequently elected the loudest and most picturesque racial agitators, regardless of their ability to govern.

The French did better because they did not practice that racial discrimination which characterized British, Dutch, and to some extent American policy. They incorporated their Caribbean possessions into the national government and sent representatives, mostly black, to Paris. Their public officials married black and brown women without losing caste. If a British or Dutch colonial official married a black woman, he was likely to lose his chances of promotion, even in a region which was ninety percent nonwhite.

Our American policy was only a little better, and in Panama it was worse. When I observed race relations in our Canal Zone I was horrified to see that racial discrimination was practiced even at our post office windows. The windows were labeled "silver" and "gold." When I went innocently to a silver window to buy two postage stamps I was told, "You belong over there at the gold window." The word "gold" was a euphemism for "white." My two letters were addressed to my two sons who were fighting at that moment in the South Pacific and Europe for "the free world."

I remember one occasion when I was returning to the United States with Charles Taussig and several associates after attending a Caribbean Commission conference. Our group included a light-colored American official who had taken part in the conference. When we landed at the Miami International Airport we went together to the main dining room to get a cup of coffee. The manager came over and said quietly: "Sorry you can't sit down together here. This is for whites only."

We were caught by surprise. Even Taussig did not know about the rule. He protested vehemently but the manager said that the rule had to be enforced. "Can we have coffee together in a side room?" Taussig asked? The manager reluctantly consented on condition that we draw a curtain so that we could not be seen from the main dining room. So we all moved into a side room, drew the curtain—and had coffee with Ralph Bunche!

In spite of this racial discrimination our total American policy in the Caribbean was far more generous than that of the European powers operating there. In Rexford Tugwell and later in Luis Muñoz Marin we had two progressive governors. We had the money and we poured it into Puerto Rico. The average worker in Puerto Rico received about twice the income of the average worker in Jamaica, and we had already given the Puerto Rican people far more self-government than the corresponding natives received in the British islands. I advertised our superior American generosity quietly in Jamaica by bringing in American government pamphlets about Puerto Rico—the British had created a legend that our Puerto Rican slums were the worst in the region—until the Jamaica governor ordered me to keep out such inflammatory material. Our Puerto Rican slums were bad enough, but the slums in Jamaica and other British possessions were worse, consisting in many cases of hundreds of huts made of tin cans, straw and wattle, and daub, with a water tap for every twenty huts. Cane-field workers in Jamaica averaged less than $4 a week.

Mary and I operated in this black-and-white paradise with a considerable sense of guilt because we were living so far above the level of the Jamaican blacks. We rented a house with five black servants from a British colonel on condition that we keep all the servants and promise not to "spoil" them by raising their wages. Their wages were about $2 a week and out of this amount they were supposed to get their own food. Two of them chased our tennis balls when we played on our private court.

Since we had diplomatic status we were invited to all the ranking cocktail parties, where we heard the white planters who owned about ninety percent of the land on the island complain about the laziness of their workers. In all the time in which I was in the Caribbean I never saw a white man doing any manual work outside of Puerto Rico. There was a saying among the Jamaican natives which ran something like this: "A white man farms with his forefinger. He says: 'Nigger, put that plant there.' "

At the first cocktail party I attended in Jamaica I fell into conversation with a wealthy lady who summed up the attitude of her class quite well. "Conditions here," she said, "are frightful. There are two men I would like to hang, Alexander Bustamante and Norman Manley." These two men, both destined to be prime ministers, were then the two most powerful and representative colored leaders in the Caribbean. During the war they had both been interned for "public safety" by the British governor.

To my horror I discovered that in Jamaica color prejudice extended among the blacks and browns themselves. The economic-color graph predominated in the professions and corresponded roughly to skin pigment. The light-colored Negroes, when they rose to positions of power, practiced color discrimination as persistently as the whites did. They often treated their blacker brothers with the utmost cruelty. Business institutions followed the color line in employment. A coal-black girl could almost never secure a position in a bank and only a few could find jobs in department stores, and one reason for the discrimination was that near-white girls refused to work next to coal-black girls. The successful professional men were nearly all light brown, and they tended to choose for themselves wives who were of an even lighter shade. The situation is better now but not much better.

All this snobbery and discrimination went back to the traditions of slavery, and the corruption spread to all branches of family life. The whites under Caribbean slavery had not permitted the black slaves to marry or to secure an education, so the vast black population had become a subgroup of illiterate animals, prized only for their manual labor and their capacity to breed more breeding animals. Powerful black bucks had been circulated in the slave quarters and encouraged to produce offspring. When a slave mother had six living children, she was allowed to "retire" to the mountains for life, but if one of the six died she was brought back again to the fields or the kitchen to breed one more item for her quota. It is not surprising that when I was in Jamaica from sixty to ninety percent of the children of the blacks were technically illegitimate. One result of the traditional breeding policy was that black society was essentially a matriarchate. The responsibility for raising the children often belonged to the mother, partly because the identity of the father might be unknown.

After the British shuffled off their world empire in the post-war period, their Caribbean colonies had the opportunity to form some kind of economic and political combination that would bring them reasonable prosperity. But localism and racial animosities triumphed over regionalism. A movement for a West Indies Federation of the British Islands, launched in 1958, failed largely because Bustamante in Jamaica, using all the devices of the racial demagogue, defeated a federation proposal in a referendum by a margin of about 10 to 9. Jamaica, Trinidad, and British Guiana moved on to complete or partial independence. Noxious trade barriers and provincial jealousies seemed to cancel out nearly all the benefits of the new democracy. Jamaica, the Queen of the Caribbean, with twenty percent unemployment, seemed only a little more prosperous than it had been in the days of all-white domination. Its basic problems remained unsolved.

The first of those basic problems is over-population. If they leave their native islands, most of the Caribbean people have no better place to go. Puerto Rico can dump its surplus on New York City. The British islands did some dumping in Great Britain after the war, but the British people soon became alarmed over the black influx and, like the United States, they have almost closed the door on nonwhite migration from the Caribbean. The economic life of the area was given a temporary boost by a prodigious flood of post-war American tourists who flung their surplus money around with reckless extravagance. One Jamaica hotel I visited graciously offered to feed and house any tourist couple for $1650 a week, enough to support a native couple for a year. It is not surprising that such a contrast between poverty and wealth is helping to win converts to the gospel of Fidel Castro, and Castro's island is actually within sight of the northern shore of Jamaica. In 1969 great "black power" riots broke out in Trinidad, Jamaica, and Curaçao, although the first two of those islands are now under black rule.

It is an understatement to say that I was restless about the alleged usefulness of the American foreign service during my four years in that service. Everywhere I saw duplication and waste in personnel, and I came to agree with that abrasive and courageous ambassador, Ellis Briggs, that most embassies could get along better with one-half of their official staff. I sent scores of reports to Washington about many vital aspects of the Caribbean and I am sure that they were read by Taussig but I remember only one that reached the policy-making level of the department. I was surprised and delighted when Mrs. Roosevelt told me that she had read it, but no one ever told me that the President had read it. Most of the employees in the department spent about half of their time adjusting themselves to the other surplus servitors on the payroll, regurgitating their own memoranda, and casually running through the memoranda of the other little guys who were caught in the same treadmill. I do not think that the situation has improved in recent years. The department has become a monster of extravagant bureaucracy manned by fairly able and scholarly men who spend their lives in decorous futility.

Because of this sense of futility I decided at the end of four years in the foreign service that I did not want a permanent *minor* career in the department. I would have accepted an ambassador's appointment, but that would have required Senate confirmation, and I knew that no Senate would ever confirm a man who had declared that no capitalist nation was worth dying for. I might have continued in the department as a well-paid labor attaché, sending in long and scholarly reports which nobody would have taken the trouble to read, but this seemed to me too dismal a fate for a man who still considered himself intellectually alive. So, again, I took my economic life in my hands and "retired" at the age of fifty-three to do what I wanted to do, write books. My new situs was that blessed Vermont farm where I am writing most of these words.

14. *AMERICAN FREEDOM*
AND CATHOLIC POWER

IN AN OLD DIARY the other day I found an annotation from the period of our Vermont "retirement" in which I estimated that we could live on our Vermont farm for about $20 a week. Blessed optimism! If we had known how much it actually cost us, we would never have undertaken the venture.

When we set out to buy our farm in 1941, we put an advertisement in *The New York Times* which read:

Wanted within 30 miles of the Dartmouth Library a farm with trees and a brook. Will pay maximum $1,500 improved, $1,000 unimproved.

The replies we received were more fantastic than the ad. We were offered $20,000 mansions two hundred miles from Dartmouth with no brook or trees, and broken-down shacks which would not have kept a cow alive in the blizzards. After touring the region in our open-top Ford, we were utterly discouraged. Then, one afternoon in Thetford, Vermont, only seventeen miles from Dartmouth, the real estate agent, after showing us many impossible properties, said: "There is an old, rather run-down wooden house out on a back road that an old lady is asking $600 for—with 55 acres of land. It doesn't have plumbing or a brook but it has trees. Would you like to see it?" We would.

The house stood there on a knoll looking down a valley southeast over the Connecticut River toward the White Mountains of New Hampshire. They told us it was more than a hundred years old. Its boards were brown and deeply furrowed by the winds of forty winters without paint. Some of its windows were broken and some of its floors were gone. There was a barrel in the kitchen and a small lead pipe through which trickled some spring water. Outside, the backhouse stank. But the house had ten rooms including, marvel of marvels, an upstairs room in the garret, separated from all other rooms, with a window that looked out over a meadow where a fox came out of its hole and gazed quietly down the valley.

We paid the old lady who owned the place the whole $600 on the spot, giving her $50 net profit. She had bought the place for $550. Then we bought her kitchen stove for $2 and began the long and expensive process of installing bathrooms, fireplaces, windows, and stone walls. (I painted the house three times myself.) When we retired there in 1946 we had no neighbors within a mile but we did not miss them, in part because we had a third person in the household, NV, a black champion standard poodle given to us by Norman Thomas and his wife Violet, for whom she was named. Soon she produced eight little balls of black fur to make our household even more lively.

"Retiring" at the age of fifty-three on $20 a week, I remarked in a diary: "I should be able to keep my faculties fairly normal for 15 years more, and in a state of survival 5 years after that." I outlined a literary program for the first of those years. There was to be a novel called *God and Samuel Seebright* about a fundamentalist evangelist somewhat like Elmer Gantry whose motto was "See bright with Sam Seebright." Another book on my schedule was to be an all-out, straightforward nonfiction attack on Christianity. Bertrand Russell's *Why I Am Not a Christian* had not yet been written and I had not seen H. L. Mencken's *Treatise on the Gods*.

My first year of writing on Sawnee Bean Hill—that was the name of our hill—was fairly easy because I had an assignment from Macmillan to write my book on the Caribbean. It came out in 1947, sold quite well, and received a kind reception from the critics. After it was finished I floundered awhile in inept fiction.

Then one day I was browsing in the Baker Library at Dartmouth, picking out a book here and there to scan casually, when I came upon a four-volume work called *Moral and Pastoral Theology*, written by one of the best-known Jesuits of England, Father Henry Davis. The work bore the imprimatur of the Archbishop of Birmingham. Leafing through it, I encountered the sections on priestly medicine. As I read, my eyes bulged with astonishment. Here was a manual for celibate priests which dared to prescribe the most detailed and viciously reactionary formulas for women in childbirth, for sexual intercourse without contraception, for the conduct of a Catholic girl who had been raped, and for the general manners of the marriage bed.

Did the public really know about this amazing stuff? Why should I not take this volume and other documents of the Catholic underworld and do a deliberate muckraking job, using the techniques that Lincoln Steffens and other American muckrakers had used in exposing corporate and public graft in the United States? Why not? This was apparently one field not yet preempted by the muckrakers.

I took home Father Davis' four-volume work, pored over its pages, and soon secured through the mails a whole shelf of priestly books and pamphlets on Catholic medicine, all published under a bishop's imprimatur. I discovered that there was a vast literature in this field, used by Catholic doctors and nurses but written in nearly every case by celibate priests. It was not surprising that this literature was voluminous because, as I soon discovered, there were 692 Catholic general hospitals in the United States with more than 3 million patients a year, with five Jesuit medical colleges in which every graduate had to pass a course in Catholic medical ethics.

The Catholic doctrine which caught my attention first was the doctrine of the equality of mother and fetus in childbirth. The Catholic rules against birth control were equally archaic and unrealistic but there was nothing novel in these rules. I had always assumed that Catholic physicians in handling childbirth were bound by the same general ethical standards followed by non-Catholic physicians, viz., save *both* mother and child but if there should be any *necessary* choice between the two, the living mother should naturally come first, even if in saving her life by therapeutic abortion the life of the fetus had to be sacrificed. I discovered that the Catholic rule was different. It was called "the equality of mother and fetus," and Father Davis had phrased it in this fashion:

One of the most distressing problems which surgeons have to face is that of saving the lives of both mother and child in difficult cases of parturition. Each has a right to life and *neither has a better right than the other* [italics mine]. Where induced abortion, *abortus provocatus*, is the procedure indicated, he [the Catholic doctor] will disregard his textbook and save the mother in some other way, and if there is no other way, he will abandon the case. In the last resort, where nothing whatever can be done to save the mother except abortion, he may not destroy a nascent life directly.

Father Davis had made the problem easier for his conscience and his Church by skipping over the most serious moral issue. What if the fetus was bound to die anyway? Under such circumstances could a nonviable fetus be directly removed in order to save a living mother? Still the answer was no. I located that answer in Father Patrick A. Finney's *Moral Problems in Hospital Practice*, reprinted in that very year of 1947 under the imprimatur of the Archbishop of St. Louis.

Question. If it is morally certain that a pregnant mother and her unborn child will both die, if the pregnancy is allowed to take its course, but at the same time the attending physician is morally certain that he can save the mother's life by removing the inviable fetus, is it lawful for him to do so?

Answer. No, it is not. Such a removal of the fetus would be direct abortion.

I found the Catholic rules on childbirth equally repulsive in those cases in which the mother died before extrusion of the fetus. Then her body must be cut open very quickly to get some water on to the head of the dying fetus before its life became extinct. Canon 746 of Catholic canon law provided that "Immediately after the death of a pregnant mother, a Caesarian section should be done in order that the fetus may be baptized." Otherwise, if the fetus had reached the sixteenth week of gestation, its soul might be consigned to limbo instead of heaven. In fact, it might be consigned to limbo for all eternity. The official Catholic booklet "Routine Spiritual Care Procedures for Laymen, Doctors, Nurses" put it this way in describing the procedures immediately after Caesarian section of a dead Catholic mother-to-be: "Here again there is the absolute necessity of baptism lest the infant be deprived of the happiness of heaven for all eternity; and regardless of the inconvenience and difficulty involved all concerned will consider it a serious matter of conscience."

After this short dip into the lower reaches of Catholic medical dogma I got on a train, went to Washington, and began that long research into Catholic documents which was to occupy much of my time and energy for several years. Securing a stack card in the Library of Congress— that rare privilege was granted because I had formerly possessed it as a State Department official—I plowed through miles of books and magazines in the gloomy and, for the most part, unused religious section of the stacks, then confirmed many of my findings at the library of the Catholic University of America. (When my books on Catholic power were finally published, this library put them behind a special metal fence so that students could not get them without permission.)

When I was through with this bit of preliminary research, I realized that I had the best story of my journalistic career, although very few journalists would have accepted it as a feasible story. Direct attacks on the Catholic Church were considered taboo by almost every editor and

publisher in the country. Who would publish an exposure
of such things? On my way back from Washington I
stopped off in New York and called on my old friend Freda
Kirchwey, who had then become the publisher and editor
of *The Nation*. She was the same charming and courageous
lady I had remembered. I said: "Look at this stuff I have
gathered and tell me if I don't have the gist of three
blazing articles on The Roman Catholic Church in Medicine, The Roman Catholic Church in Sex, and The Roman
Catholic Church in Education. Would you dare to publish
the stuff?"

She looked over my material and said: "Yes. We would
not only dare to publish this. *The Nation* wants these
articles." I do not believe that she ever regretted her decision, although her magazine was subjected for years to one
of the greatest counter-attacks ever directed against an
American journal.

My three articles, running in November 1947, were
featured with striking drawings on *The Nation* cover, and
the reverberations were startling. Great piles of the magazine were sold out on the newsstands within a few minutes of their arrival. I think it was the first time in
American history that the church had been attacked so
systematically from the left in a journal of general circulation.

Although *The Nation* carefully explained that I was
attacking not "the faith" of Catholic Americans but the
political and social policies of their church's hierarchy, the
distinction was not accepted by Catholics, even liberal
Catholics. And in truth, as I soon admitted, there was no
real distinction since the hierarchy controlled the whole
complex and dictated every policy and doctrine. For Catholics, even liberal Catholics, I became the leading "anti-
Catholic" in the United States, a distinction which I have
never relished.

That revelation about the equality of mother and fetus
shocked Catholic intellectuals, and perhaps they were even
more shocked when I quoted the extreme statements made

about birth control and venereal disease in the highest
Catholic journal in the United States, *The American
Ecclesiastical Review,* published by the Catholic University
of America:

Question. Would a husband ever be justified in using a
condom when having relations with his wife—namely, if his
only purpose is to protect his wife from a disease with which
he is afflicted, and there is absolutely no possibility that she
will ever again become pregnant? Could he argue in such a
case that what he is doing is no sin inasmuch as he is not
preventing conception?

Answer. . . . Even if his only purpose in performing the act
in this manner is to protect his wife from disease, he would
still commit a grave sin, for a good end does not justify the
commission of an intrinsically evil act.

A political counter-attack on *The Nation* began almost
immediately in those cities which had Catholic-dominated
machines. Newark led off. Four of its five city commissioners were Catholic and its Catholic superintendent of
public schools sent his children to parochial schools. He
announced that *The Nation* was a "dirty rag" and he
banned it from the school libraries of his city because it
had published three "virulent anti-Catholic articles attacking the fundamental religious principles of the Catholic Church in the areas of marriage, birth control, and the
family." Trenton followed suit by using scissors to cut out
the offending articles from copies in the school libraries,
and in Massachusetts five state teachers colleges banned
the magazine from their libraries because, as Director Patrick J. Sullivan explained, "I read in the newspapers that it
contained anti-Catholic articles." Mr. Sullivan confessed
that he had not had time to read the articles himself.

The contagion soon spread to New York City, where the
board of superintendents tried to impose a ban in secrecy,
dropping the eighteen subscriptions for *The Nation* in
school libraries. When a reporter for the *Herald Tribune*

discovered the eighteen cancellations and broke the story, a great uproar followed. By this time the critics had a stronger case against me. I had followed my three original articles with nine more, and in two of the later articles I struck at the heart of Catholic religious exploitation, the use of relics, saints, and apparitions of the Virgin Mary. From long experience I have discovered that no other type of comment on Catholicism arouses such white heat as an alleged slur on the Virgin Mary. Is this because celibate priests have developed a substitute sexual fixation on the Virgin Mary? I suspect so, and later on I was to say so.

Two of these later articles, said Superintendent of Schools William Jansen, were definitely "anti-religious," and officially it was this attack on faith which caused the *Nation* ban in New York City. In the excitement the public did not notice that at no time were *The Nation* or my articles used in classrooms. The material was not forced upon the students directly or indirectly. The use was confined to high school libraries where reading was entirely voluntary.

The New York ban produced a national reaction in the form of an Ad Hoc Committee to Lift the Ban on *The Nation*. Headed by Archibald MacLeish, the committee enlisted the support of several hundred nationally prominent intellectuals and opened a campaign to lift the ban. The members who attracted the most attention were Eleanor Roosevelt, Governor Herbert H. Lehman, President Charles Seymour of Yale, and Robert Hutchins, chancellor of the University of Chicago. There were others of equal eminence, including Adolf Berle, Leonard Bernstein, Van Wyck Brooks, Henry Steele Commager, Truman Capote, Bernard De Voto, Marshall Field III, Harry Emerson Fosdick, Oscar Hammerstein II, Mrs. J. Borden Harriman, Moss Hart, Hamilton Holt, Ralph McGill, Lewis Mumford, Edward R. Murrow, Reinhold Niebuhr, Elmer Rice, and Edward Weeks. More than thirty labor, religious, and welfare groups joined in the appeal. Not all of these defenders of *The Nation* agreed with me but they all spoke out for my right to speak out. They said:

The argument advanced in defense of this revolutionary proposal [the ban] is apparently that religion cannot be criticized in American education. There is nothing in American law or in the American tradition which says that religion cannot be criticized in education, nor does the principle of the separation of church and state involve any such consequence. On the contrary, the American Republic was founded, and the American continent was settled, by people whose actions were in large part an expression of their criticism of certain established religions. . . . The American people have never felt that it was the purpose of education to teach their children to be blind.

The New York Times and the *Herald Tribune* gave the appeal solid editorial support, while the Hearst press adopted the line of the Catholic diocesan journals and spoke of "the Hitlerian impact" of my articles, "motivated by malice and calculated to inflame religious distrust."

Many of the signers of *The Nation* appeal were hounded for years in the Catholic press as enemies of the Church. Mrs. Roosevelt suffered the most, although she had explained in one of her columns, in discussing the *Nation* ban, that she did not agree with all that I had said. I stayed away from her scrupulously during this period, although she knew Mary quite well. I did not want to embarrass her. Once several years later she attended a meeting where I spoke and afterward she walked up to me and said, "Mr. Blanshard, I want you to know that I am a great admirer of yours." By that time her quarrel with Cardinal Spellman over tax grants to parochial schools had made her "anti-Catholicism" world famous.

Freda Kirchwey and *The Nation* fought the New York City ban clear through the New York courts but failed to win a revocation because of the presumption that the administrators of a school system have the option to choose all books for school libraries. The ban was not lifted for fifteen years, and then only after the magazine had changed ownership.

During the bitter fight over the *Nation* ban in New York

I had been busily stretching my articles to twelve, adding a great deal of new material and producing the book which came to be known as *American Freedom and Catholic Power*. Innocently I thought that it would be fairly easy to place it with a large New York publishing house. The uproar over *The Nation* had given it invaluable advance publicity. But I did not then know of the overwhelming censorial influence of Catholic schools as potential purchasers of textbooks. I found that most of the big New York publishers were simply afraid of a Catholic boycott of their textbook business if they dared to publish what I had written. I secured the services of one of the best of New York's literary agents, Elizabeth Otis of McIntosh and Otis, and she peddled the manuscript from door to door without success. Ten big publishers refused it.

Then a young publisher, Melvin Arnold of the Beacon Press of Boston, accepted it. At that time he was relatively unknown; later he was to serve as president of Harper and Row. His publishing house, Beacon Press, was owned by the American Unitarian Association, the most advanced denominational group in American religion, wholly untainted by any anti-Catholic fundamentalism. But even in this sophisticated liberal group Arnold and his associate Edward Darling, after accepting the book, were confronted with an attempt by Unitarian conservatives to prevent publication because they feared the repercussions in Catholic-dominated Boston. Arnold and Darling scored a victory for free speech by blocking a conservative attempt to get the approval of the controlling board of the Unitarian denomination to override Beacon's editorial independence. Two leading members of the board, including one of the nation's most prominent university presidents, resigned in protest.

By pure chance I had come with my rejected manuscript to one of the most courageous publishing houses in America and my associations with that house during the twenty-five years since then have strengthened my faith in human integrity. The Beacon Press has steadily pursued a policy of truth-telling even when the risks were great. In the era of Joseph McCarthy it took a leading role in challenging mass hysteria. In the great scandal of the Pentagon Papers in 1971 it was to the Beacon Press that Senator Mike Gravel of Alaska turned for the publication of those "secret" memoranda which documented the deception on Vietnam perpetrated by the Kennedy-Johnson administrations.

In 1948 Melvin Arnold realized that his first hurdle in publishing my book was credibility. He took special precautions to make every paragraph foolproof. The entire manuscript was mimeographed before publication and sent for scrutiny to a group of experts in history and ecclesiastical affairs, including two eminent former priests and a popular Catholic author. One distinguished scholar double-checked obscure references in the Vatican library. A few minor changes were made, and I accepted them all because they were only incidental and the alterations strengthened the text.

Would the great newspapers accept advertising for such a book? Incredible as it seems in the light of later freedom of advertising for the most extreme attacks upon Catholic policy, the first response of several journals was in the negative. The most important refusal came from *The New York Times,* which had been so generous in supporting *The Nation*'s right to publish the controversial articles. (It had also been very generous to me personally in the La Guardia days, calling my record "brilliant" when I retired from public office.) The *Times* advertising ban caught me by surprise, although I had heard of strong Catholic influence in both the advertising department and the news departments. Cyrus Sulzberger in his memoirs and diaries in a 1946 entry had accused his own newspaper of having a "heavily Catholic bullpen" which blacked out one of his dispatches from Spain exposing Catholic textbooks in that country as opposing "naturalism, Darwinism, atheism, pantheism, deism, rationalism, protestantism, socialism, communism, syndicalism, liberalism, modernism and

masonry." Arthur Hays Sulzberger rejected all advertising
for my *Nation* articles and *American Freedom* on the
ground, as he explained in answer to a protest from
Norman Thomas, that

Our department of advertising acceptability was of the
opinion that they constituted an intolerant attack on the
Catholic Church and its clergy. One of the articles, "The
Sexual Code of the Roman Catholic Church," now repeated for
the most part in the book under the title "Sex, Birth Control
and Eugenics," was considered to be particularly objectionable
since it involved highly controversial matters of a religious
nature.

Norman struck back at Sulzberger with much gusto. In
a second letter to the *Times* publisher he wrote:

Is our democracy so immature that we must not discuss the
effort of a powerful Church to impose its own standards on
divorce and birth control on the rest of us through the power
of the state lest we stir up religious hate? Is the virtue of
Catholic opposition to communist totalitarianism so great that
its own authoritarianism cannot even be discussed calmly and
with documentation?

Probably Sulzberger, an intelligent and sensitive man,
was fearfully embarrassed by the decision he had made
concerning my book. He was certainly not a religious conservative or an opponent of free speech. Although he was
buried as a Jew in 1968, he was more humanist than Jew.
James Reston has described his attitude toward religion.
"I have no personal God," Sulzberger once wrote. "No one
who watches over me. . . . If I deserve punishment, it will
be meted out to me by my fellow men or by my own
conscience." He had accepted the prevailing advertising
code of the 1950's without careful reflection. Under that
code it was quite common for publishers to refuse to advertise any work criticizing any particular sect if the author
was not a member of that sect.

When the *Times* refused to accept dignified advertising for the book, quietly quoting prominent authorities such as John Dewey, Beacon sent them a small "tombstone"-style ad containing not a word of comment or salesmanship . . . just listing the titles, authors, and prices of its series, "Beacon Studies in Freedom and Power." *American Freedom and Catholic Power* was one of a half-dozen titles listed in small type; the others included a biography of Thomas Jefferson.

When the *Times* refused to publish even this subdued listing, Beacon calmly instructed them to run the prepared plate, mortising out the reference to my book—leaving blank space in the center of the listing. The *Times* refused even to do this, but realized the ridiculous nature of its position, and invited Beacon officials to a private session with Mr. Sulzberger. The discreet Beacon staff will only say that Mr. Sulzberger spoke frankly of his problems "over there," pointing in the direction of Cardinal Spellman's headquarters, popularly known in New York as "The Power House." The Beacon officials told me that they left the session with the strong impression that the head of the world's most influential newspaper was indicating to them that small Beacon had greater freedom of action than the giant *Times,* and was adroitly encouraging them to make full use of their freedom.

In the case of my book, the *Times* reversed its policy in 1958 and accepted advertising for later editions of *American Freedom and Catholic Power* and for my subsequent publications in this field. In 1949, however, the rejection by the *Times* influenced a number of other journals, notably the *Cleveland Plain Dealer* and the *Buffalo Courier-Express,* to join in an advertising ban.

The Catholic press, of course, refused all advertising because at that time there was general Catholic acceptance of Canon 1399 of Church law which forbids the promotion of any work directly attacking Catholic doctrine and policy. The two most intellectual of the Catholic journals, *America* and *Commonweal,* were quite frank about it. When Beacon Press submitted dignified advertisements to both of these journals, they replied promptly. Said *Commonweal:*

We believe that the Blanshard book is in error in its over-all effect and many of its particulars. Since the book attacks the operation of the Catholic Church, and since the very reason for publishing *The Commonweal* is to foster the Faith which the Church espouses, it would be defeating our basic purpose to print advertising for the book.

America, in rejecting an advertisement, declared that the book "directly conflicts with the editorial purpose of our publication." Melvin Arnold heaped coals of fire on *America*'s head by buying up twelve hundred copies of a bitter pamphlet by Father George H. Dunne, S.J., issued by *America* as an answer to me, and sending them out free with the next twelve hundred purchases of *American Freedom and Catholic Power.*

Public censorship of my attacks on Catholic policy did not hurt me in any way. On the contrary, it helped immensely in the sales of books because the American people do not like anything that savors of official and especially clerical censorship. When the Knights of Columbus and other Catholic organizations succeeded in persuading Macy's store in New York to boycott *American Freedom and Catholic Power* for a short time, the uproar was tremendous and pickets marched in front of Macy's carrying signs: "Blanshard's Book Tells Facts; Who Is Afraid of Facts—Macy or Spellman?" Although the book soon became a national library favorite and was listed among the fifty outstanding books of 1949, many librarians were intimidated by the pressure of what the *Library Journal* called the greatest "display of critical vitriol during this generation." Scores of copies of the book disappeared from open library shelves throughout the country or were seriously mutilated. Ten years later the head of the Boston Public Library told me that, although the library had bought nineteen copies of the book, it could not keep them in open circulation because so many copies were stolen or mutilated.

The incident which lifted *American Freedom and Catholic Power* to the best-seller list and kept it there for seven months was entirely fortuitous. It was Cardinal Spellman who made the book a real national success. He was not only the most prominent cardinal of the American Catholic Church, very close to his chieftain, Pius XII, but he was also the most violent and passionate advocate of tax support for all parochial schools. At the Fordham University commencement in 1947 he had attacked the leading Protestant journal in the country, the *Christian Century*, and had declared that "the attack of today is directed not at Catholicism but at the patriotism of American Catholics. . . . Bigotry once again is eating its way into the vital organs of the greatest nation on the face of the earth, our own beloved America."

It was in the midst of this controversy, about two months after the publication of *American Freedom and Catholic Power*, that Mrs. Roosevelt published in her column "My Day" a quiet affirmation of the traditional American principle of tax levies for public schools only, mentioning Cardinal Spellman's position:

Those of us who believe in the right of any human being to belong to whatever church he sees fit, and to worship God in his own way, cannot be accused of prejudice when we do not want to see public education connected with religious control of the schools, which are paid for by taxpayers' money.

Spellman chose to strike back with a blistering public letter, declaring: "Your record of anti-Catholicism stands for all to see—a record which you yourself wrote on the pages of history which cannot be recalled—documents of discrimination unworthy of an American mother!" There were, of course, no "documents of discrimination" in Mrs. Roosevelt's record, although she had, as a consistent liberal, supported birth control and opposed Generalissimo

Franco. As far as the general public was concerned there was only one alleged "document of discrimination" which seemed pertinent in the controversy and that was Mrs. Roosevelt's public statement defending the right of *The Nation* to publish my articles. Instantly the book which grew out of those articles, *American Freedom and Catholic Power,* became a popular weapon in the controversy. "Pass the ammunition," said the public, and sales jumped to six thousand a week, ultimately reaching a total in excess of three hundred thousand. *Publishers Weekly,* the "Bible" of the book trade, reproduced its cover, prominently, in a display of the ten largest-selling books of the year.

Spellman's phrases were quite appalling and their intense emotionalism surprised the public. He ended his attack by saying:

Why, I wonder, do you repeatedly plead causes that are anti-Catholic? . . . America's Catholic youth helped fight a long and bitter fight to save all Americans from oppression and persecution. Their broken bodies on blood-soaked foreign fields were grim and tragic testimony of this fact. . . . Would you deny equality to these Catholic boys? . . . Would you deny their children equal rights and benefits? . . . I shall not again publicly acknowledge you.

Mrs. Roosevelt answered the cardinal with unimpeachable dignity:

If you carefully studied my record, I think you would not find it one of anti-Catholic or anti-any-religious group. I assure you that I have no sense of being "an unworthy American mother!" The final judgment, my dear Cardinal Spellman, of the worthiness of all human beings is in the hands of God.

The public verdict on Mrs. Roosevelt was so overwhelmingly favorable that Cardinal Spellman felt obliged to call on her personally in Hyde Park, ringing the door bell without notice and offering his humble apologies.

But there were no humble apologies for me in the Catholic press, and there were very few gracious words for me in the book reviews. The *Christian Science Monitor* was an exception. Lewis Gannett wrote a fairly favorable review in the New York *Herald Tribune* but he told me later that he had had to argue with his publisher for a whole hour to get it accepted and then the publication of the review was delayed for many weeks. The Sunday *New York Times* carried a summary slaughter written by a Catholic reviewer—but not identified as a Catholic—describing me as a "prejudiced" purveyor of "old wives' tales." The New York *World-Telegram* carried a brief hostile note by a reviewer who later told us that he had been enthusiastic about the book and had said so emphatically but that all the enthusiastic sentences had been sliced out of his review.

Nevertheless, many editors were reasonable in their treatment, including the editors of liberal publications such as the Minneapolis *Star* and *Tribune* and the St. Louis *Post-Dispatch*, while the Book-of-the-Month Club placed the work on its recommended list with a ringing endorsement from J. P. Marquand.

My experience during these years in dealing with the press made me feel very much as John Crosby felt when he wrote a column for the London *New Statesman* about Catholic censorship in America. (His column was occasioned by a BBC public apology offered to a priest because this publicly owned broadcasting organization had used a less-than-respectful sketch about the Catholic gospel on birth control.)

This is a form of Catholic terrorism that has paralyzed and throttled criticism in my own country, the United States. I'm saddened to see Britain yield to it. The Catholic technique is simply to kick up such a storm that next time the writers, the editors, will be too terrified to comment or criticize anything

Catholic. This works very well in America. . . . A column I
wrote discussing, very mildly, the effect of Catholicism in
Ireland was suppressed. . . .

In America, Catholic pressure suppressed discussion of the
Aid to Education Bill, the most important piece of social
legislation since the abolition of slavery. . . . The Catholic
position is fully printed in all newspapers. . . . The Protestant
arguments never get printed. . . . The Catholic parochial
schools in America (as any liberal Catholic will tell you) are
not only flat broke but they are the worst schools we have, far
worse than our state schools. . . . They [the Catholics] have
been legally restrained from torture which they practised so
skillfully in the Inquisition. Now they are practising a sort of
editorial Inquisition.

Some writers declare that they do not care about what
critics say concerning their writings and that they never
even read the reviews of their own books. I have never
believed such claims. Any author worth his salt is sensitive about his reputation, and usually he suffers excruciat-
ing agony when he is held up to public ridicule. That has
been my fate. It caused me special agony whenever I was
described as a bigot, even when the charge was published
in a disreputable and partisan sheet that embodied all the
worst features of Catholic bigotry.

I was to learn later that the Catholic press often treated
non-Catholic authors in similar fashion even when they
published only tangential criticisms of the Church in fiction form. James Gould Cozzens published his outstanding
novel *By Love Possessed* at the height of the controversy
about my books on Catholic policy, and he earned the same
kind of vituperation that I had received because of an inimitable portrait of a soft-headed female convert to the
Church who finally slept with the hero. Cozzens had been
even more devastating in revealing the weaknesses of a
leading Protestant lawyer, but this did not excuse him from
the charge of being an anti-Catholic bigot. Father Paul
Mohan, writing in the most official of the American Cath-

olic Church magazines, branded the Cozzens' book "a one-
dimensional, relentlessly anti-Catholic polemic," and added:
"Mr. Cozzens' religious portraiture has none of the mis-
chievous adroitness of Roger Peyrefitte, nor the sneering
urbanity of Paul Blanshard. It is rather the old naturalis-
tic idiom of a Maria Monk delivered in tones less shrill."
Bishop Robert Dwyer of Reno called Cozzens' book "Blanshard refined by Pulitzer."

Such vicious misrepresentation of critics of Catholicism
was very common in those days. The non-Catholic critic
was the institutional enemy and no words were too bitter
to describe his moral turpitude. In dealing with me through
the years, Catholic editors deliberately chose to brand me
as a Protestant extremist although they knew that I belonged to liberal and tolerant religious groups far removed
from the intolerant Know Nothing school of thought. In
the 1950's I had joined the All Souls' Unitarian Church
in Washington where the great liberal preacher A. Powell
Davies held forth, and for nearly ten years I was active in
the American Humanist Association, lecturing for that
organization and producing the church-state column for
The Humanist magazine. But in the diocesan Catholic
press I continued to be a sample of "the New Nativism"
because it suited the Church editors to present this image
of "Blanshardism" to their readers.

15. THE HOLY YEAR: 1950

AFTER THE FIRST FUROR over *American Freedom and Catholic Power* had died down a bit, I continued to do some minor writing for *The Nation*. Two articles I produced in Washington were called "Billions for Brass" and "Pork Barrels in the Pentagon," and I never enjoyed writing any articles more than these two exposures of reckless military spending. Freda at that time asked me to be Washington correspondent for *The Nation* and I should have accepted the offer. But I was, for the moment, hell-bent on continuing my anti-clerical exposures of Catholic power from a new angle.

I said to Freda: "The Catholic Church is about to have one of the greatest celebrations of all Church history, the Holy Year of 1950. Why not send me to Rome as your special correspondent?" Her reply was to publish in the next issue of the magazine a large advertisement in the fancy style of a wedding announcement: "The Editors take pleasure in announcing that Mr. Paul Blanshard, author of *American Freedom and Catholic Power,* will be *The Nation's* special correspondent in Rome during The Holy Year." Freda coupled my Roman trip with a proposed trip to Israel, and I gladly accepted the extra assignment, although I had no special fitness for it. I had never made any study of Judaism and I had no firsthand knowledge of Zionism, but I was tremendously curious about the new Israel and I knew that as a representative of *The Nation* I would receive a warm welcome there because the magazine had done so much to promote the national cause.

So Mary and I closed up our house in Thetford Center, Vermont, boarded a boat in New York, landed in Naples in time for the chief celebrations of the Holy Year, and holed up in a small apartment on the Viale Vignola in Rome rented to us at an exorbitant price by an Italian "countess." Mary drove our small Fiat serenely through the insane traffic of Rome, and I, when I was not keeping my sacred 8 to 3 vigil at my typewriter, was trying vainly to get an accurate picture of the Catholic world structure of power.

It was an almost hopeless assignment. The Vatican at that time had no adequate mechanism for keeping reporters informed even about major events. Camille Cianfara of *The New York Times*, the best of the American Rome correspondents, helped me a great deal. (Later on he was to die tragically in the collision of the *Andrea Doria*.) In spite of the great prestige of the *Times* he could not dislodge from the Vatican even an hour in advance of its release any copy of a papal encyclical, and then it was all in Latin. He had to rush through an imperfect translation as best he could and get off a few paragraphs by cable.

Pius XII never held a press conference and his minor officials were very reluctant to give out any interpretation of his heavy, ambiguous phrases. At that time seventy-five years of age, Pius had not yet begun to go to pieces mentally as he did in the last years of his pontificate. He was a handsome, magnetic man looking like a theatrical saint, and no one ventured to call him an opportunistic politician. His unholy silence about Hitler's anti-Semitic policies had not been exposed. His reputation was protected by tradition and by Italian law.

The sexual life of the priests was subject to the same taboo. I heard all sorts of sexual scandals about the allegedly celibate priests—a Roman whore house reserved for them, their flight to South American posts where they could have concubines openly, the annual resignation of seven hundred priests in order to marry—but I resolved that I would leave this whole area of priestly scandal alone. If I dipped into it my status as a serious critic of institutional power would be destroyed.

But there was one sexual subject on which both Mary

and I spoke out publicly; that was birth control. Mary made one of the first public speeches for birth control ever made in Italy, in the Palace of Leonardo da Vinci in Florence, and I wrote an article against the papal policy on the subject in the magazine *Il Ponte*, sponsored by Peitro Calamandrei, Ignazio Silone, and other liberals. After Mary's speech the Vatican felt obliged to notice us. The official Vatican daily *Osservatore Romano* declared that my ideas would lead to a "freedom" similar to that achieved under Hitler.

I felt even in those days that the most serious flaw in Catholic policy was sexual hypocrisy and suppression. The enforcement of birth control laws was a farce. Mary and I visited many drugstores in Rome, some of them within a few rods of the Vatican, where condoms were sold under conspicuous advertisements: "Have a happy week-end." There were said to be twenty thousand prostitutes in and near Rome, and the nation had the second highest venereal disease rate in the world. Perhaps one million couples were living outside of marriage because they could not free themselves from separated spouses. The Vatican insisted that under the Mussolini-Vatican treaties of 1929 the Italian people could not adopt any divorce laws without Church sanction.

Even the saint-making ceremonies (which I attended) of the Holy Year dramatized the anti-sexual fixations of the hierarchy. The star saint of the Holy Year was Maria Goretti, an eleven-year-old Italian girl who had resisted an attempt to rape her and had been stabbed to death in the encounter. Pius XII was not content with this dramatization of purity; he went on to further glorification of self-flagellation. His second female saint of the year was a nun from Ecuador, Maria de Paredes, who virtually achieved self-destruction at the age of twenty-seven by self-torture and starvation, presumably in remorse for her sexual thoughts. She had slept for two or three hours a night, her body wrapped in strands of thistles, and had clung to a cross on the wall of her room for many hours each day.

During the Holy Year I saw these and many other things in Italy, and later toured France, Belgium, and the Netherlands to pick up material for *The Nation* on Catholicism and the schools in those countries. I welded all this material into another book called *Communism, Democracy, and Catholic Power*, which, like its predecessor, soon made the best-seller lists and stayed there for several months. It was a simplistic, straightforward summation of the elementary facts about the two greatest dictatorships in the world, the Vatican and the Kremlin, stressing their structural, not their ideological, resemblances. One of my basic purposes in the book was to deprive the Catholic Church in the United States of its shopworn claim that because it was such a bitter enemy of communism it was therefore entitled to respect as a friend of democracy. My rather transparent conclusion was that democracy should eschew both manifestations of totalitarian rule.

Naturally, the Catholic press reacted violently, pretending that I had charged individual American Catholics with disloyalty. One New York monsignor publicly advocated a book-burning to get rid of the offending tome. When *Newsweek* praised the new work, crediting me with "evident sincerity and considerable scholarship," the Boston *Pilot*, organ of Cardinal Cushing's archdiocese, published an editorial headed: "Please Cancel My . . . ," urging its readers to cancel their subscriptions to *Newsweek*. (About the same time the *Reader's Digest* was removed from 113 parochial schools in Wisconsin because of a favorable article about Margaret Sanger.)

Because I flayed communism for about 150 pages in the new book, I lost many of my left-leaning friends. The Communist *Daily Worker* topped its review with heavy block letters: "Blanshard Makes Faces at Vatican but Wants Holy War on Socialism." "What Mr. Blanshard has done," said the reviewer, "is to repeat every Trotskyite, fascist and otherwise slander against the Soviet Union. . . . Poor Mr. Blanshard! . . . he exposes the fact that he, like J. P. Morgan and Harry Truman, identifies capitalism with democracy."

My parallels between Vatican and Kremlin organization extended into the fields of labor unions and political parties, and they were based on long private talks with the leaders of the International Confederation of Christian Trade Unions in Utrecht and the Nouvelles Equipes Internationales in Paris. I was amazed at the extent and power of the Catholic labor and political networks in Western Europe. In Italy the Christian Democratic Party under Alcide de Gasperi had made Italy into a confessional state operating under a Vatican Concordat, with Catholicism as the state religion, some financial support for the clergy, and the recognition of Catholic marriage law for all Catholics. In the Netherlands the Catholic Party had become the largest party in this non-Catholic state, and the public school system had been decimated in the process. In West Germany, where the Catholic and non-Catholic populations were about equal, the representatives of the predominantly Catholic Christian Democratic Union outnumbered non-Catholics in the Bundestag by about 2 to 1.

I concluded after my surveys in Western Europe that "Self-interest is the Vatican's primary motive for being in politics, and in practical operation it is as consistent in pursuing that end as Tammany Hall." I noted that two objectives were always present in the demands of every Catholic party, opposition to the Kremlin and public money for Catholic schools. If these two concepts were firmly held, a local Christian Democratic Party could be almost as socialistic as it wished. In describing the priest-diplomats who were most influential in manipulating Catholic political movements, I mentioned a young diplomat named Giovanni Montini and I added, "Monsignor Montini, although still too young to succeed Pius XII, is considered by insiders as a possible future pope."

In the middle of the Holy Year *The Nation* sent me to Israel. It was a blessed interval because it gave me the chance to be enthusiastic about something. I was enormously impressed with the new nation, with its spirit and its accomplishments. My hostile criticisms of Catholic policy did not constitute any handicap in Israel since the Jews at that time considered the Vatican their No. 2 enemy, second only to the Arab states. It was Vatican influence that had swung the vote in the United Nations Assembly in favor of the internationalization of Jerusalem, and there was a widespread belief that, as one Roman journalist put it, the "real villain in the piece was Monsignor Giovanni Montini of the Vatican Secretariat of State."

The Vatican based its anti-Israel policy on a demand to preserve the sanctity of the "dozens" of Christian shrines in Jewish-controlled Jerusalem, but I showed that there were exactly two such Christian shrines in Jewish territory while there were thirty-four in Arab territory. It was obvious that the Vatican was using "endangered" Christian shrines as an excuse for a power ploy. Israel guaranteed most favored trusteeship for the shrines of all faiths in the Middle East.

Behind the artificial anxiety about Christian shrines was the Vatican's obvious fear of the development of a modern, non-Christian semi-socialist state which might be unfriendly to Catholic clerical policies. "Israel," I said in *The Nation,* "is an infection-point in the Middle East for new ideas. Islam has none of these shortcomings. . . . In many ways Catholicism and Mohammedanism are brothers under the skin: both have their roots in a feudal structure of power which can survive only so long as social ferment is repressed."

But I was surprised and horrified to see how much power had been surrendered by Ben-Gurion and his socialistic followers to the Orthodox Jewish extremists who were trying to make the new Israel into a clerical state. Although these Orthodox extremists comprised no more than twenty-five percent of the population, they had maneuvered themselves into a decisive position in the Knesset, between Ben-Gurion's Mapai and his leftist rival, Mapam. In order to hold power Ben-Gurion had guaranteed not to disturb the laws which gave Orthodox Judaism a favored position in the new commonwealth. The Orthodox religious courts controlled all divorces; no nonreligious marriages were possible; the school system was divided largely along religious lines; and Reformed synagogues were nonexistent. It was impossible to get a bus or attend a sporting event or a cinema on the Jewish Sabbath.

In describing these things in *The Nation,* I said that they were not "to be taken too seriously, and growing enlightenment will rapidly eliminate them." I fear now that I was too optimistic. The barnacles of Jewish fundamentalism have clung to the new ship of state for an unconscionable period. In December 1968 Horace Kallen and Alex Hershaft, as officers of the American Friends of Religious Freedom in Israel, publicly protested that Israel was violating the United Nations Declaration of Human Rights because "selected state-sanctioned religious hierarchies have exclusive jurisdiction over all matters of personal status. . . . Orthodoxy is the only sanctioned Jewish denomination. . . . Orthodox religious observance is imposed on all citizens, regardless of their own belief, in the nation's public institutions, its schools, and even its armed forces." The restrictive power of the Orthodox rabbinate in Israel is all the more amazing because it has lasted so long in a nation in which, apparently, the majority of citizens do not accept the whole Orthodox code.

If I was surprised by the relative power of Jewish Orthodoxy in the new Israel, I was horrified by the "Christian" exploitation of so-called Christian Holy Places. I expected to find a measure of reverence and dignity in those Holy Places. I found, for the most part, noisy rackets, fake history, and bitter sectarian rivalry. If there is any place in the world where a Christian who wants to preserve his faith should *not* go, it is to the Holy Land. There he will find the whole Christian story debased by swindle and commercialism.

16. "THE ANTI-CATHOLIC BIGOT"

PROPAGANDA HAS BEEN DEFINED euphemistically as education with a purpose. Education presumably must be objective to be pure. If it becomes partisan it sinks to a lower level. I have never accepted this distinction, and I am happy to see that it is being rejected by increasing numbers of scholars of the new generation.

After the amazing success of my first two books on Catholic power I had to face the question of whether I would become an active propagandist on speaking platforms. Shortly after the appearance of *American Freedom and Catholic Power* many university student groups asked me to appear in lectures or debates and I accepted several invitations. Overflow crowds came out almost everywhere. Two very exciting debates with Jesuits took place at the Harvard and Yale Law Schools. I decided that I might as well desert my desk for a while and become a platform muckraker again. I announced that I was ready to debate any priest anywhere in the United States, but after the two engagements at Harvard and Yale the hierarchy suddenly decided that it was unseemly for a priest to appear on a public platform with me, and all future engagements of this type were refused.

Then a new Washington-based national organization known then as Protestants and Other Americans United for Separation of Church and State asked me to serve it as lecturer, lawyer, or what-have-you, giving me the option of setting my own time schedule. I finally accepted the invitation and served the organization for about ten years intermittently as lecturer and special counsel, never devoting more than half-time to its work and allocating the rest of my time to the production of five books.

The organization finally had the wisdom to change its clumsy name to Americans United for Separation of Church and State, although its governing boards continued to be overwhelmingly Protestant. It had been founded by some of the best and most liberal Protestant leaders of the country, including my old friend and London tennis partner, Bishop Bromley Oxnam of the Methodist Church, the man who had successfully challenged Senator Joseph McCarthy at the height of his power. The two leading executives of the organization, both very competent in their fields, were Glenn Archer, a former law school dean, and C. Stanley Lowell, a former Washington Methodist clergyman who became editor of the lively and very valuable magazine *Church and State*.

The organization scored a quick success in the 1950's, attaining at one time a membership of about two hundred thousand. Its primary purpose was to block the Catholic drive on the public treasury for tax funds for parochial schools, but its leaders were just as zealous in promoting two other causes dear to my heart, birth control and firm opposition to the appointment of an American ambassador to the Vatican.

I regarded this last issue as relatively trivial but I had a personal interest in it because of special inquiries I had made in Rome during the Holy Year. President Roosevelt had appointed the Episcopal steel magnate Myron Taylor as his special representative to the Vatican from 1940 to 1950. Taylor was never a legal ambassador because Roosevelt did not dare to send his name to the Senate for confirmation. So cleverly—and, I thought, unscrupulously—Roosevelt bypassed the Senate without telling the public that many of the expenses of the Taylor mission would be paid for out of the State Department budget. Taylor drew no salary for himself, but he occupied a seven-room suite in a State Department building in Rome, and two foreign service officers on the State Department payroll did nearly all his work for him. He was present in Rome for about ten percent of his time. While Roosevelt persisted in speaking of him as merely a personal representative, the Vatican made no attempt to preserve the illusion. Taylor was received with full ambassadorial ceremonies and listed among the regular members of the Eccelentissimo Corpo Diplomatico.

After Roosevelt had died and Taylor had resigned, President Truman sent to the Senate the nomination of General Mark Clark as an authorized and official ambassador to the Holy See. Suddenly, on this relatively minor issue, all the dormant pride of American Protestantism seemed to burst into flames. Who said this was a Catholic country? Why should *one* church be singled out for such recognition? What had become of the traditional policy of the separation of church and state?

Americans United seized the opportunity to stage a series of thirty mass meetings clear across the country in which I spoke for thirty consecutive nights to the largest audiences of my life, some of them ranging up to six thousand. The meetings produced a flood of mail protests which ran about 6 to 1 against Mark Clark's appointment. In the face of such opposition, the general quietly withdrew.

Although the issue was trivial, the victory was sweet. The voters' reaction, as I pointed out in a two-part discussion of the subject in the *Atlantic Monthly* with Arthur Schlesinger Jr., "was a spontaneous and amazingly powerful reaction in defense of the American tradition of the separation of church and state." The public debate also illuminated the fact that the Vatican did not accept the American interpretation of church-state separation. The church still clung to the traditional privilege of naming the heads of the diplomatic corps in Catholic countries.

Later on, leaders of the American Catholic Church, notably Cardinal Spellman, continued to favor the appointment of a full ambassador to the Vatican in spite of the opposition in Congress. When President Nixon finally sent Henry Cabot Lodge as a diplomat to the Holy See in 1970, he imitated the strategy of FDR and adroitly bypassed

Congress, giving Mr. Lodge no official status as an ambassador. Although Nixon's act was technically an act of discrimination against all non-Catholic faiths, since he did not give such recognition to any other ecclesiastical establishment, his action caused little stir. Did not approximately seventy other countries send diplomats to the Vatican? And should not all good politicians, especially Protestant politicians, curry favor with the Catholic voters?

The period of my lecture tours was the period when the hottest attacks against me appeared in the Catholic press. I was denounced with appropriate fury as an "anti-Catholic bigot." The fury spread to any public figure who endorsed me. When I was speaking to a crowded meeting at Princeton one night, there shuffled into the hall a frail old gentleman with white bushy hair, wearing carpet slippers. I was nervous in his presence and doubly anxious for his approval. At the end of my address, during the question period, Albert Einstein stood up and said: "I wish to express my gratitude to a man who is fighting the abuses of a powerful organization. We are grateful to him for his efforts." Later, in a public statement, he was much more specific in supporting me.

The anti-Einstein reverberations in the Catholic press continued for months. The right-wing editors took advantage of the situation to couple their denunciations of Einstein as a supporter of Blanshard and their denunciations of Einstein as a person of doubtful loyalty whose alleged sympathies with communism had aroused their suspicions. One New York Catholic journal said: "We doubt if any intelligent person will be fooled by this . . . foe of religion, applauder of bias and member of pro-Red fronts, who urges witnesses to defy our Congress." Einstein struck back in several public statements. In reply to one published letter attacking him he wrote:

I am convinced that some political and social activities and practices of the Catholic organization are detrimental and even dangerous for the community as a whole, here and everywhere. I mention here only the fight against birth control at a time when overpopulation in various countries has become a serious threat to the health of people and a grave obstacle to any attempt to organize peace on this planet.

I shall not go into discussion of other points because Mr. Blanshard has treated everything exhaustively in his publications. Reading your letter, I cannot help to doubt whether you have really studied Mr. Blanshard's publications. If I am not mistaken your Church has forbidden Catholics to read any books the content of which does not completely agree with the interests of the organization.

Einstein was not a traditional "foe of religion," although, after experiencing a brief surge of Jewish faith at the age of eleven, he had abandoned all loyalty to the concept of a personal God. In using the word "god" in later life he accepted it only as a term defining the superior order of nature. He had specifically praised the Catholic Church during the dark days of Hitler's rule for its courage in opposing some features of that rule.

It was about this time that both John Dewey and Bertrand Russell came to my support against the Catholic critics. Dewey went far beyond a perfunctory endorsement and described the Catholic Church as a "powerful reactionary world organization promulgating principles inimical to democracy." He pictured the fight against the Catholic power structure as "essentially a conflict of claims to exercise social authority."

When *Communism, Democracy and Catholic Power* was published and a copy had been sent to Bertrand Russell, I was delighted to receive right out of the blue from Lord Russell an original poem "to express the gist of your work in immortal verse." He called the poem "The Prelate and the Commissar," with apologies to Lewis Carroll and "The Walrus and the Carpenter." He gave me permission to have it published, and later on he described it in his autobiography as "my only venture into verse." "May you have all success," he wrote me, "or, alternatively, not live long enough to be burnt at the stake! . . . When the McCarthy-Malenkov Pact has been concluded, you and I will be stood up between the two armies and co-operatively shot as proof of perfect harmony."

Here is the Russell poem:

THE PRELATE AND THE COMMISSAR

The Prelate and the Commissar
    Were walking hand in hand:
They wept like anything to see
    Much laughter in the land:
"If this could but be turned to tears,"
    They said, "it *would* be grand!"

"If Commissars with Cardinals
    Swept it for half a year,
Do you suppose," the Prelate said,
    "That they could get it clear?"
"I think so," said the Commissar,
    And did not shed a tear.

"O Workers, come and walk with us!"
    The Prelate did beseech.
"A pleasant walk, a pleasant talk,
    Along the briny beach:
We cannot do with more than four,
    To give a hand to each."

And four young Workers hurried up,
    And many more behind:
Their coats were brushed, their brains were washed,
    Their thoughts were clean and shined—
And this was odd, because, you know,
    They hadn't any mind.

"The time has come," the Prelate said,
   "To talk of many things:
Of bombs—and ships—and aeroplanes—
   Of presidents—and—kings—
And how to make the sea grow hot—
   And give policemen wings."

"A sacred book," the Prelate said,
   "Is what we chiefly need:
Rubrics, and commentators, too,
   Are very good indeed—
Now, if you're ready, Workers dear,
   We can begin to feed."

"It seems a shame," the Prelate said,
   "To play them such a trick.
After we've brought them out so far,
   And made them trot so quick!"
The Commissar said nothing but
   "The butter's spread too thick!"

"O Workers," said the Commissar,
   "You've had a pleasant run!
Shall we be trotting home again?"
   But answer came there none—
And this was scarcely odd, because
   They'd starved them every one.

In his correspondence with me Russell mentioned the
reaction of the audience at Columbia University when he
attacked Catholicism in a famous lecture. "For a moment,"
he said, "the whole audience gasped in amazement that
anybody should dare to attack so powerful an institution,
but the next moment practically everybody burst into passionate applause. I felt that they were living under a reign
of terror and were enjoying the breath of freedom from
abroad."
Here is the passage in that Russell lecture which produced the audience response:

It is dangerous error to think that the evils of communism can be combatted by Catholicism. The evils of communism may be outlined as follows: adherence to a rigid and static system of doctrine, of which part is doubtful and part demonstrably false; persecution as a means of enforcing orthodoxy; a belief that salvation is only to be found within the church and that the True Faith must be spread throughout the world, by force if necessary; that the priesthood, which alone has the right to interpret the Scriptures, has enormous power, physical east of the Iron Curtain and spiritual over the faithful *in partibus;* that this power is used to secure an undue share of wealth for the priesthood at the expense of the rest of the population; and that bigotry, and the hostility that it engenders, is a potent source of war.

Every one of these evils was exhibited by the Catholic Church when it had power, and would probably be exhibited again if it recovered the position it had in the Middle Ages. It is therefore irrational to suppose that much would be gained if, in the defeat of communism, Catholicism were enthroned in its place.

Russell, of course, was openly and vigorously anti-Catholic, and he publicly scolded the Catholic hierarchy for bringing about his removal from a professorship at New York's City College in 1940, ostensibly for the views he expressed on sex in his *Marriage and Morals.* But in that particular period he was even more caustic in his opposition to Stalin. In a 1953 letter he said:

I have been saying for the last thirty years that the ultimate contest will be between the Vatican and the Kremlin, and in that contest I shall side with the Vatican. My ground for preferring the Vatican is . . . that religions, like wines, mature with age. I should on this ground prefer Buddhism to Christianity if it were a practical alternative, but I should desert logic if asked to back fetishism. I do not think that either the Nazi or the Communist religion embodies the religious needs of the population. I think both express merely the will to power of governments, and the incapacity of subjects to stand up against modern governmental techniques.

In spite of the large crowds at my crusading mass meetings, the local newspapers and radio stations rarely gave me a straight and fair news story. Often I was able to trace the policy of silence to the pressure exerted by local chapters of the Knights of Columbus or the Holy Name Society. Mass meetings of from three thousand to five thousand in Chicago and Los Angeles were completely ignored in the press. When a local radio station in Fort Wayne, Indiana, had the temerity to broadcast my speech before eight hundred people in a local church, the counter-pressure was so great that the station manager felt obliged to publish a notice saying that the station "wishes sincerely and humbly to apologize" for carrying such a speech. In requital, the manager gave to the local Catholic leader, Bishop Noll, a full and unrestricted hour to answer me. Noll charged that I had been for "eleven years associate editor of *The Nation*, a socialist periodical which has little use for religion." Socialism, he said, was atheistic. Noll had published the leading anti–public school pamphlet of the American Catholic Church, "Our National Enemy No. 1—Education Without Religion."

The reaction of that radio station manager in Fort Wayne was more or less typical of the American reaction to any interdenominational religious controversy in the years before the Second Vatican Council. The word "tolerance" had been redefined in the press and on the air to mean evasion. There were almost no frank editorials or broadcasts about the fundamental issue of the separation of church and state. In this atmosphere the Catholic hierarchy had an immense advantage because, while the standard media of press and radio avoided searching analysis, the diocesan newspapers of the Church poured fourth almost every week streams of emotional propaganda which convinced their readers that they were the victims of atheists, Communists, and apostles of hate who sought to deny their constitutional rights. One result of this one-sided propaganda battle was that nearly all members of Congress were frightened away from any frank discussion of Catholic tax demands.

The decade of the 1950's was marked by the greatest struggles over the separation of church and state in our history, and during almost all of that decade I was a part-time lobbyist in Washington on matters such as parochi-aid and birth control. Yet I never heard more than two good speeches on the floor of Congress during those years which revealed any candor or courage in analyzing Catholic policy. When Catholic schools were under discussion, the evasive term used was "private schools." When priestly lobbyists appeared before congressional committees they were treated with conspicuous deference. When the opposition appeared, Congressmen found that they had engagements elsewhere. Among timid Congressmen the exception was Senator Ernest Gruening of Alaska who, as chairman of a Senate committee on population problems, produced a set of massive volumes of facts about the need for birth control in an overcrowded world.

During those years my impression of the religion of members of Congress could be summarized in the single word "hypocrisy." A prayer room was provided in the Capitol and almost nobody used it. Tax dollars were used to pay for chaplains in both houses and very few Congressmen arrived on the floor in time to hear the prayers which ascended to heaven. The one institution in Washington which faced the issues of the separation of church and state was the Supreme Court. Beginning in 1947 it handed down a series of decisions on the issue which, although equivocal in some respects, did more to preserve the American principle of separation than any act of Congress. But then, of course, any eulogy of the Supreme Court's courage should be tempered by the thought that the justices did not need to run for re-election.

17. GENETICS—AND THE IRISH

ALTHOUGH, ON THE WHOLE, I enjoyed the pitched battle with Catholic power, I was anxious to avoid the exclusively anti-Catholic stereotype. I thought of myself as primarily an all-around liberal writer, and I began to look for areas of endeavor outside the Catholic orbit. For two short periods I did break away, once in Boston and once in London. During one winter at the Harvard library I turned out a book on literary censorship, *The Right to Read*. It was well received but it sold only about eight thousand copies, and this seemed to me rather trifling when compared with the hundreds of thousands of my books on Catholic power. Then I went to London with Mary. We rented an apartment in a cold mews, and Rufus joined us for several months. He was studying on a Fulbright fellowship after receiving his Ph.D. at Harvard. I called this London period in my life my "human quality" period. My interest in eugenics was closely bound up with my interest in Catholicism and my increasing doubts about the validity of my earlier and rather naïve socialism.

In an old notebook the other day I found a quotation I had once extracted from Romain Gary's *The Roots of Heaven:* "The only revolution I still believe in is biological revolution. One day man will become a possible thing. Progress can only come from the biological laboratories." I was not ready to go quite that far. I still wanted a socialist society but I could not visualize a successful socialist society unless the population problem could be solved first.

I saw two almost insuperable obstacles to economic progress in the population crisis, the quantitative production of unwanted children, particularly in the underprivileged nations, and the qualitative overproduction of inferior types. I felt that modern medicine with its humane but undiscriminating policy of saving every possible human life was actually diluting human quality at an alarming rate. The declining death rate—the United States death rate had declined forty-five percent during my first fifty years—was a mixed blessing unless it could be coupled with a program for human quality as well as human survival. T. H. Huxley had calculated that nature at the lower levels did its own eliminating of the unfit very effectively since one single green fly produced in a single summer enough descendants to weigh down the entire population of China. But nature conveniently killed off the surplus flies. Could man produce for humanity an intelligent alternative to the green-fly pattern?

I had been drawn into this area of thought partly by the stupidity and cruelty of the Catholic policy in eugenics. In a standard Catholic textbook for doctors, the movement for eugenical improvement in the human stock was called "a most dangerous movement." Pius XII in a bitter public statement had denounced the practice known as AID, artificial insemination of a woman by the use of semen not donated by her husband. He had even outlawed husband-donated semen when it was obtained by clinical masturbation.

Although I was a complete tyro in the field of genetics I was encouraged in my new enterprise by my old friend and Nobel Prize winner, Herman J. Muller of the University of Indiana, who had probably gone further in imaginative genetics than any other American writer. (He was serving as president of the American Humanist Association.) He advocated the creation of frozen semen banks for possible future breeding. Beacon Press gladly signed a contract with me for an imaginative book to be called *Preface to Human Quality*.

It was never written. After six months of research in the British Museum and elsewhere I decided that I did not know enough even to popularize the thought of other men in this field and that the geneticists themselves were so divided and uncertain about the practicability of any scheme for genetic improvement that a book of this kind could not be written for another generation. Nevertheless, Mary and I had a lively six months in London, taking in its marvelous theaters and meeting many of its most interesting people.

Among our close friends were Jennie Lee and her husband Aneurin Bevan. Mary and Jennie had marched on American picket lines together and Jennie had visited our farm in Vermont. Ni and Jennie were probably the two most colorful people we had ever known, she from Scotland and he from Wales, both from mining families, both convinced revolutionists. She was a raving beauty with coal black hair and pink cheeks; he was a great burly man with a lilting Welsh accent. I saw him one day in the House of Commons stand up and give an ad-lib reply to Winston Churchill on an intricate phase of British diplomacy and he demolished Winston so brilliantly that even the Tory benches cheered. Once, several years later, when he was visiting our house in Washington, I heard him perform another oratorical feat, this time in poetry. He spied on my book shelf a copy of Dylan Thomas' *Under Milk Wood*. He walked over to the book shelf, pulled it out, and for half an hour read it out loud as he paced up and down. His Welsh rhythms matched the words perfectly.

I think there was a little envy in his worship of Dylan Thomas. He told me once that he would rather write books than hold public office, although he had served with distinction as minister of health in a Labour government and he might have become prime minister if cancer had not struck him down in mid-career. Jennie, after serving successfully in Harold Wilson's Cabinet, ultimately became a baroness in the House of Lords, a fate which seemed supremely bizarre for the socialist daughter of a Scotch coal miner who had specialized in attacks on the upper classes.

Perhaps the most significant man I came to know in

England in my human quality period was J. B. S. Haldane. He was a woolly bear of a man who hated the British Establishment, the American Establishment, and the Military Establishment—everywhere except in the Soviet Union. His hates included all organized religion. He had once taken the affirmative in a public debate on the question, "This house has no need for a god." He was a Communist and had served as chairman of London's *Daily Worker* until he felt obliged to resign from the party when the Soviet Union—particularly Stalin—promoted the absurd fallacy of the geneticist Trofim Lysenko that nearly all acquired characteristics were inheritable.

Although he had done more than any other human being to debunk the white racial supremacy theories of Hitler, he was still working under the shadow of Hitler's fanatical "eugenics." Hitler had set back the movement for human quality for a generation by advocating the extermination of the "unfit" and by defining unfitness in such a way as to include Jews and liberals. Ergo, anybody who suggested tampering with the species genetically must be Hitleresque. (Catholic propaganda in the United States frequently resorted to this analogy.) Haldane finally fled from Great Britain to India "as a refugee from the American occupation of my country." "American soldiers," he declared, "have turned my home into a brothel."

My own inquiries into "the unfit" during this period filled me with unalloyed dismay. Before I went to England I had visited many leading American institutions for defectives. In England I visited many more. I saw long corridors of slobbering, grimacing, urine-smelling monsters in wheelchairs and coffin-length baskets. In the largest home for defectives in Surrey—it was operated by the National Health Service—I saw in the infant ward babies with swollen heads and twisted faces fed pap by nurses spoonful by spoonful, unable to walk, talk, or handle their own evacuation. Across the corridor, in the adult ward, I saw the prototypes of these same infants, now thirty years old or older, still in baskets and diapers, cackling, eyes staring, loose lips gaping while nurses fed them spoonful by spoonful. "We have 1400 here," said the medical super-intendent. "There in the corner is the child of a wing com-mander: that is the child of an Oxford don. No, we do not believe in euthanasia under any circumstances." I figured that every monster exhibited there cost sixty per-cent of the energy and time of one human life.

So it was with immense relief that I abandoned the horrors of human quality and returned to the horrors of Catholicism. Mary and I crossed the Irish Sea, rented a flat in a beautiful but very cold Georgian house in Dublin, hired a very dirty but cheerful charwoman, and I set out to write a new book, *The Irish and Catholic Power*.

An Irish Jesuit scholar had challenged me to take Ire-land as a "pilot model" for a future Catholic America. I accepted his challenge with alacrity. The Irish Republic was not only the most priest-ridden country in the world but it was also the chief biological source of supply for the clerical machine that dominated the American Catholic Church. At the time of my arrival in Ireland every Ameri-can cardinal was of Irish extraction. My new study em-braced the whole field of Irish Catholicism on both sides of the Atlantic.

We were much worried about our reception in Ireland. The uproar over my books had preceded me and my name was instantly recognized when I started my studies in the frigid rooms of the Central Catholic Library of Dublin. But the Irish have an inimitable warmth about them, and the librarian, smiling, declared, "We don't have any of your books, Mr. Blanshard, but here is the reply to you by James O'Neill and I hope it will correct some of your errors."

Before my study was completed I was able to discuss my "errors" with nearly all the most important leaders of Irish life, North and South, including Prime Minister De Valera, Lord Brookeborough in Belfast, the chief under-ground terrorists of the Irish Catholic rebels in London-derry, the head of Ireland's chief Catholic seminary, May-nooth, and the chief literary figures of the country. We came to know Frank O'Connor, Sean O'Faolain, and Brian

Inglis; we received immense help from two courageous fighters for intellectual freedom in the Republic, Hubert Butler and Senator Owen Sheehy Skeffington.

The battle for intellectual freedom in the Republic interested me more than anything else. The Republic had a Censorship of Publications Board which seemed to operate in the spirit of the Inquisition. (Even De Valera seemed somewhat ashamed of it when I raised the subject with him, and he implied that if he could ever get Northern Ireland to unite with the Republic he would be willing to abandon the censorship system.) The board had only one priest as a member, but that priest was chairman and he directed the official policy on all moral matters so obviously that the whole board had been identified in the public mind as a Church enterprise. Its members were appointed by a Catholic minister of justice, it was composed entirely of Catholics, and all its employees were Catholic. Its two favorite villains were Sex and Unbelief.

"There is no reason," said Bishop Lucey of Cork, the Republic's chief specialist in blasphemy, "why it [the state] should tolerate unbelief or, at any rate, open propaganda on behalf of unbelief." The ban on sex was more difficult to enforce, especially since London sent in its Sunday papers and travelers brought in sinful novels from both London and Belfast. "In Ireland," said Sean O'Faolain, "a policeman's lot is a supremely happy one. God smiles, the priest beams, and the novelist groans."

The groaning was justified. Almost every Irish author worthy of respect had at least one book on the banned list of 4,057 titles. That list included four Nobel Prize winners and the outstanding successes of the American Book-of-the-Month Club, the Literary Guild, and the British book clubs. Aldous Huxley had four banned titles, William Faulkner six, Ernest Hemingway three, and Somerset Maugham seven. Of course such heretical works as Bertrand Russell's *Marriage and Morals*, Sinclair Lewis' *Elmer Gantry*, Joseph McCabe's *The Popes and Their Church*, and H. G. Wells' *The Work, Wealth and Happiness of Mankind* were all banned. In addition the Church had a supplementary banned list for public county libraries. The last Protestant county librarian had been forced out of her position just before I arrived. This supplementary list included Dorothy Canfield's *The Bent Twig,* Arnold Bennett's *Imperial Palace,* and even the works of such "Catholic immortals" as Sigrid Undset and Sheila Kaye-Smith.

I was somewhat abashed when I found that my own books were not on the official lists, but I soon discovered that they were banned most effectively by private censorship. If one of them appeared in a book shop in the Republic, a priest would soon arrive and ask for its removal. The bookstore owner knew that if he did not comply with the request he would face a Catholic boycott.

The formal censorship system was only one phase, and not the most important phase, of a whole system of clerically controlled culture which began with the elementary schools and continued into the universities. More than ninety-five percent of the Republic's children attended Catholic schools, supported by public revenue, in which the parish priests were the bosses, with power to remove all teachers for any theological deviation. "Lay education is poison," shouted a priest at a great mass meeting I attended in Dublin. "The government should stay away as far as possible from education." But the priest did not want his government to stay away from Catholic education financially. The church received nearly ninety-eight percent of its educational costs from the public treasury.

The Protestants had their small schools also, supported out of public revenue, and there were a few tiny Jewish schools to complete the picture. Both the leading political parties, the Fianna Fail and the Fine Gael, were essentially Catholic parties. The Church's prohibitions against birth control, divorce, and abortion were written into the nation's laws, and the hundreds of Irish girls who were producing illegitimate children had to be rushed to hospitals in England for their secret accouchements.

I found one hospital near London where 290 illegitimate babies had been born to Irish mothers in a single year. In Ireland the drugstores did not dare to sell condoms because of priestly threats. The priests instructed Irish wives to resist all condomistic intercourse up to the point of "the greatest actual danger," and for a time these priests even banned the use of tampons during the menstrual period as a "grave source of temptation"—until the ruling was drowned out in a wave of public laughter. The Archbishop of Dublin in announcing his opposition to birth control proclaimed: "Keep your young married life unstained by this crime. . . . The one who desires to limit the number of his children will come under God's anger. There may be very serious reasons for limiting the number of children. . . . In such a case the married pair must use their will-power and prudence, and live as brother and sister." Rules were announced for living successfully as "brother and sister." When, because of poverty and crowding, the man and the woman had to sleep in the same room, it was suggested that they should never sleep in the same bed. They should not undress in each other's presence!

The man who presided over this cultural and political mess, Eamon de Valera, had already become only a symbolic shadow of Irish nationalism and Catholic faith. He was seventy years of age at that time and so blind that when I held out my hand to shake hands with him our hands passed without touching. He wanted desperately to bring Northern Ireland into his Republic but he had no intention of making those basic concessions to liberal and Protestant thought which would have made reunion possible. To my surprise, he talked to me quite frankly, perhaps because I had been one of the editors of *The Nation* and *The Nation* had supported his crusade for Irish independence with great vigor.

He visualized a united Irish island without divorce, without birth control, without abortion, and without any departure from the Catholic rule in mixed marriage which committed all the children of such marriages to his Church. He saw nothing inappropriate in going to the Dublin airport as head of the state when Archbishop D'Alton of Armagh was made a cardinal, twice genuflecting before him and kissing his ring before the motion picture cameras as a symbol of his own allegiance and that of a state which made Catholicism the state religion.

When I got to the six counties of Northern Ireland, I found there an anti-Catholic militancy that was almost as fanatical as the pro-Catholic militancy of the Republic. The big difference was that in the North the Catholic third of the population challenged the very existence of the Stormont government while in the South the Protestants were quiescent and aloof in their upper-class dignity. The Catholic rebels of the North were working-class rebels, occupying the poorest houses, often barred from employment by Protestant discrimination. Hence the Catholic-Protestant war had become to a certain extent a class struggle.

This Northern Irish state was the only state I had ever seen where religion and politics had developed completely parallel antagonisms. The Protestants were nearly all loyal to the British nation, of which their Northern Ireland was a part, while the Catholics were openly subversive in their allegiance to the Republic to the south. The Londonderry walls were scrawled with Protestant-Unionist graffiti: "To Hell with the Pope" and "No Popery." The answering taunts read: "Up the Pope" and "Up the IRA." The leaders of the Northern Irish Catholics talked to me with the utmost frankness, readily confessing their plans for taking over the North through violence and chaos. For them this was the highest form of dutiful patriotism. For the Protestants it was papal imperialism plus treason to their majority rule. The Irish Republican Army was still very much alive as the underground guerrilla organization that blew up Northern bridges and even London mail boxes. The militant Protestant units were more orderly but equally determined. In County Down, where my Grandfather Coulter had been born and where there were many surviving traces of Coulter history, the Protestants had even dishonored the alleged grave of Saint Patrick by refusing to cut the weeds around the huge, dirty boulder on that grave.

I left Northern Ireland in complete despair about the

conflict which divided the North and the Irish Republic. I found many local examples of Protestant discrimination against Catholics, particularly in employment and housing, but I saw little hope that the violence-prone Irish Republican Army would permit any settlement short of complete conquest of the North. And I felt that the North had a right to exist. Two-thirds of its people wanted to be part of the British nation and they had entered into a treaty guaranteeing their protection in that status. At the parliamentary level—*not* the local level—their regime was quite democratic. If a minority, headed by guerrilla extremists, could overthrow a parliamentary regime through terror, what did democracy amount to? The Southern Irish did not seem to me to have any more right to conquer the North than the United States had to conquer Canada.

My worst fears were realized in the great "troubles" of 1968–1972 when Northern Ireland exploded in a series of riots. They were described as Catholic-Protestant riots, and there was some truth in the description, but the motivation on both sides was largely political and national. Nationalist fanaticism was inflamed with religious emotion, and it would be difficult to find a worse combination. Technically the Northern Catholics were correct in charging that they had suffered from discrimination but they were brutally wrong in resorting to wholesale murder as their remedy.

My own gloomy prediction is that the "troubles" in Northern Ireland will go on for a long time to come no matter what framework of political power is adopted. Religious fanaticism has poisoned national sentiment. The children have been taught to hate each other from the cradle up, partly because they have been trained in hostile school systems. If they could grow up together in one common, nonsectarian system and learn to accept the separation of church and state, they might ultimately find a solution. As it is, Northern Ireland is almost certain to continue as the world's worst illustration of religious conflict.

18. FRANCO, SALAZAR, AND FATIMA

Later on, long after I had produced my Irish book, I decided to explore Catholic power in Spain and Portugal. For muckraking purposes Spain might be described as wide open. It was the most flagrantly fascist area of the Western world and it was the most rigidly Catholic in the operation of its laws. The two forms of authoritarian rule, that of church and that of state, were completely coordinated. The coordination had been formalized in the 1953 Vatican-Franco Concordat, which said: "The Catholic Apostolic Roman religion will continue to be the sole religion of the Spanish nation."

In this Catholic state Jews were second-class citizens and Protestants were fourth-class citizens. The distinction was not based on any love for Jews. At that time the buildings of the two "synagogues" in Spain, which I visited, were not allowed to look like synagogues, and their congregations were not allowed to print their own literature. The Protestants were rated below the Jews simply because the Jews did not proselyte whereas the Protestants did.

The Spanish Protestants were pathetically weak, with only about eleven thousand members in a population of thirty million, but they were very militant and they were largely financed by American Protestant money. These two facts were enough to make them alien subversives in the eyes of the Spanish authorities. They had the right of "private" worship but the Spanish law curtailed all public activities by providing that "No other outward ceremonies or demonstrations than those of the Catholic religion shall be permitted."

The key word in this law was "outward." In most parts

of Spain it was interpreted in such a way that no Protestant church was permitted to have a steeple, an apse, or a large cross; no Protestant preacher could carry a professional card; no Protestant schools were allowed to function; and no Protestant funeral processions were permitted in the streets. No Protestant marriage ceremony involving a baptized Catholic had any legal effect. I ferreted out the names of twenty-eight Protestant churches and chapels that had been closed by the police and photographed the ruins of many of them. Some of them had been wrecked by Catholic mobs and by the police. Often the mobs had been encouraged by local priests.

Although liberal Catholics in the United States vigorously opposed such religious discrimination, our government accepted it in silence. We had made a military deal with Europe's leading fascist and we kept our part of the bargain. (Nixon's administration renewed that deal, with handsome financial grants, in 1970.) In our great military bases on Spanish soil we instructed American military chaplains never to make any contact with Spanish Protestant churches for fear of annoying the Franco regime. While I was in Spain, a Protestant picnic group composed entirely of members of the American armed forces and their families was broken up by the Franco police because a priest had complained that the holding of such a picnic in a Madrid park was an illegal "public manifestation" of a non-Catholic faith. Our embassy and our military authorities maintained silence.

This permissive silence under Catholic pressure has been a characteristic of American policy in dealing with Franco since he overthrew the elected government of Spain in 1939. Indeed, it is doubtful whether Franco could ever have risen to power if he had not possessed the support of the American Catholic hierarchy in their crusade against the shipment of arms to Spanish loyalists. John W. McCormack, then the chief spokesman of the Vatican on Capitol Hill, led the fight in Congress for an arms embargo, and he was backed by the leading American cardinals. Harold Ickes in a 1938 entry in his diary noted: "He

[Roosevelt] said frankly that to raise the embargo would mean the loss of every Catholic vote next fall. . . . This proves up to the hilt what so many people have been saying, namely, that the Catholic minorities in Great Britain and America have been dictating the international policy with respect to Spain."

In American Catholic propaganda during that period the whole struggle in Spain was represented as a struggle against God by Communist and anti-Catholic forces bent on destroying democracy in Spain. In Spain I took pleasure in ferreting out a famous church textbook for use in Spain's national schools, *Nuevo ripalda*, and I quoted some of its choicest passages, among them these:

Is it true that man may choose the religion which pleases him best?

No, because he must profess the Catholic apostolic Roman religion, which is the only true one.

What does "freedom of worship" mean?

That the Government must protect the free practice of all faiths, even if they are false.

What then is the Government's duty in this respect?

The Government itself must profess and then protect the only true religion, which is Catholicism.

What does "freedom of the press" mean?

The right to print and publish without censorship all kinds of opinions, no matter how absurd and corrupt they may be.

Should the Government repress this freedom by means of previous censorship?

Evidently yes.

What is so-called civil marriage?

The kind celebrated in front of a civil authority without the intervention of Church authority.

Is civil marriage a real marriage?

No, only obscene concubinage.

In recent years there has been a slight increase in religious freedom for Protestants in Spain but the military alliance between Franco and the United States has become more open and more costly to American taxpayers. Our American military bases, ostensibly established to protect "the free world," have continued to serve as outposts of strength for an essentially fascist regime. When our military agreements with Spain were renewed in 1970, Senator Fulbright pointed out that the direct and indirect costs might come to $400 million.

A "religious liberty" law was passed by Franco's henchmen in 1967 but it scarcely conformed to democratic concepts of genuine liberty. Non-Catholics were given the right to worship publicly, but their Spanish clergymen were not exempted from military service, as the priests are, and the Catholic catechism remained obligatory in all the national schools.

I found that Salazar's Portuguese regime was a fascist twin of Franco's Spain but it was not an identical twin. Salazar permitted slightly more religious freedom in his territory. Protestant churches were allowed to look like churches and Protestant members could walk proudly to their meetings on Sunday mornings with black Bibles under their arms. Portuguese Protestants could even get a divorce under some circumstances if they had not been married in a Catholic ceremony. There was in the country some slight residue of religious liberalism left over from that sixteen-year period between 1910 and 1926 when the republican regime had been anti-clerical and mildly socialistic.

But the Portuguese-Vatican Concordat of 1940 had given the Church the exclusive right to teach religion in the national schools and it had granted a monopoly to the Church in certain missionary territories overseas. Portuguese imperialism in Africa was a joint accomplishment of church and state, and later on I was to discover that it was almost as bad as South Africa's apartheid. Salazar could veto the appointment of any bishop if there were "any objections of a general political character." Under the circumstances, only one bishop in Portugal challenged the Salazar dictator-ship and he had been shipped out of the country just before I arrived.

To me the most interesting thing in Portugal was a special propaganda gimmick, the miracle of Fatima, which had been used for years by the Catholic Church as a kind of anti-Communist come-on, blessed by the popes and ex-ploited in the United States by a great McCarthyite organi-zation known as the Blue Army of Fatima. This Blue Army of Fatima flooded the country with pro-Salazar publicity, collected huge sums of money, and guaranteed to every repentant enrollee who wore a Brown Fatima Scapular that he would be assured of heaven on the Saturday after death when the Virgin Mary would personally rescue him from purgatory.

I plunged into a study of the mechanics of this racket with all the zest of an ecclesiastical detective. How could a great church create such a myth and win millions of Fatima believers in the broad daylight of the twentieth century? The core of the myth was the legend that on a certain day in 1917, at the height of World War I, the Virgin Mary had appeared to three little shepherd children of Portugal and had given them a special message against Russian communism. Fatima was a tiny rural village about seventy miles north of Lisbon, located in a dreadfully poor region where nearly all the peasants were illiterate. We visited it three times and watched the hordes of cripples, idiots, and very old persons march out on to the plaza, beg the priests for special miracles, and drink the magic "Fatima Water," which was simply local tap water. Al-though Fatima was not quite as repulsive as Lourdes, it was more tragic because almost no pilgrims seemed to be rewarded with the hoped-for healings.

The Fatima legend began when the three children in-volved, who were only ten, nine, and seven at the time, said that they saw in a field a vision of a "Beautiful Lady" who told them to come back to the same spot on the same day each month and they would ultimately see something wonderful. The word of the "vision" was spread around the district, and when the children returned each month to the same spot, increasing crowds came to observe the "something wonderful." On the fifth month they saw a "great miracle" in the sky, a rift in the clouds where the sun seemed to whirl like a "silvery disc." The oldest of the three children, Lucia, said she saw Saint Joseph, the child Jesus, and the Virgin Mary. The Virgin Mary—in vision form—said something to Lucia. But the other children did not claim that they heard or saw such things and there was no report about Russia or communism. The two younger children died soon afterward in the world influenza epidemic, and Lucia, a frail neurotic girl suspected of epilepsy, was sent to a convent as a Carmelite nun. She was so carefully guarded that no journalist or independent investigator was allowed to approach her without special written permission of the Pope. About twenty-four years after the event, Lucia for the first time "revealed" that the Virgin Mary had given her a message about communism and Russia. It was a vague, platitudinous message which had no particular significance. The Vatican seized upon the "revelation" and made it the center of a campaign against communism.

Actually, the earliest records show that the alleged message of the Virgin to Lucia did not concern Russia at all but predicted the end of the war. In fact the Virgin was said to have predicted the end of the war on the very day of the message, but this mistake was omitted from most of the Fatima literature. The alleged whirling of the sun seemed to have a perfectly natural explanation. Many persons present on the day of the great wonder saw nothing more miraculous than an unusually beautiful cloud formation following a rainy squall, with great streaks of light coming down through the mist. Driving out to Fatima one day, and not looking for any special miracle, we saw for ourselves something quite as striking. The Fatima region was a region of whirling clouds and magnificent light effects where the fog poured in from the sea and temporarily worked wonders with the sun. (The other day I read a sentence in a story by John Updike which seemed to epitomize our own experience at Fatima: "He glanced upward to measure the day and noticed, on gauzy cirrus clouds near the sun, the explicable but eerie phenomenon of iridescence.")

With the help of an interpreter we located the man who had been described as the chief "independent" witness of the original miracle. He turned out to be an emotional retired grocer without any scientific training who had kept silent about his version of the great event for twenty years. Then he had come forward with a version which "verified" that of the Church authorities. He had written a volume of very bad poetry about the event and he was trying to support himself by selling it.

With the help of some older Portuguese scholars who had lived through the original Fatima period I built up what I considered the natural explanation for the myth. The three little children of Fatima were illiterate but their mother was not. She read to them frequently. One of the favorite stories which she read aloud was the story of the Catholic miracle of Our Lady of Salette, a direct parallel to Fatima, in which a "Beautiful Lady" had given "a very special and important secret" to a shepherd boy and girl in the French Alps. Shortly afterward the Fatima children had seen, crossing the open fields near their home, an officer's wife who was dressed in unusual elegance in a golden dress that glistened in the sun. The rest was easy. The anti-Communist stuff was an afterthought, produced by suggestion in the troubled mind of the neurotic Lucia.

19.   J.F.K. AND THE CONSTITUTION

As the 1960 presidential campaign approached I was intensely unhappy. My muckraking attack on Catholicism had been steadily directed against certain anti-social policies of the Church, not against Catholics as individuals or Catholics as candidates for public office. Now, with the appearance of a Catholic presidential candidate who had a reasonable chance of election, discussion of the issues was personalized in a way I had tried to avoid. Could a particular Catholic named John F. Kennedy be elected President without injury to the national welfare?

All things considered, I was inclined to answer that question in the affirmative. Certainly I wanted to destroy the Protestant monopoly on the White House if a Catholic could be elected without strengthening the reactionary hierarchy of his Church. And I had no use for Nixon.

Characteristically, Nixon manufactured during the 1960 campaign an oratorical evasion of the church-state issue. "There is only one way," he said, "that I can visualize religion being a legitimate issue in an American political campaign. That would be if one of the candidates for the presidency had no religious beliefs." Evidently Mr. Nixon did not think that the "equal protection of the laws" in the Fourteenth Amendment protected unbelievers.

I liked John Kennedy from the first. He had style and his mind seemed to work swiftly and precisely. He wrote fairly good books, although I never thought his *Profiles in Courage* deserved a Pulitzer Prize. When, in 1959, I was writing *God and Man in Washington*—later it was chosen by the Book Find Club—I had interviewed Kennedy in his office and he had surprised me by his utter frankness and his freedom in discussion. After all, I was at that time the nation's chief critic of his Church and when I went in to see him I might have encountered a shorthand secretary, a recording machine, and even a definite written promise not to quote from him directly.

There was nothing like this in our interview. He talked with me alone about the whole range of Catholic policy and did not once forbid quotations even when he was talking about such delicate matters as birth control. As we sat down, he said, "See, I have two of your books over there and I have read them both." When my *God and Man in Washington* appeared, he sent me a special message to tell me how much he appreciated my fairness in describing his ideas.

During his early years as a Congressman, Kennedy's record on matters of Catholic policy had been somewhat spotty. In 1949 he had helped to introduce a bill which would have given federal money to parochial schools for bus transportation. This move attracted little attention because many Congressmen, both Catholic and non-Catholic, had also favored it. The Supreme Court had ruled 5 to 4 that such a use of tax funds did not violate the federal Constitution. Later on, Kennedy privately favored an appropriation bill supported by the National Education Association which omitted any potential grants to parochial schools. But suddenly, during the debates, he called the association on the telephone and said frankly that he would have to change his position because of pressure from Cardinal Cushing's office. (This story was denied during the campaign but I had traced it down and was quite satisfied that it was true.)

Apparently this was the last time that Kennedy ever followed the hierarchy of his Church blindly. Until then he had coasted along without thinking much of the underlying issues involving church and state. He had not gone to a Catholic school for more than two or three months in his life and he had been spared the pro-Catholic pressures often exerted by Catholic bishops on the poor. He had not, for example, ever been ordered to boycott non-Catholic schools under Canon 1374 of his Church's Canon Law although Cardinal O'Connell, the boss of the Massachusetts archdiocese when Kennedy was a youth, had issued flaming denunciations of Catholic parents who sent their children to non-Catholic schools. Kennedy, in fact, told me that he had never heard of Canon 1374 until he was seventeen years old and then his father had ignored it. Old Joe Kennedy was so powerful in Massachusetts Catholicism and so generous with his Church donations that the Church unofficially approved his decision to send his girls to Catholic schools and his sons to non-Catholic institutions.

As the campaign year of 1960 approached, Kennedy became increasingly careful about endorsing any legislation that could be called Catholic. When, early in 1960, an amendment to an educational bill came up in the Senate which would have granted loans to parochial schools for buildings, he was the only Catholic in the Senate to vote against it. When he stated his principles in an article in *Look* magazine he said: "There can be no question of Federal funds being used for support of parochial or private schools. It's unconstitutional under the First Amendment as interpreted by the Supreme Court."

The Catholic hierarchy did not like this but the masses of the Catholic people did not seem to object; they were willing to settle for a Catholic of Irish extraction in the White House even if he seemed somewhat anti-Catholic. The Catholic masses did not endorse the view of the Baltimore *Catholic Review* when it said, "He appears to have gone overboard in an effort to placate the bigots."

There was, of course, plenty of bigotry on both sides in the 1960 campaign and some of it made very good copy. A fake Knights of Columbus oath pledging K of C members to "hang, burn, waste, boil, flay, strangle, and bury alive" their heretical enemies reappeared along with the old canard that Catholics had assassinated Abraham Lincoln. I was glad that I had long ago condemned these tales.

The most colorful anti-Catholic to put in an appearance in the campaign was a little old lady in her eighties, Mrs. F. M. Standish of San Francisco, to whom *The New York Times* gave eleven inches. She proclaimed:

If the Hierarchy, which knows how to eliminate its political opponents with speedy finality, gets possession of our government, it would take hundreds of years and rivers of blood to get back American freedom. To avoid going back to the Dark Ages and burnings at the stake, we must keep Catholic Commanders-in-Chief out of the White House. If we had a Catholic Vice-President, the non-Catholic President would not live to serve out his term. We must consider history —Presidents Lincoln, Garfield and McKinley were all assassinated by Roman Catholics educated in parochial schools.

Kennedy himself and his liberal advisers—both Theodore Sorensen and Arthur Schlesinger Jr. were Unitarians —realized that it would be political suicide to pretend that popular anxiety about a Catholic in the White House was based entirely on bigotry. They knew that there were certain policies of the Catholic Church which no Catholic could endorse if he wanted to reach the White House. They were horrified when two bishops from the American mainland operating in Puerto Rico ordered their constituents not to vote for the liberal party of Governor Luis Muñoz Marin because his regime was a regime of "license, denying Christian morality." (The attack, which failed miserably, was based on Muñoz's support of birth control and his opposition to the teaching of Catholicism in the public schools.) Some Catholics tried to turn Catholicism back upon Kennedy by picturing him as a bad Catholic. In New York James L. Buckley, later Conservative Senator from New York, published "An Open Letter to American Catholics" arguing that "there *is* a Catholic issue" in the campaign, the Catholic opposition to communism, and "Kennedy has chosen to identify himself with that segment of American society which is either unwilling or unable to regard Communism as more than a childish bugaboo."

The big faux pas in the campaign was produced by America's greatest Protestant phrasemaker, Norman Vincent Peale, who was persuaded to act as temporary chairman of the Washington conference of an organization calling itself Citizens for Religious Freedom, created to "express the national anxiety" about a Catholic in the White House. The Peale group's statement questioned whether Kennedy would be able to resist the pressure from his Church's hierarchy in matters such as aid to parochial schools and our national policy in dealing with countries such as Spain. The anxieties expressed by the group were legitimate enough but it was not the proper moment to express such anxieties without assuring the public at the same time that Kennedy had clearly renounced the most objectionable policies of his Church. The Peale group was overwhelmed by the public counter-attack and poor Mr. Peale hurriedly withdrew as chairman, apologizing to his congregation for his "unwise" action. Quipped Adlai Stevenson, "I find Paul appealing and Peale appalling."

I decided to stay out of the presidential campaign and finally scratched in a protest vote for my old friend Norman Thomas. I knew that if I supported Kennedy openly I would be accused of renouncing my criticisms of Catholic policy. Also I was sufficiently uncertain about Kennedy to wait and see. I was angered, too, by the tricky evasions of some liberal Protestant supporters of Kennedy who pretended that Catholicism did not offer a challenge to our Constitution. In an article in *The New Republic* just three weeks before the 1960 election Reinhold Niebuhr absolved the Catholic Church of all intent to disturb our separation of church and state by quoting a general statement of one Jesuit scholar to that effect. Neither he nor the Jesuit scholar he quoted mentioned the stepped-up drive of the Catholic hierarchy to raid the public treasury for tax support for its schools or the great network of papal nuncios and concordats operated by the Vatican State. Although I liked Kennedy, I did not want to be associated with that kind of misleading propaganda.

Kennedy's strategy in the campaign was brilliant. He decided to challenge his right-wing Protestant opponents at the seat of their power. With perfect effrontery he chose a meeting of the Houston Ministerial Association to discuss religion and the presidency. At that meeting he declared, "I believe in an America where the separation of church and state is absolute—where no Catholic prelate would tell the President (should he be a Catholic) how to act and no Protestant minister would tell his parishioners for whom to vote—where no church or church school is granted any public funds or political preference." And then he added: "Whatever issue may come before me as President—on birth control, divorce, censorship, gambling, or any other subject—I will make my decisions in accordance with these views, in accordance with what my conscience tells me to be in the national interest, and without regard to outside pressures or dictates."

The Protestant preachers at that Houston meeting were unprepared for such a frontal counter-attack on their prejudices. Their questions were clumsy and involved. They had not even asked Americans United for carefully prepared ammunition for the question period, so they revealed both ignorance of the law and anti-Catholic prejudice. That Houston meeting, plus the first television debate with a wry-faced Nixon, probably supplied Kennedy with the hair-line margin by which he became a minority President.

I was greatly relieved, although I continued to have the most grave anxieties about the potential influence of the Catholic hierarchy after such a victory. The Catholic press jubilantly pretended that the Kennedy victory had refuted all "bigotry" concerning Catholic policies in the field of church and state. The "bigots" had been wrong and the American people had given them their comeuppance. Speaking at a mass meeting of four thousand people in Constitution Hall in Washington just after Kennedy's inauguration, I rather presumptuously warned the new President to keep his pledges to the letter. "We are watching you," I said, "and we want to say this to you, Mr. Kennedy. If you so much as crook your little finger in the direction of a single public dollar for Catholic schools, you will not return to the White House in 1965." I described the Catholic Church as "still the baldest, most unashamed, most absolute dictatorship in the world."

After all this I was rather surprised to be treated by the Kennedy administration as a friendly adviser. One day when I was talking on the telephone to Theodore Sorensen at the White House, he seemed much interested in my ideas and said that "they" would like me to come in and discuss my point of view. It should be confidential, of course. I readily accepted.

After a long conversation in Sorensen's office, I was taken into a smaller office and, without warning, in walked the President of the United States, looking like a young athlete in his well-pressed brown suit. He shook hands cordially and we immediately plunged into a frank discussion of aid to religious schools. He made it clear that he agreed with most of my thoughts about the Constitution and parochiaid. He was in the final stages of preparation for the issuance of his first message on education. What did I think of this and this passage in the document? He handed me the papers. I looked them over and told him what I thought. Later, at White House request, I submitted a memorandum on the law which may have had some influence.

Kennedy talked freely about Cardinal Spellman, who had greatly embarrassed him by demanding even before his inauguration absolute financial equality in government grants to Catholic and public schools. (About three months later the Catholic bishops of the United States made this demand official.) Kennedy not only turned down this demand by the leader of his own Church but he was equally firm in rejecting the idea of a Vatican ambassador because it seemed to him to constitute favoritism to a single church. He would not even grant a public audience at the White House to Rome's Apostolic Delegate to Washington. And, later on, when Kennedy visited Pope Paul in Rome in 1963, he was equally careful about any special recognition to the Catholic sovereign. By pre-arrangement he shook hands with His Holiness in a somewhat awkward manner.

The American hierarchy did not appreciate such conduct on the part of the first American Catholic President, and Church leaders expressed their displeasure in many ways. Getting wind of my private visit to the President, the Jesuit magazine *America* accused me of "peeking over the White House fence" while the first Catholic President was pursuing a non-Catholic policy. By the end of Kennedy's first year in office the Jesuits were so angry that they published in *America* a general attack under the heading "Church and President."

> Surely no one who is not misled by the charged rhetoric of such assorted commentators as Mr. Blanshard and Co., the editorial writers of the *New York Times*, Drew Pearson and *Look* correspondent Fletcher Knebel can fail to see that Catholics could not in conscience have done other than protest the undeniable discrimination of such public laws as would effectively deprive them of rights guaranteed under the Constitution. Of what value is the right of personal freedom of education if the exercise of that right has been priced out of existence by massive Federal grants to one school system to the detriment of others?

This quotation is a perfect illustration of the way in which Catholicism has undertaken to reach the public treasury by twisting the meaning of the Constitution. The Constitution in the First Amendment prohibits the establishment of religion, and the Supreme Court has said over and over again that the prohibition applies not only to a single established church but to all churches. Since 1947 it has reiterated the concept that government may not directly aid religion by tax support.

The Catholic bishops of the United States have steadily and repeatedly defied this interpretation of the Constitution, beginning in 1948. The Jesuits have supplied the necessary legal double-talk. They have pretended that the "rights guaranteed under the Constitution" include the "right" of tax subsidies for their Church's most important branch when the very purpose of the no-establishment clause of the First Amendment was to prevent just such tax subsidies to religious institutions. In Jesuit hands "freedom" has become a claim to sectarian privilege.

I confess that I would not take this Catholic claim to public funds so seriously if I did not regard the tax-supported public school as the most important thing in our democracy. I regard the public school as the natural place in which the children of all faiths and races can learn to live together. As Felix Frankfurter has said: "The public school is at once the symbol of our democracy and the most persuasive means of promoting our common heritage." As James B. Conant of Harvard has put it: "To my mind, our schools should serve all creeds. The greater the proportion of our youth who attend independent schools, the greater the threat to our democratic unity. Therefore, to use taxpayers' money to assist such a move is, for me, to suggest that American society use its own hand to destroy itself."

Many of my liberal friends fail to see the importance of the parochiaid issue because they have been won over by the plea for ethnic sympathy for a "minority." Sympathy for the Catholic minority was in order a hundred years ago when Protestant bigotry infiltrated public education. But not today when any expression of anti-Catholicism is very rare in public classrooms and the Church itself has become the largest and most powerful religious institution in the nation. In many of our communities the public schools are on the defensive and the Catholic hierarchy is more powerful than local public school boards.

My liberal friends who are moved by ethnic sympathy rarely stop to examine the real nature of the Catholic school system. The Catholic school is not a free school; it is a fee school. Although it helps some poor students it is not, like the public school, open to all the poor. It is usually supported by the same collection plate as the local church, and in practice any aid to the parish school is essentially aid to the church. The Catholic school is doctrinally a part of the Catholic Church, managed and taught primarily by priests and nuns who may be dismissed if they publicly disagree with Catholic teaching. Its primary purpose is to keep the Catholic child faithful to his Church.

This purpose is a worthy purpose and no democratic society has a right to thwart it by suppression or discrimination. But it is not suppression or discrimination to limit tax support to public institutions when the children of all faiths and races are admitted to such institutions free of charge. If Catholic parents decline the invitation to accept the benison of free public education, they cannot logically plead that they have been treated unfairly.

For me there are three extra reasons why believers in American democracy should support the separation of church and state in education. (1) Compulsory tax support for a religious school system impairs that principle of personal religious freedom which Madison and Jefferson asserted in 1785: "To compel a man to furnish contributions of money for the propagation of opinions which he disbelieves and abhors is sinful and tyrannical." (2) Complete tax support for sectarian systems would not only be more expensive than our present system but it would ultimately result in fragmenting the public school system. It would create many competing systems, wrangling with each other and with local school boards for a larger share of public money and public power. The sour experience of the Netherlands, Northern Ireland, Canada, Australia, and many other countries underscores this prophecy. (3) In our own Southern states, in spite of the sincere protestations of Catholic leaders against racial segregation, a Catholic, tax-supported school system is bound to be overwhelmingly white—only about four percent of American Negroes are Catholic—and the end result of government subsidy for private schools would be a white racist school system using the Catholic label.

The majority of American Catholic parents—some say two-thirds—have now accepted the healthful religious neutrality of our public schools by enrolling their children in those schools. However, the dwindling hard-core Catholic minority, backed by the American Catholic bishops and their overlords in Rome, continue the old struggle for tax grants. The Church's present campaign is based on a dialectical artifice, the claim that the demand is for "aid to the child and not the school." It was doubly fortunate, therefore, that in June 1971 the Supreme Court, with only one dissenting vote, struck down as unconstitutional two favorite devices for subsidizing church schools with public money—the purchase of teachers' services in parochial schools and the payment of a percentage of teachers' salaries. Catholic lobbyists immediately began to re-group their forces around two other seductive devices for subsidies— the so-called voucher plan under which tax grants would be given to all parents and then passed on to "the school of their choice" and the tax credit plan under which parents would be allowed to deduct part of their parochial school tuition from their income tax payments.

On the surface the Catholic arguments are persuasive. The parochial schools are dying in many localities and parents who must pay public school taxes are complaining that it is unfair to tax them twice. But they are not taxed twice. They are taxed once as all citizens, including bachelors, are taxed for the maintenance of our greatest public institution, and their payments to a private, church institution are voluntary. The serious compulsion involved in the Catholic plan is that unconstitutional compulsion which Jefferson and Madison deplored.

Moreover, there is, for enlightened and progressive parents, a supplementary reason why they should not support a Catholic school system. That system is part of a great conservative complex centering in Rome which, without giving American Catholics the power to disagree effectively, stands for no birth control, no divorce, no abortion, and the promotion of many anti-scientific ideas which liberals find repugnant. If we must have a rightist bloc in American elementary education, let the rightists pay for it!

20. VATICAN II AND "THE CATHOLIC REVOLUTION"

ONE REASON I did not participate actively in the 1960 presidential campaign was personal and tragic. During that summer we were staying in Thetford while I worked on my book about Spain and Portugal. When we had traveled in those countries during the preceding year, Mary had seemed in normal health. During our years in Washington she had become executive director of the national organization known as the Unitarian Fellowship for Social Justice. In that capacity she had organized a series of very successful Workshops for Religious Liberals, edited a special monthly bulletin, and produced a monthly column for a time in the national journal of Unitarianism, *The Register*. She had always been far more energetic than I was and she seemed to be the very picture of healthy womanhood.

But, during our stay in Spain she had missed her annual physical checkup by our beloved personal physician, Dr. Sven Gundersen of Hanover. When she went again to the Hanover Hospital in 1960, she came up the steep driveway to our house weeping. The doctors had found possible cancer in her rectum. It was only very tiny, they said—they always say that—and it could undoubtedly be eliminated, and so forth. Mary was carried along by their practiced optimism but I was not deceived. I remembered Julia.

Fortunately, there is some magic resource of nature that helps the doomed to face life cheerfully. The will to live overcomes the pessimism of even the most sophisticated persons. Mary knew all about the evasions and circumlocutions practiced by the doctors treating incurable cancer. At our house in Washington Jennie Lee had told us in great detail how the London surgeons had eased her husband, Aneurin Bevan, toward death with cheerful evasions. But when it came to herself, Mary somehow accepted the illusions of the doctors and talked about the pain from her "sciatica," telling her friends that the fatal traces of cancer had been completely eliminated. She lived for five years and during most of that period she worked cheerfully.

When Mary reached the last three months of life in Thetford, it was impossible to get nurses to our farmhouse in the snowdrifts. I served as nurse and cook until she mercifully died in her sleep.

Before Mary's death there had occurred, in 1962, something which changed the whole position of the Roman Catholic Church in the world scene. Until then critical discussion of Catholic policy had been taboo in most journals and publishing houses. Books by ex-priests were classed as gutter literature. I, having produced my tenth book on my old typewriter in the upstairs study at the Sawnee Bean Farm, confessed to myself that my stereotype was not flattering and that it would be difficult to revise my reputation. I had become branded as a muckraker, an apostle of "Blanshardism," which the Catholic press, and many of the secular editors, translated as "bigot." My ultra-liberal past had apparently been forgotten.

Had I painted myself into a literary corner? Could I ever get out of that corner? My gloom was accentuated by the fact that Mary had undergone that year her second operation, emerging barely alive after eight hours on the operating table. My pessimism about the possible reform of Catholicism was complete. At that time no one could have made me believe that within three years the whole area of Catholic policy would emerge into the public forum and that many of my allegedly partisan criticisms of Catholic reaction were destined to be repeated and emphasized by Catholics themselves.

The thing that brought about this astonishing transformation in public attitudes was the Vatican Council of 1962–1965. It had been announced in January 1959 by Pope John XXIII, the Bergamo peasant who had begun life as Angelo Giuseppe Roncalli and then moved up through the Vatican diplomatic apparatus as Papal Nuncio to France and finally Cardinal Archbishop of Venice.

There was nothing in his record to indicate that he was a conscious or unconscious revolutionist, or even an advanced liberal. He had helped to kill the worker-priest movement in France, and he was seventy-seven years old when he ascended the throne of Saint Peter, hardly an age appropriate for vigorous reform. When I read John's first announcement of the Council I was inclined to dismiss the whole thing as ecclesiastical eyewash, not worthy of serious consideration. The coming assembly, I noted, was to be made up of members of the Establishment, appointed bishops and religious-order bureaucrats. How could anything progressive come out of such a nonrepresentative group?

After the first session in 1962 my attitude began to change. This looked like something potentially explosive, particularly after Xavier Rynne's brilliant articles in *The New Yorker*, which made the whole affair look like a third party political convention. Mary, temporarily recovered, thought that I ought to be in on such an event. "You belong there," she said. "You helped to start all that ferment. Now you can see if the ferment is working." She wanted me to produce a book on the Council.

I called up Arnold Tovell at Beacon Press and asked, "Want a book by P. Blanshard on those doings in Rome?" The reply was instant: "Of course, we do." After all, although the field was being cultivated intensively by some of the best journalists in the world, I had spent as much time in exploring the background of Catholic policy as any of them and my seventy years did not seem to weigh too heavily upon me. As it turned out, both Mary and I had a physically good time at the Council. We rented a rather elegant and cold apartment in downtown Rome in the very building where Pius XII had been born, and every day I walked across the Tiber several times to attend the press conferences and other meetings at the Vatican where the theological experts transmitted and interpreted the dull homilies spoken in Latin at the "private" sessions in the great aula of St. Peter's. The place was swarming with nine hundred journalists who hungrily pounced upon every fact and rumor which could possibly serve as the basis for a story. I was delighted to see that some of the most penetrating and critical questions were asked by liberal Catholics.

I had some misgivings about my own reception at the Council but there was no basis for worry. When I registered at the Vatican Press Office an archbishop with a broad Irish brogue caught sight of me and rushed up shouting: "Hello, Paul. I am delighted to see you here." He was the same archbishop, then a lowly monsignor, who had treated me so coldly in 1950 when I had tried to see Pius XII. Even when Sanche de Gramont produced an article about me in the *Herald Tribune* headed "Professional Anti-Catholic at Vatican Council," it did not seem to dampen my welcome. The Church of Rome was on its good behavior. Perhaps some optimists hoped to make a convert out of a notorious sinner. A widely distributed Associated Press article pictured me as "mellowed" in my attitude toward Catholicism. I admitted that I had mellowed some but only after Pope John had done some mellowing himself.

I am reluctant to downgrade Pope John in any way because he was such a genuine and warmhearted man and because on at least three issues he was a progressive in his own Church, the issues of war, poverty, and racial justice. He published two magnificent encyclicals, *Mater et Magistra* and *Pacem in Terris*, in which he expressed a broad humanity that was far removed from the institutional dogmatism of most papal encyclicals. He had expressed a willingness to talk to Communists and unbelievers as human beings, which was quite refreshing after the rigid—and futile—anti-communism of Pius XII.

But the image of Pope John that was created by writers inside and outside the Vatican during the years of the Council was at least fifty percent synthetic. He was a humane individual; he was the world's grandfather; he wanted to get rid of some of the formalism of his Church. But he was far from being an all-around liberal who wished to deal with other religions on a basis of equality. Liberal Catholics throughout the world seized upon him as a dialectical launching pad. His name was used to support many, many reform notions which he never espoused. The "spirit of Pope John" became a loosely defined slogan adopted by all those who wanted to reform the Church for any reason. (American reformers are fond of using the "spirit of Abraham Lincoln" in the same way.)

John showed no inclination to reform the power structure of his own Church or the Church's antiquated sexual code. He continued to support imposed celibacy for Western priests, and he continued to oppose birth control and liberal divorce laws. Just before the opening of the Council, he had called together, for the first session in many years, the synod of his own diocese of Rome. He treated the priests in that synod like children, denying them the most elementary rights of participation. In a Palm Sunday homily in 1960 he exhorted Catholic parents to have many children. "Don't be afraid of the number of your sons and daughters," he declared. "On the contrary, ask Divine Providence for them so that you can rear and educate them to their own benefit and to the glory of your fatherland here on earth and that one in heaven." (Ten years later, in November 1970, Pope Paul, desperately defending his own reactionary opposition to contraception, quoted Pope John's intransigent and equally conventional position on the same subject.)

Having taken for his motto when he became Pope "Obedience and Peace," John seemed to honor both equally, assuming that he could make friends with non-Catholics without modifying the autocratic supremacy of his papal throne. Although he spoke charitably of heretical Protestants as "our separated brethren," he never even suggested that they were entitled to equality with Catholics in

mixed marriage. This concession seemed to me the absolute minimum required of the Catholic hierarchy if its proclaimed effusions about "brotherhood" were to be taken at
their face value.

The Church was in a terrific slump when the Council
was called. It claimed nearly six hundred million members
throughout the world; careful Catholic analysts put the
membership at four hundred million, and not more than
half of these were active, practicing Catholics. In Italy
itself the Catholic population was largely indifferent to
church principles. At least eighty percent of the men did
not even perform their Easter duties and about twenty-five
percent of them voted with the Communists on election
day. Between the first Vatican Council in 1870 and the
second Vatican Council in 1962 the number of priests in
Italy had declined seventy percent while the population
had doubled.

At first this depressed state of the Church was concealed
by the gaudiness of the display. This was the greatest
show on earth and it was given the largest audience in
religious history by world television. But the combined
image of medievalism and elegance was not altogether
pleasing, and the clerical class distinctions seemed utterly
out of place in a world of democratic institutions. The
assembly of some twenty-five hundred bishops was completely nonrepresentative of the Catholic people of the
world. At first there was not a single layman or woman in
evidence, and, of course, all the bishops present were
chosen by the Pope, not by the people of the various countries. The cardinals with their gaudy robes—they were
said to cost about $3000—arrived in St. Peter's Square in
their limousines and entered the aula by separate doors
while the ordinary bishops and theologians came in buses.
The cardinals sat in red upholstered seats while the rest sat
in green upholstered seats. When a mere bishop wanted to
speak he might have to wait for days or weeks for his
turn. When a cardinal wanted to speak, his name went
to the head of the waiting list. Above them all, of course,

was the Pope, too sacred and important to attend regular sessions or give press interviews or answer any embarrassing questions directly.

When the Pope attended the extraordinary open sessions of the Council he usually appeared on his swaying *sedia gestatoria,* carried by fourteen scarlet-clad henchmen. During the ceremony of the obediences he sat in his gold-trimmed white robes on a high throne while the cardinals, many of them limping with rheumatism and old age, trundled across a great open space in St. Peter's, climbed up three steps, and kissed his hand as a symbol of their abject obedience. (The bishops kissed his knee while the abbots kissed his foot.)

The Council delegates were all male, almost all old, and almost all celibate. Many of the cardinals were in their eighties. Pope John was in this category and so were his Secretary of State Amleto Cicognani, and his chief ecumenical negotiator Cardinal Bea. Largely because of age, sixty-three of the delegates died during the first Council year. The average bishop was appointed to his post only ten years before his death, at an age when the average American businessman was almost ready for retirement.

All things considered, it was miraculous that this Council accomplished as much as it did accomplish in its four sessions. Technically it was bound by the fantastic claim that the Church's doctrine never changes. A large part of the time of the *periti* (theological experts) was spent in devising ways to change outworn and incorrect assertions about life without admitting that any change was taking place. Often as I sat listening to such intellectual manipulations I felt that these men were committing what Sherwood Anderson once called the real sin against the Holy Ghost, "believing your own bunk."

Pope Paul was a typical product of the system. He was saturated with institutional loyalty, having come up to the papal throne through the diplomatic bureaucracy, where he had served for twenty-nine years, fifteen of them directly in the service of Pius XII. He always refused to sit down in the papal presence and always insisted on standing up at the telephone when the Higher Authority called him in his apartments.

The word "balance" was the key word to describe him. During the stormy first session of the Council he had managed to be adroitly noncommittal about all the controversial issues arising in debate. No one knew at the end of that session whether he was a liberal or a conservative. Ultimately, like Pius IX, he moved to the right after becoming Pope and turned out to be a genuine reactionary, using his influence to fight against nearly all priestly reform movements throughout the world.

At the Council I was chiefly interested in four things— the struggle of some of the relatively liberal bishops against papal dictatorship, the demand of a few of them for more religious liberty, the policy of the Vatican on church and state, and the Church's sexual code. The struggle over papal dictatorship took three years and the end result was as ambiguous as an American political platform. Even the most liberal bishops from such semi-rebellious countries as Holland, France, Germany, and Belgium did not dare to assail papal rule directly, so they concocted what they called "collegiality," a theory that the Pope under Catholic tradition shared his rule of the Church with the bishops. The advocates of collegiality produced a few phrases from the records of the First Vatican Council of 1870 to support their ideas but they had no real authority for their challenge to papal power. The outcome of the long debate was almost total futility. The sharing reforms adopted turned out to be entirely paternalistic, a little like nineteenth-century imperialism. The Pope promised to consult the bishops but he felt no obligation to follow their advice. In the end the final Dogmatic Constitution of the Church, which came out of the Council, abjectly proclaimed that "a religious submission of mind and will must be given to the authentic teaching of the Pope, even when he is not speaking *ex cathedra.*" The synods of selected bishops which came after the Council were not even free to act on either birth control or celibacy, the two most important controversial issues of this era.

The Council did a little better in facing the issue of religious liberty, although even in this area the internal censorship system of the Church was only slightly changed. After a two-year battle the Council adopted a declaration which asserted that "the human person has a right to religious freedom" and "no one is to be forced to act in a manner contrary to his own beliefs."

Although this sounded like substantial progress, the conservatives triumphed at the final session of the Council when they forced the addition to the religious freedom declaration of a paragraph limiting the new liberty to civil society, leaving the hierarchy's internal dictatorship over its own people still unchanged. Said the statement: "Religious freedom . . . which men demand as necessary to fulfill their duty to God, has to do with immunity from coercion in civil society. Therefore it leaves untouched traditional Catholic Doctrine on the moral duty of men and societies toward the true religion and toward the one Church of Christ." Although internal censorship in the Church has been relaxed, all priests who write about religion must still submit their writings to a diocesan censor.

The touchy and vital subject of the separation of church and state was almost ignored. No one listening to the debates in the aula would have realized that there was any conflict between the American Constitution and Vatican policy. No one in the discussions pointed out that the Vatican was both a church and a state with sixty nunciatures or diplomatic representatives functioning in the world's leading capitals, concordats with many countries giving the Church special political and legal preference, a whole string of Catholic political parties and a system of state subsidies for Church schools in those countries where the Church had the political power to win such favors from civil parliaments. The Council, with almost no debate, continued its claims on the public treasury as a "religious right," and the Declaration on Christian Education affirmed the proposition that "the office of educating belongs by a unique title to the Church."

The great unfinished business of the Council was sex. I suppose that those twenty-five hundred celibate bishops, sitting in their upholstered bleachers in their lace-trimmed robes, constituted the most powerful anti-sexual body in the world. They had been nurtured on Saint Paul and Saint Augustine, two of the worst anti-sexual mentors in history, and they had a long record of anti-female prejudice to overcome before they could look Freud in the face. They were steered away from liberalism in sexual matters by the new Pauline Paul, whose papal pronouncements on sex reached absurdity, after the Council sessions, in the encyclical against birth control.

Pope Paul VI was obviously frightened of sex. We may assume that his utter lack of sexual experience contributed to the fright. His predecessor, Pope John, was alleged to have had two mistresses briefly when he was very young before he became a priest, but no such rumor ever circulated about Paul. He was true to the spirit as well as the letter of the Church's celibate code for Western priests and his attitude toward birth control might have been borrowed from Anthony Comstock. Joy in sex, he seemed to believe, was not seemly for a Catholic woman. A good wife submitted as a duty. After the Council he told an Italian women's congress that "conjugal chastity throughout the centuries has redeemed woman from the slavery of a duty submitted to through force and humiliation."

Paul would not even let the Fathers of the Council discuss the birth control issue thoroughly. When the growing discontent of Catholic laymen and a few bishops threatened to open up the whole subject on the Council floor in the third session, Pope Paul calmly took the problem (along with some other marriage problems) away from the Council and put it into the hands of a commission appointed by himself. Then he kept the names of the commissioners secret so that they could not be reached with petitions. He pursued the same policy in regard to celibacy. When I asked Cardinal Heenan why a poll of all the priests in the world could not be taken to see whether they actually favored celibacy, I received the reply that such a poll would take too long. (An air-mail poll could have been taken in three weeks.) Only one bishop dared to twit his celibate associates on their celibacy, suggesting that the Council's attitudes on sex came perhaps from "a bachelor psychosis on the part of individuals unacquainted with this sector of life."

Pope Paul's "bachelor psychosis" was underscored when, refusing to wait for the report of his own commission on contraception, he insisted on condemning birth control in his dramatic appearance before the United Nations in October 1965. As millions watched throughout the world he inserted into his address his personal anathema: "You must strive to multiply bread so that it suffices for the tables of mankind, and not rather favor an artificial control of birth, which would be irrational, in order to diminish the number of guests at the banquet of life."

The Pope even had the temerity to maintain his dog-matic position on birth control when he went to India. I talked over the Church's policy in India with India's senior churchman, Cardinal Gracias, reminding him of his gov-ernment's program to distribute 144 million condoms a year at a cost of one cent each. (Contraceptives can be bought at post offices in India along with stamps.) What would he do to further this program? His answer was that as a Catholic who was loyal to the Pope, he would do everything in his power to block the government program. At that time India was gaining one million mouths a month while millions were living and dying in the streets.

The things that happened to world Catholicism after the Council adjourned were very much more important than the events in St. Peter's. In spite of the queasy am-biguity of its statements on religious freedom, the Council unlocked the doors of censorship throughout the world.

In the United States Catholic policy suddenly became debatable without taboos. The great magazines and newspapers, and even the television networks suddenly burst forth in candid descriptions of reactionary Catholic policies, often written without apology by ex-priests who had previously been members of an untouchable caste. One of these ex-priests, after drawing a capacity audience of cheering students at Notre Dame, reached the best-seller lists with an attack on his Church that was more caustic than anything I had ever written.

Even the Catholic seminaries and convents joined in the new exposures. Pictures of former priests with their new wives began to appear in conservative journals, with no disapproving captions underneath. Some progressive nuns marched on picket lines and raised their hemlines; many more left their profession altogether. Some American convents and monasteries were forced to close for lack of recruits. The Catholic schools lost nearly a million pupils in one year, and the convents lost thirty-three hundred nuns. The Vatican admitted that it had at least ten thousand requests from priests to be dispensed from their anti-marriage vows, and it was evident that thousands of other priests were ready to ask for the same release if and when the compulsory celibacy rules were lifted.

Progressive rebels within the Church tried to organize the new discontent into an effective reform movement, and many of them singled out the defects in the Catholic establishment that I had underscored in *American Freedom and Catholic Power*. Said John Cogley, who had written a whole series of attacks on me when he was editor of *Commonweal*:

It would be hard to find a single charge made by Mr. Blanshard that has not since been made against the clergy, the hierarchy or "the system" in the pages of Catholic magazines and newspapers. . . . If he takes some pride in his prophetic talents, who is there to fault him? Perhaps unwittingly he blueprinted the future of the Church much better than those of us who earnestly defended pre-conciliar Catholicism against his attacks.

On the whole the liberal Catholic protests were stronger in Europe than in the United States because the Irish bishops continued to dominate the American hierarchy and Pope Paul was careful to favor them in appointments. One liberal Catholic theologian, the bouncy and courageous Father Hans Kung of Tubingen, gained great influence on both sides of the Atlantic—he was most cordial and frank in discussing with me the shortcomings of his Church at the Council. He produced without Imprimatur an open challenge to papal infallibility in his book *Infallible? An Inquiry.* "The Roman system," he declared, "is the sole absolutist system that has survived the French Revolution," and he proceeded to denounce that system in terms of democracy and freedom of thought. If the Church is ever redeemed from within, the redemption will come from men like Father Kung who cling to the mystical aspects of their faith while repudiating the Church's papal machinery.

It became evident soon after the Council that the chief obstacle to Church reform was Pope Paul himself. In spite of overwhelming evidence that the younger Catholics of the world favored the right of birth control and the right of priests to marry, Paul issued two ultra-conservative encyclicals, *Sacerdotalis Caelibatus* in 1967 and *Humanae Vitae* in 1968, in which he went against the whole trend of modern scientific thinking about family life, psychology, and overpopulation. He upheld compulsory celibacy as "a brilliant jewel" for those in the Western church, and he banned all contraception as immoral. In 1970 he issued a fifteen-page instruction to all papal nuncios and apostolic delegates in the world to fight every government-supported birth control program.

To maintain his ultra-conservative position on birth control and celibacy Pope Paul was obliged to manipulate the agenda at the first two synods of bishops, which he called together in 1967 and 1969, in such a way that these subjects never reached the floor for value judgments. When the third post-Council synod met, the progressives tried to discuss the celibacy issue, but they were defeated by a wide margin because the synod membership had been stacked in favor of the Establishment.

The Church's unrealistic and unreformed sexual policies became especially evident in the United States in the 1970's when the whole power of the hierarchy was thrown into the battle against more liberal abortion laws. Some seventeen states and the District of Columbia had liberalized their abortion laws and the new permissiveness had resulted in the development of safe and low-priced clinics in several states, notably in New York. Then, with the direct aid of President Nixon, a great Catholic campaign against "murder of the innocent" began. It was a very ugly and hysterical campaign, ignoring the suffering of female victims of illegal abortion mills and the whole problem of unwanted children and centering all attention on "the destruction of human life" involved in terminating the existence of the fetus. The hierarchy announced that "life begins at the moment of conception," an ecclesiastical theory which has no support in common law since English law has never rated a fetus in its early stages as a whole human being. In any case, it cannot be forgotten that only a few years ago Catholic leaders in the battle against birth control branded advocates of contraception as "murderers of the innocent." And Catholic Canon Law still provides no mercy for the mother who needs an abortion, not even when the abortion might be considered necessary to save her life. Canon 2350 still reads: "Those who procure abortion, not excepting the mother, incur, if the effect is produced, an excommunication *latae sententiae* reserved to the Ordinary (bishop); and if they be clerics they are moreover to be removed." In effect the celibate priests are compelling thousands of unwilling Catholic mothers to have unwanted children.

In the new worldwide turmoil over Catholicism, some non-Catholics have been deceived by the volume and quality of the rebellious noise coming from liberal Catholics. They have wondered whether any further criticism of Catholic policy by non-Catholics is wise or necessary. Why not let Catholicism take care of itself? Hasn't there been a Catholic revolution?

Yes, there has been an *attempt* at a Catholic revolution by courageous liberal Catholics who deserve the admiration of all liberals. But it was never more than a minority rebellion, a defeated rebellion. The sources of power in the Church have remained firmly in the hands of the Vatican Establishment and that Establishment is still a papal autocracy which acts as a colonial power, operating its branches as imperial enclaves on foreign soil. Until the anti-democratic Roman power center is defeated and democratized it is not reasonable to talk of a Catholic revolution.

One significant test of the extent of change within the Church came in 1970 and 1971 when drafts of proposed changes in Catholic Canon Law were made public. A Catholic commission on canon law had been working for several years, supposedly in the direction of fundamental reform. Here was the opportunity to show that the papal machinery of power could be changed to grant to the Catholic people and ordinary priests some of the rights of ecclesiastical citizenship. When the editors of the *National Catholic Reporter*, the best of the liberal Catholic journals, got hold of the preliminary draft of Canon Law revisions, they said:

What stands out glaringly after this document is read in the year 1970 is that no bishop or combination of bishops, whether in conference, council or synod, is granted any independent authority whatever, however minor. . . . What we have here is a system which is not merely authoritarian but absolutist; or to use the ugly (but accurate) 20th-century word, totalitarian.

21. PERSONAL—AND
JOURNEY THROUGH APARTHEID

MARY'S LONG ORDEAL with cancer had ended early in 1965 between sessions of the Council. I was left alone in my great empty house on a Vermont hillside. I thought for a few days that I could not stand the new loneliness. I had no one to wake up to in the morning except our new black poodle, Sawnee Bean, and her desperate search for Mary brought more tears than anything else.

Everybody was kind but at such a moment kindness is not enough. I fried my hamburgers, whipped my mashed potatoes, and gagged at my TV dinners. I sat at my typewriter in the upstairs study and tried to concentrate on another chapter of my book on the Vatican Council. My sons were the soul of kindness but I could not bear to think of accepting any hospitality from them. The vision of an old man sitting beside a fireplace, somebody else's fireplace, while the younger generation went out to work did not appeal to me.

At first, also, the idea of re-marriage did not appeal to me. What was an oldster of nearly seventy-two doing with dreams of a new wife? Like most conventional people I had learned to think of Indian-summer marriages as a trifle ghastly and in bad taste, especially if they were entered into quickly by aging widowers. But when I was faced with the prospect of years of compulsory loneliness I lost all thought of proprieties. My new mood was based also on two other factors. My sexual desire, having been starved completely during the five years of Mary's illness, reasserted itself, and the thought of one woman kept recurring.

The lady was Beatrice Mayer, who had served as secretary of my department under La Guardia. She had worked with me for six of the most exciting and exacting years of my life. I remembered her as warm, intelligent, and beautiful in a sylphlike way. She had been a newspaper reporter in Tampa and Richmond, Virginia, and had married a New York doctor who, I knew, had died. I had not seen her in ten years when suddenly in the mail of condolences after Mary's death came a short and rather prim little note from Beatrice in New York expressing sympathy. She had evidently not expected any reply, for her note was written the day before she sailed for the Canary Islands and she sent no forwarding address.

Suddenly I knew that I was going to ask Beatrice Mayer to marry me, and to hell with bourgeois conventions. I was a free man and a very despondent man. I found out the address of Beatrice's daughter in London and in a long air-mail letter I poured out my longing. No response for weeks. Then another letter, more urgent than the first and just as sentimental. Still no answer. Then suddenly on the telephone up there in the Vermont woods a voice: "London calling, Mrs. Mayer will speak to Mr. Blanshard." God bless the telephone! Beatrice had just arrived in London from the Canary Islands to find my letters waiting for her.

It was a very quick and sweet wooing. I would not take no for an answer. Beatrice flew back from London, looked me over to see whether I still resembled her old boss, and we were married at Brand's big house in New Haven by a leader of the Ethical Culture Society. That seemed to be the best compromise for two unbelievers from, respectively, the Jewish and Protestant traditions. Beatrice, a native of New York, came from a middle-class family of Russian extraction which did not accept religious Judaism. She told me that her grandfather, one of the rare Jews who held an official post in czarist Russia, openly protested against all organized religion and showed his particular disdain for Jewish Sabbath rules. On Saturday mornings he would sit at his large window enjoying a big black cigar

while his fellow Jews, aghast at his blasphemy, hurried by
on their way to the synagogue.

Our life since our Indian-summer marriage has been full
of ease and joy and good comradeship—and sex. Let no
one say that sex stops at seventy! With a new wife I have
acquired a beautiful and gifted daughter, Marcia Gregg
Mayer, and two sprightly new grandsons, bringing my total
subprogeny to nine. Marcia, who scored a great success in
the modern dance in London, has now joined the dance
faculty at Washington University in St. Louis, and her
Australian husband, Ross Winter, is adding to the family's
artistic accomplishments by serving as both architect and
choreographer. Beatrice has added to my puritan-starved
intellect a new dimension, the awakening love of art. An
avid student of art history, she had spent the later years
of her widowhood traveling around the world savoring its
artistic treasures. She has gradually aroused my interest
and appreciation in a hitherto undiscovered world.

We flew off to Rome for the final session of the Vatican
Council immediately after our marriage, and I confess that
I was somewhat maliciously amused to walk into the press
conference with a wife who was serving as a correspondent
for the American Jewish Congress while I was listed as a
correspondent for the national Unitarian magazine. (I
had become a Unitarian about five years before.) The
Unitarian-Jewish combination must have been somewhat
puzzling to those Catholic critics who had described me as
the founder of a new Protestant nativism.

In that fourth session we walked right into the middle
of the great battle over the alleged anti-Semitism of the
Vatican. The Vatican, of course, had a long record of anti-
Semitic innuendo and prejudice to overcome. The statement that "the Jews killed Christ" could still be found in
many approved Catholic books, and the Vatican had consistently opposed recognition of Israel. For political as well
as religious reasons it seemed necessary for an ecumenical
council to say something nice about Jews.

Cardinal Bea, leader of the goodwill forces in the Council, prepared an adequate resolution on anti-Semitism, but reactionary leaders of the Curia thought that it might offend the Arabs, so they changed the wording in the most tactless way. In the original resolution the Catholic anti-Semitism of the past was "condemned"; in a revised version the Fathers merely "deplored" it. The Curial leaders did not seem to realize what that one verbal change could mean in a world which remembered the six million Jews who had been murdered by Hitler. And those Curial leaders made matters worse by squeezing into the revised resolution the old inference that the Jews had actually killed Christ. Although the resolution contained many strong denunciations of anti-Semitism, the harm had been done.

At about this time several plays and books appeared which exposed Pius XII as a careful, suave politician in dealing with Hitler's anti-Jewish policy. This was in the years when the former Pacelli had been Papal Nuncio to Germany and then wartime Pope. Pius had been silent at the wrong moment, and Rolf Hochhuth in his play *The Deputy* dramatized the papal weakness with fearful emphasis. If the case against Pius XII as a calculating anti-Semite was overstated—and I think it was—neither Pius XII nor Paul VI came out of the controversy with improved reputations. Montini, on the very day he ceased to be archbishop of Milan and became Paul VI, had a letter published in the London (Catholic) *Tablet* declaring that Hochhuth's play "entirely misrepresents" his old chief, who had never been "inspired by a calculating political opportunism." Paul was doing his duty. The world respected his loyalty but it did not believe him.

After the Vatican Council and the publication of my book on that subject, Beatrice and I were very tired of popes, cardinals, and theologians. We wanted to get away to some corner of the world where we could confront an entirely new scene. (Beatrice had worked very hard for me at the Council translating French newspapers and documents in her fluent French.) Back in Vermont again, with no unfinished book on the horizon, we felt also the urge to get away from Johnson's America where, it seemed to us, the Vietnam war spirit enveloped us like the effluence of a poisoned swamp.

Why not Africa as our next target and haven? We had both been there briefly but only in the northern parts. Why not see for ourselves the most God-awful citadel of racial discrimination in the world, South Africa?

By a combination of circumstances I was given a special opportunity to answer two questions about South Africa. How do three and one-half million whites rule over thirteen million nonwhites without being murdered? And how does a man murder a racist Prime Minister while the Prime Minister is sitting in his own Parliament?

The first question concerned both Beacon Press and me; they wanted me to produce a short book to be called *Journey Through Apartheid*. The second question led to an arrangement I made with the London magazine *Encounter* to represent that journal as a correspondent at the Cape Town trial of Demetrio Tsafendas, the man who had murdered the South African Prime Minister, Hendrik Verwoerd, in the fall of 1966.

In the packed courtroom at Cape Town—packed with an audience that was nine-tenths white, with all-white lawyers and three all-white judges—I watched the drama of the Verwoerd murder unfold. Tsafendas, a swarthy native of Mozambique, the child of a Greek father and a half-Negro mother, had somehow wormed his way into the holy of holies of white supremacy. He appeared on the scene as a uniformed white messenger in the national Parliament. Although he was a man of sallow complexion with some obvious mixture of Moorish blood, he had passed himself off for many years as white, carrying a white seaman's employment card and belonging to a predominantly white Protestant church. By accumulating six passports and using four different names in different countries, he had confused many immigration authorities.

Was he a Communist or was he crazy? These were the

first two questions that the public asked about him after the murder. Although he had demonstrated some fleeting sympathy for communism, he was not a serious social revolutionist. He was, rather, a fundamentalist Protestant fanatic, a Catholic-hater who relied on the Old Testament instead of on Karl Marx to express the alienation of a schizophrenic mind.

One morning while working in the South African Parliament he had asked for thirty minutes leave to go shopping. He went down to the business district of Cape Town, bought two kitchen knives, stuck them in his belt, and returned to the Parliament. Protected by his messenger's uniform, he walked into the Parliament chamber as the members were streaming into the opening session where the Prime Minister was already seated, leafing through the notes for a speech he was about to deliver. Tsafendas stepped to his side under pretext of delivering a message and drove a knife downward into his chest four times, his powerful arm moving like a piston. At least one of his four stabbing strokes reached Verwoerd's heart and he died instantly.

The Nationalist regime handled the crisis with considerable restraint. Their leaders were relieved, I think, that the assassin was not a racial hero or a leader of the black majority. Under the circumstances they decided to give him his full rights under the Mental Disorder Act, which provides that a defendant pleading mental incapacity can have a full and separate trial on that issue alone. There was no real doubt about Tsafendas' condition. Abundant proof was supplied that he had been in and out of asylums as a schizophrenic in four different countries, including the United States. In the end he was sent away for life as mentally incompetent.

For that brief interval of the Tsafendas trial, while all the world was looking on, the racist regime of South Africa was on its good behavior. It wanted to demonstrate that with all its limitations it was a regime of law rather than lynching. To one insane, semi-white victim it gave justice with British punctilio. Then it went back to the routine of injustice as usual. One morning while we were in South Africa I read in the newspapers the story of how nine black men were hanged for the murder of one white man. That story seemed to dramatize mathematically the apartheid system.

The Tsafendas trial marked for us only the beginning of a fruitful and fascinating seven months in South Africa. They were seven months of mixed horror and delight. Finding a small furnished apartment over a hardware store in downtown Cape Town, we reveled in the beauties of the region. The Table Mountain area with its blue seas, its flowering jacaranda trees, and its eternal gardens is one of the most picturesque places in the world. And unconsciously we found ourselves day by day accepting more readily the position of privileged visitors in a white heaven located over a black hell. How easy and natural it is to fall back into the smugness of a ruling racial caste if you are a member of that caste!

Around us was the most completely organized and legalized four-layer system of racial discrimination in the world, all stratified on the basis of skin color. On top were the whites, called Europeans—although the Japanese were given a special status of "honorable Europeans." Then came the coloreds of mixed blood, mostly descended from those early Dutch seamen who had slept with black women in the days when no white women inhabited the area. Then came the Asiatics, mostly East Indians, who have their own special type of racial hell in Africa. At the bottom were the majority of the people, the Bantus or blacks, the lowest legalized caste in the world.

We saw for ourselves that a black man in South Africa could not vote in a national election or sit in the national Parliament or attend a school with whites or sleep with a white or marry a white or use a public general toilet or enter a railroad car with a white or attend a theater with a white or even buy a postage stamp at the same post office window with a white. Nor could a black man live in the same area with a white except as a servant in the white man's back yard. He could buy goods at a white man's counter but the white man was not obliged to provide a toilet for him. He could not see black men fraternizing with white men on television because there was no television. He could buy some cheap books but all racially "dangerous" works were forbidden by an all-white censorship board. Any book with the word "black" in it was likely to be banned. One censor had banned *Black Beauty* until he was told that the hero was a horse.

The most obnoxious feature of the whole apartheid system was the law condemning the black man to live in a restricted area and accept exclusion from the jobs for which whites were eligible. Great special cities for the blacks had been constructed outside of white cities such as Johannesburg and Cape Town. They were cesspools of crime as well as poverty. Soweto, the black city of a million near Johannesburg, had the highest murder rate in the world. The system meant that thousands of black workers had to rise at 4 A.M. to get to employment in the white man's city, reaching work in overcrowded black buses or arriving at a railroad station where they were not even permitted to disembark except in a remote area away from the white man's waiting rooms. When they got to work, their pay might be about one-fourth of the white man's average. Black leaders claimed that the whites in the mining industry averaged ten times the wages of the blacks. All black workers were forbidden to strike.

The chief mechanical device for the surveillance of this system of racial serfdom was the pass book. Every black was compelled to carry a pass book with his vital statistics and tax records in it, and woe be to that Bantu who was ever caught without his documents! More than a million blacks a year were arrested and penalized by white judges for pass-book violations. In Sharpeville in 1960 the blacks staged a brief rebellion against the system. When the police stopped firing, seventy-two blacks lay dead on the ground.

In a Cape Town court I saw long lines of Bantu defendants on trial for pass-book violations. They were run through the "trial" without counsel at the rate of one a minute. Usually they were given reasonably small fines and warned not to break the law in the future, but if they were repeaters or "agitators," they faced the awful fate of being "endorsed out" to some barren, native reservation where employment was almost impossible to find and where the government's old-age pension was $4.20 a month.

The most interesting trials I observed in Cape Town were not, strictly speaking, trials at all but secret preliminary hearings before a racial classification board which had power to permit legally colored persons to "pass over" into the white community. I was admitted to some of these hearings through the good offices of a friendly solicitor.

Some 350 appeals for racial re-classification of coloreds as whites were being heard in Cape Town alone when I was there and, surprisingly, many of them were being granted. The reason for this leniency was obvious. The racial line between whites and coloreds involved many very respectable people. As one local historian told me: "I have studied the history of this region for many years and I have yet to find a single Afrikaner family which does not have some strain of nonwhite blood." All sexual intercourse across racial lines in South Africa is now illegal, but for almost three centuries after the white man arrived in this region there were no such barriers. The first generation of white settlers had no white women at all.

In the racial pass-over hearings which I witnessed, the questions and the inspections were merciless. Each applicant was greeted with a hard stare, a white man's stare appraising his color tinting. If the skin was conspicuously dark, his case was ordinarily hopeless. If his skin color was somewhat doubtful, sharp questions followed. What toilet do you use at the place where you work? Why did you carry a colored card for a time? How were your father and mother classified? Are these persons your father and mother? What does your brother look like? Why did he not appear at this hearing? Do you ever eat lunch at a white restaurant? Which church do you belong to? Does it ever permit mixed congregations? (Churches are the only organizations in South Africa which are permitted to have mixed assemblies under certain circumstances.)

One young man, slightly swarthy, testified anxiously. He was an artisan who claimed that he had been wrongly classified as colored and that the mistake would cause him to lose his job and his substantially higher "white" pay. Also it might lose him his "wife." They were not yet legally married because of the cloud on his racial status but the white "wife" and the reasonably white child were there in the courtroom with him asking to be made respectable. He asked for the privilege of marrying legally and of legalizing his child. He could not legally continue to live with her if his application failed. He sat there blinking under the long scrutiny of the all-white board. Application denied.

The dominant Nationalists—they have been dominant for about twenty-five years—have developed a public relations artifice which they call a Bantustan to create the illusion that they are planning to give the blacks self-determination in part of South African territory. Their paper program calls for eight reserved areas (Bantustans) where blacks are scheduled to go freely and "develop their own way of life." Only one forlorn and mountainous section in the eastern part of the country, the Transkei, has been even partially developed for this purpose, and thousands of the poor and the old have been sent there to live in near-starvation with only local self-government. I found that their capital, Umtata, was itself a racially compartmentalized city where the best land belonged to the whites. The black voters were allowed to vote on some local issues but they were not allowed to challenge the apartheid system itself.

The whites do not hold authority by terror alone. They have developed an advanced industrial system which grants even to the blacks the highest incomes they receive anywhere in southern Africa. The Nationalists grant freedom of the press—limited—to great English-language

dailies which oppose the government openly, and this freedom is more than the black nations of the north allow to
their critics. (In a visit to six of these northern black nations I did not find a single one which allowed a genuine
opposition press or a genuine opposition party.)

The dominant Nationalists of South Africa base their
regime quite soberly on the Bible. They profess reactionary Protestant Christianity as expressed in the South
African Dutch Reformed Church, whose pastors are fluent
in quoting all the passages in scripture which divide the
human race into ethnic groups and assign a minor role to
those of darker skin. God, it is clear, intended that white
men should rule. Fortunately at least two Christian
churches oppose this convenient gospel, the Roman Catholic Church and the Anglican Church. The Afrikaners are
particularly suspicious of the Roman Catholic Church. I
was somewhat embarrassed to find that Bertrand Russell's
Why I Am Not a Christian and many other anti-Christian
books were banned by government censors though the
South African libraries were full of my books. Rome is next
to Moscow as a villain in Dutch Reformed churches.

I never wrote my book on apartheid for several reasons.
One of them was that I could not contact the leaders of
black revolutionary groups without endangering their freedom. I knew that I was watched everywhere whenever I
tried to get information about the world of black revolution. I knew that "suspicious characters" could be held
without trial for 180 days, and thereafter they could be
re-arrested and held for 180 days more. In a United Nations hearing in Tanzania I heard black revolutionists from
South Africa tell of the treatment they received in prison.
"They beat me on the testicles until I was ready to say
anything." "They kept fifteen of us in a cell seventeen by
eleven with one open toilet bucket for us all." "They kept
me standing for seventy-two hours."

In spite of these horrors the black revolutionaries of
South Africa and of the Portuguese colonies of Angola and
Mozambique keep on trying. I met many of them in Zam-

bia, Tanzania, and Rhodesia, and they talked to me freely because I bore personal introductions from my old friend Ralph Bunche. On a plane flying over Zambia we met a black revolutionist with a high price on his head who told us calmly that on such and such a date such and such a department store in Rhodesia would go up in flames. And, sure enough, when we got off the plane in Salisbury the embers were still burning.

I left Africa in a state of profound discouragement because I saw so little hope of the defeat of apartheid in the near future. In South Africa itself there are three hopeful phenomena but they should not be overrated in importance. In the English-speaking universities students who come in contact with the outside world have begun to demonstrate against the worst forms of racial discrimination, and the movement is spreading a little even among Afrikaners. In the sporting area South African whites have been humiliated by the exclusion of their national athletes from the Olympic games and, for a time, from Davis Cup tennis. Such an exclusion shocks a white upper class which has prided itself on high sportsmanship. And, in the political arena, one woman leader of the tiny Progressive Party, Mrs. Helen Suzman, stands up all alone in the Parliament at Cape Town and fights against the apartheid system with enough factual ammunition to keep the world informed.

But these are pretty feeble tokens of that basic reform which the situation demands, and I cannot imagine that such minor modifications and criticisms of the *apartheid* system will long appease the black majority. That majority, with all its shortcomings, represents Africa, and Africa belongs to the black people. It seems to me that a white upper class which attempts to hold such a majority in humiliation and serfdom is bound to perish under the terrible swift sword of black rebellion.

22. AN ATHEIST'S APOLOGY

WHEN A MAN approaches his ninth decade, he feels Something or Somebody looking over his shoulder. He knows that his summing up is his last hurrah.

Does the sense of termination make him any wiser? I think not, but it helps to eliminate petty things. The whole human race seems a bit unimportant, and the unimportance includes himself. The thought of death is not so unwelcome because death gives richer meaning to time. As Tennyson has put it: "Old men must die or the world would grow mouldy."

A man's real apprehension concerns not death itself but the slow decay of old age. He may even picture a withered patient lying in the corridor of a nursing home, rolling in the remains of his own dung, pleading for a release which does not come because "the sacredness of life" still gains nominal lip service from a convention-bound medical profession. He may wish that he could be an animal, for animals have no apprehensions about the end.

Looking back, I am interested more in the fate of my ideas than in my own career. What can I say about those three things which I mentioned as the foci of my young fervor—religion, politics, and sex?

As to politics and sex, I have pretty well set forth my views in telling the story of my past. I, who entered my youthful crusades as a bouncing and sentimental revolutionist, seem now to be nothing more extreme than a standard, socialistic pragmatist, infected with some non-violent dreams, non-Marxist dreams. This is partly because the world has almost caught up to some of my dreams, and partly because, like all men faced with the necessity of overcoming obstacles, I have had to hone down my theories to suit my immediate objectives.

On the whole, I am an optimist about my country and the material world. I do not agree with the doom-sayers. Even if our nation has become the most dreaded military monster in the world, and even if nuclear war should come, the remainder of the human race could re-populate the earth in a few generations. In spite of its ugly triumph in keeping us in the Indochina war, the military-industrial complex is losing ground. The concept of government by the people, not by the militarists, is still vigorous in our society. We are confronted, of course, in the Soviet Union with a power able to destroy us, but we have an even greater power to destroy the Soviet Union. We do not want world suicide, and neither do the Russians. That simple truism may be too simple in a world where some push-button maniac may start the final holocaust, but it seems to me that the common sense of self-preservation will ultimately bring the human race to something approximating enforced peace by a world government.

The technical progress of mankind during my life span seems to argue that, in the long run, success in controlling the environment is probable. Someday there will be perfect and cheap birth control, ending the threat of an over-crowded world. We should remember that ninety-nine per-cent of the history of science, including the wonder-tale of scientific medicine, has been compressed into the last three hundred years, and, spurred on by our new explosion of knowledge, the pace of scientific progress in the future will be geometric rather than arithmetic.

While still believing in a worldwide socialistic drift, I have become increasingly skeptical about any ideological system. Henry George, Karl Marx, and Lenin had their uses in inspiring men to rebel against injustice but their systems have never actually worked completely anywhere. A commitment to economic dogma may inhibit men who have a practical task to accomplish. The greatest achievers of the future may be men who know how to take fragments of ideal systems from the great social philosophers and adapt those fragments to a pragmatic pattern. I see no absolute contradiction between reform within capitalism and the movement toward some kind of socialism. The one may very well lead to the other as production for private profit proves unworkable in a complex society. Indeed such production has already proved unworkable. Capitalism could not exist without a protective and regulatory network of state controls.

If we must emphasize some ultimate goals, I would prefer piecemeal moral goals to full-blown utopias. If I were both an economic dreamer and a political dictator, I think I would begin with two dreams—(1) the strict control and ultimate national ownership of all land, designed to stop the most inexcusable form of profiteering in our society, the capture by land manipulators of the unearned increment of land values; and (2) a national policy of income limitation which would bracket all working citizens between the lower limit of $5000 a year and the upper limit of $50,000. I have long felt that the riches of the super-rich constitute the greatest disgrace in our society and that no man has a right to call himself moral who receives a large income in a society where millions are starving.

Fifty years ago I would have said that organized labor must play the chief role in the reform of our economic system. Now I am not so sure. Although American labor can claim a rightful place at the bargaining table, has it demonstrated any capacity to govern? Big labor under such leaders as George Meany—I knew him years ago when I chaired a La Guardia committee that included him —has allied itself with the military-industrial complex in the Indochina conflict. Big labor has destroyed many newspapers by the use of nonwork requirements and featherbedding, and it has undermined the whole building industry with craft restrictions, unjustified pay scales, and some outright loafing. Granted that Wall Street can produce proportionately more villains of unearned wealth than all the labor unions of the world, this comparative innocence does not establish labor's right to govern.

This leaves us with the intellectuals to fall back upon. I shall not try to define the fuzzy word, or draft a platform for the intellectuals' revolution. Let the new generation write its own platform! It cannot be worse than the brand of waste, war, and poverty produced by my generation. And it might be much better. With all the unjustified extremism of the student generation of the 1960's and 1970's, that generation has demonstrated a moral seriousness which is quite incomparable. It *might* produce in the twenty-first century an American society more interested in social service than in self-service.

I am more definitely sanguine about the future of sex than about the future of socialism. In spite of the so-called breakdown in the morals of the young, I believe that the new frankness has brought an increase in human happiness. Men want women and women want men, and now both men and women are willing to say so, and to act accordingly. The bashful female has gone out with the whalebone corset and swooning. She never was an authentic person to begin with. If newspaper polls can be believed, the majority of our "best" young people endorse or practice copulation outside of marriage at some time during their youth.

Of course, no one can deny that the new permissiveness strikes at the institution of marriage itself. It may even lead to a reorganization or partial dissolution of the thing we call the home. But will monogamy endure? I think so, at least as an institutional norm, perhaps with occasional and forgiven excursions into dalliance. There is something so natural and solid in the one-man-one-woman relationship that I think it will always be the primary form of sexual association, at least in the West. Men and women need to overcome that worst of all afflictions, loneliness, and children need a loving father and mother for sustenance and survival. If every phrase in this judgment is a cliché, who can claim that old wisdom is necessarily nonwisdom? I have always scorned those effete critics who scorn clichés.

As to the larger scientific uses of the new sexual knowledge, I am as stubbornly utopian as I was in my human quality period. After birth control, voluntary sterilization, liberal abortion laws, and easier divorce—all developments of my life span—there must come, I believe, the planned tailoring of the human gene to produce a superior form of human life. I am still so much enamored of the possibilities of this new eugenics that if I had my life to live over again I would be a geneticist.

When it comes to any final judgment about religion, I must approach the area with circumspection because of the prodigious verbal confusion which surrounds the subject. There are very few people in the world who are able to discuss their own religion rationally because self-interest and emotion are stronger in most men than the reasoning faculty. This is particularly true in the sunset of life when we are afraid to be realistic about death. Since I am destined soon to join what J. P. Marquand has called "the big parade to oblivion," I need to assert a special determination to be honest and definite about religion. It is too late for perfumed lying. How do I vote on religion? Yes or no. Then it must be no.

Of course the greatest difficulty in passing any judgment on religion is that the term wriggles and wobbles like a politician's campaign promises. In common usage it means anything from worship of a genuine deity to reciting of the pledge of allegiance to the flag. A "Christian gentleman" may be in practice one who dumps napalm on Vietnamese babies. The obfuscationists have captured the popular use of the word "religion" so completely that it has become an all-purpose synonym for honesty, cheerfulness, and clean underwear. Even Bernard Shaw, who was an outstanding enemy of all supernatural twaddle, fell into the prevailing verbal trap and declared that "Society cannot be held together without religion." He should have said that society cannot be held together without a set of moral ideals. The power of orthodox religion has been kept alive for an extra century by just such off-center manipulations of language as that of Bernard Shaw.

When I say that I vote against religion, I do not wish to belittle the auxiliary accompaniments of religion—decency, kindliness, and hope—but I do deny that these things have any necessary connection with the elaborate frauds of organized religion, the galaxy of saints, miracles, messiahs, heaven, hell, prayer, dogmas, and God which comprise the *distinctive* elements in religion. I would like to see the human race freed from all these basic, surplus over-beliefs so that men can live in a realistic and adult moral climate, divorced from illusion. As it is, we have produced in our religion a monstrous amalgam of goodness and fraud, the most spurious part of our Western culture. And the amalgam is promoted for clerical profit by our anointed spiritual leaders, who serve as both sky pilots and professional liars.

It seems to me that the most spurious of all the great religions is Christianity. Its biblical miracles are childish, pre-scientific myths. Its theology has been taken right out of the caldrons of blood sacrifice and appeasement. For God so loved the world that he allowed the crucifixion of his only son to appease his own wrath, and then he denied eternal life to billions of human souls who refused to accept the gory myth. Hitler murdered six million Jews. The Christian God, in continuing genocide, has denied life to many times that number because of failure to "accept Jesus Christ as Lord and Savior." That last phrase is the standard description of the required ticket to heaven in nearly all Christian sects.

One reason why it is fair to call Christianity the most spurious of the great religions is that it has continued to flourish in nations of the West after whole libraries of criticism have exposed its shortcomings. Medicine, engineering, geology, and astronomy have abandoned their primary superstitions in the new explosion of knowledge. The disciples of Crosstianity still cling to concepts appropriate to an age of bloodletting.

There have been two centuries of scientific thought since Voltaire, Hume, and the Enlightenment, and during that time the case against orthodoxy has been documented to the hilt by scholars within and without the Christian community, ranging from Johannes Weiss to David Strauss to Adolf Harnack to Albert Schweitzer to Rudolf Bultmann, with prodigious scientific assists from Darwin, T. H. Huxley, and Albert Einstein, and very valuable hortatory assists from Robert Ingersoll, Mark Twain, Bertrand Russell, H. L. Mencken, and Walter Kaufmann of Princeton. The sky pilots who ignore this mass of destructive truth deserve the rebuke of Tom Paine in *The Age of Reason:*

It is impossible to calculate the moral mischief, if I may so express it, that mental lying has produced in society. When a man has so far prostituted the chastity of his mind as to subscribe his professional belief to things which he does not believe, he has prepared himself for the commission of every other crime. He takes up the trade of a priest for the sake of gain, and, in order to qualify himself for that trade, he begins with a perjury. Can we conceive anything more destructive than this?

The sky pilots who ignore Tom Paine may have some excuse, since Paine wrote so long ago. But they have no right to ignore the profusion of exposés of Christianity written in this century. Two books, still current, contain enough scholarly dynamite to blow all Christian orthodoxy to oblivion—Walter Kaufmann's *Critique of Religion and Philosophy* and Jabez Sunderland's *The Origin and Character of the Bible.*

The Christ who occupies the central position in the Christian amalgam is a synthetic product with very little historical substance. Jesus of (perhaps) Nazareth was probably a footloose young Jewish prophet of considerable charisma who may not have intended to establish any new religion at the beginning of his ministry. He (probably) expressed in unsystematic parables some very useful moral generalizations which showed no great comprehension of the problems of poverty, war, or slavery, all very real problems in his time. Then he (probably) perished in pitiful agony on Calvary, apparently convinced that somehow he was the embodiment of the dream of the Jewish Messiah and that during a fast-approaching Judgment Day he would return to the earth in regal glory.

That, at least, is one guess we can make about the fragmentary and ambiguous teachings which have survived to us in a language which Jesus never spoke, recorded by writers who had never met him. Although he lived centuries after the great intellectual leaders of Greece, he showed no sign of understanding or appropriating the fruits of an advanced culture. He borrowed most of his slender ethical code from earlier Jewish sources. He left not a single sermon or book to sum up any distinctive message. The so-called Sermon on the Mount is now recognized by scholars as a literary meld, nothing more than a collection of fragments concerned chiefly with the interim morality required for men approaching an imaginary end of the world.

This misty semi-historical Jesus was built into a magic part of the Godhead almost accidentally by Saint Paul, who had never seen him, and by the authors of the Greek-language gospels who had likewise never seen him. The expanded magical story of the magical Messiah of the New Testament was produced long after Jesus' death by several of his followers and put together by men without scholarly training who lived in a pancake Mediterranean world where scientific standards in historical research were unknown. Not a single independent contemporary witness has been found to confirm the propaganda tracts which were ultimately bound together and called the New Testament. As Mark Twain once remarked about the Bible: "It has noble poetry in it and some clever fables;

and some blood-drenched history; and some good morals; and a wealth of obscenity; and upwards of a thousand lies." It is, as one noted Catholic scholar, Dom Aelred Graham, has recently declared, "the world's most overrated book."

I know that it is fashionable in these days to avoid discussion of such "simple" things as the *truth* of Christianity. When theological argument starts in liberal circles, a kind of glaze comes over the eyes of the younger participants. Why kick a dead horse? Why not let organized superstition die out gradually? The favorite escape word is "irrelevant." As if a fraudulent theory of the nature of the universe could be irrelevant in any part of that universe!

When such sentiments are expressed, I feel an old-fashioned, some would say naïve, resentment. I feel like shouting: Quibbler! Coward! You know that the universe of laser beams, galaxies, light years, and chromosomes is not built on a Christian or Jewish or Mohammedan pattern! Why allow such patterns to masquerade as actual truth? Why allow Christian salvationism to flourish side by side with scrupulously accurate science as if they were legitimate twins in our culture when you know that the Christian doctrine of salvation is untrue?

Such pointed questions must be addressed to Protestant leaders just as vigorously as to Catholic leaders. Billy Graham cannot be exempt if Pope Paul is held responsible. In fact, I can see little to choose between Catholicism and Protestantism *theologically*. Catholicism is more dangerous than Protestantism to democratic institutions because it stands wherever possible for state religion and a reactionary family code, but the intellectual credentials of both major branches of Christianity are equally defective. There is no point in a man being halfway honest when he commits himself to the search for truth.

Aside from the untruth of Christianity there is another reason why tolerant men should question it. It tends to divide men who are in pursuit of a better world. Why should we be segregated according to competing myths which are largely irrelevant to modern social needs? Why should there be Christians, Jews, Mohammedans, Hindus, Catholics, Protestants, Buddhists, all emphasizing their archaic sectarian differences as if they were both true and important? There is a humanitarian core, of course, in all these faiths, but that is not the property of any one faith or of all faiths. It belongs to humanity and it would exist without any supernatural sanction.

I think it is necessary to repeat these basic, destructive truths over and over again because nearly all the institutions of our society are arrayed against complete honesty in this field. There is a kind of economic as well as social determinism that supports the orthodox myths, and no one is *naturally* on the de-mythologizing side. No one likes to add disillusionment to the other agonies of agonized man. Preachers and priests are not only professional salesmen selling illusions to their congregations but they are also entrepreneurs of psychological magic, selling cheerful merchandise to themselves. There is no Consumers' Religious Bureau in heaven, earth, or hell to check the merchandise for the pollution of over-belief, since over-belief seems to bring happiness to an immature human race.

The mystics and the neo-orthodox, from Kierkegaard and Karl Barth down, have argued that God can be apprehended directly and that the ordinary processes of perception and reasoning can be bypassed. Odd that in millions of years of human history no one has seen or heard or smelled this over-arching Deity in such a way as to convince the followers of competing sects. In my own early days of yearning prayer I thought I was apprehending that Deity directly, but I think now that I was merely looking at the blood in my eyelids.

The truth is that very few men ever analyze their religious beliefs with their minds. They accept an institution, and their loyalty to that institution is based on tradition and association. A few years ago my brother Brand wrote a review of Barrows Dunham's *Heroes and Heretics* for the *New York Times Book Review* and it so neatly summarizes the case against orthodoxy that I shall quote it here. Although the words are Brand's, the ideas summarized are Dunham's; Brand's own comprehensive and devastating rational analysis will presently appear in the third volume of his Gifford Lectures, *Reason and Belief*.

Orthodoxy is not loyalty to truth but loyalty to an organization. Suppose, for example, that you believe in the creation story, or in miracles, or in the Trinity; why do you do so? Is it because you have looked at the evidence and found it compelling? Almost certainly not. It is because you belong to a church whose power and prestige are behind these beliefs and presses them upon you with a force that is hardly resistible even when unperceived. And where did the organization itself get the beliefs? From science? From critical history or critical reflection? Not at all. It drew most of them from primitive poetry and the rest from expediency. The men who wrote the creation story knew nothing of critical history; they imagined how things might have happened and wrote it down in all innocence as what presumably did happen.

Should an honest man call himself an agnostic or an atheist? I think it is largely a matter of glands and personal taste. Both terms are realistic if honestly applied. The trouble is that the atheist is rarely granted an honest appraisal of his views. He is a devil by presupposition.

The agnostic, looking out into the dark, says: I do not know about God, so I will not commit myself one way or another. The atheist, looking out into the same darkness, says: I positively (or negatively) reject the whole idea of God as contrary to my knowledge of reality. Although I admit that I do not know everything, I do know enough to affirm my unbelief.

This does not mean that the atheist is any more dogmatic than the agnostic. He may welcome new knowledge just as eagerly. But, when he has finished his current analysis, he refuses to stop with a question mark. He chooses to end with an exclamation point! If the extant facts seem to indicate that God is a myth, why not say so?

He puts the burden of proof on God, and not hearing any convincing reply to his questions, he says that for the present at least God does not exist. If God should appear to some new Moses in some new burning bush, the atheist would be interested in examining the new phenomenon, but he would bring along three television cameras to photograph the divine revelation from the backfield, the scrimmage line, and the goalposts.

Even Bertrand Russell did not bother to make the distinction between the agnostic and atheist labels as applied to himself until late in life. He said once in reply to a correspondent, "I call myself sometimes the one and sometimes the other." Then he added:

> For all practical purposes I am an atheist. I do not think the existence of the Christian God any more probable than the existence of the Gods of Olympus or Valhalla. To take another illustration: nobody can prove that there is not between Earth and Mars a china teapot revolving in an elliptical orbit, but nobody thinks this is sufficiently likely to be taken into account in practice. I think the Christian God just as unlikely.

I would be perfectly willing to say that I believed in God if, like Einstein, I could confine my belief to a superior order of nature. But a superior order of nature is not God within the limits of meaning of that word as used by ordinary men, and I think it is dishonest to play carelessly with ambiguous terms in order to bolster unverifiable faiths.

Similarly, the people who argue for God on the ground that there must be a First Cause should be told that if they rely on causality to establish the existence of a Creator, there must be a Cause Behind the First Cause, and a Cause Behind the Cause Behind the First Cause, and so on. If we ask, "Who made me?" we must also ask, "Who made God?" In any case if a Causeless First Cause should ever be located, he would be confronted by the comment of H. G. Wells' Mr. Britling: "Why! If I thought that there was an omnipotent God who looked down on battles and deaths and all the waste and horror of this war—able to prevent these things—doing them to amuse himself—I would spit in his empty face."

So, when I am called upon by conscience to vote on the categories of unbelief, I will vote atheist because I think it is the most honest vote. I do not relish the awful associations of that word in an allegedly pious society, since I am not yet a murderer, a Communist, or an all-around blackguard. In fact I still believe enough in ethical associations to be a creedless Unitarian, Ethical Culture, and Humanist atheist because men who defy the dragons of orthodoxy need mutual support. I am allergic to the whole Russian pattern of atheist promotion because of the element of coercion involved, although I must admit that the wholesale rejection of the supernatural by the Communists may someday be hailed as a vital advance in human culture.

I am inclined to think that millions of alleged orthodox believers actually agree with my atheism but are afraid to announce their unbelief because of social pressures. It is more than a century since John Stuart Mill said in his *Autobiography:* "The world would be astonished if it knew how great a proportion of its greatest ornaments—of those most distinguished even in popular estimation for wisdom and virtue—are complete skeptics in religion." The word "skeptics" in Mill's statement could be replaced by the word "atheists," and the assertion would still be true for our time. Perhaps that is one reason why, if this century ever bears a distinctive, descriptive label for its religious condition, the label should be "hypocrisy." We profess to believe not because we actually believe but because pretense is more socially acceptable.

My Indian-summer arrival at the port of atheism has brought me great psychological release. I feel mentally clean, free from hypocrisy and superstition. Now I can be honest about life, death, and morals. I can reject openly all the semantic jugglery of over-belief. There is no longer up in the sky even the shadow of a vengeful Old Man telling me what to think in the field of conduct. Morality is made by man, and all the pratings of the preachers and priests are only human footnotes, not divine revelations. In my new Kingdom of Honesty the brotherhood of man does not flow from the fatherhood of God. We who are pilgrims on the long journey to oblivion may love and serve our fellow pilgrims without any supernatural intervention. We can do whatever needs to be done. It has always been that way, since God has never been anything more than a helpful psychological crutch created by the human imagination for its own comfort.

I suppose that religion, rigidly orthodox and permissively vague religion, will continue for many centuries to command the loyalty of some men. General faith in the supernatural is declining rapidly, along with church attendance, but preachers and priests can be counted on to seize the latest and most popular emotional and moral novelty and bring it within the range of their particular creeds. Social activist principles which have no necessary connection with religion will be appropriated boldly by men who require something constructive to talk about and who realize that they cannot indefinitely maintain themselves by the use of a vague supernatural jargon.

Will the human race be any happier when these votaries of faith have been exposed as word-jugglers? I do not know. Freud rejected the idea that "man cannot in general do without the consolation of the religious illusion," but he admitted that it will be a long, long time before he reaches that stage of maturity when religious childishness is overcome. Meanwhile, those of us who favor integrity to the bitter end will prescribe for that end no funeral, no cant about survival, no pretense that Somebody Up There cares anything about any sparrows or pilgrim muckrakers.

So endeth the chronicle of Paul Blanshard. It began on an $8 table in a room over a hardware store in Cape Town, South Africa. It ends on an $8 table in Florida. Is there some magic talisman for me in the number 8, coming at the end of my eighth decade? Perhaps. I am favored with a good wife, good health, and a modest but certain income. This detestable American capitalist system which I have scolded all my life sends me each month a Social Security check for $227.50 without any notation about treason or ingratitude. Beatrice, who does the useful work of the establishment, gets a check for $110.90 for "minor" services. Some book royalties keep rolling in.

I have learned to play and read and relax. Robert Benchley once said that he read four books at once, keeping bookmarks in each. I have almost equaled his reading pace. For conscience sake I serve as a local officer of the American Civil Liberties Union, and I have resumed some writing for a column on church and state in the *Humanist* magazine. My mind is still alive.

I have no final words about the meaning of life which might masquerade as wisdom, no buildup for applause before the curtain falls. I am relaxed. Outside the soft wind flows gently through a hedge of poinsettia plants. A squirrel romps up the trunk of a giant live oak tree happily unaware of nuclear fission, napalm, and the Pope.

INDEX